D0850218

God, Humanity, and History

God, Humanity, and History

The Hebrew
First Crusade Narratives

Robert Chazan

UNIVERSITY OF CALIFORNIA PRESS
Berkeley · *Los Angeles* · *London*

*The publisher gratefully acknowledges
the generous contribution to this book
provided by the following organizations:*

DAVID B. GOLD FOUNDATION
LUCIUS N. LITTAUER FOUNDATION
SKIRBALL FOUNDATION
S. MARK TAPER FOUNDATION

University of California Press
Berkeley and Los Angeles, California

University of California Press, Ltd.
London, England

© 2000 by the Regents of the University of California

Library of Congress Cataloging-in-Publication Data

Chazan, Robert.
God, humanity, and history : the Hebrew First Crusade narratives /
Robert Chazan.
    p.   cm.
Includes bibliographical references and index.
ISBN 0-520-22127-3 (cloth : alk. paper).
    1. Jews—Germany—History—1096–1147—Sources. 2. Jews—
Persecutions—Germany—History v Sources. 3. Jewish martyrs—
Germany—Biography—Sources. 4. Crusades—First, 1096–1099—
Sources. 5. Germany—Ethnic relations—Sources. I. Title.
DS135.G31 .C53 2000
943'004924—dc21   99-050352
                                                        CIP

Manufactured in the United States of America

09 08 07 06 05 04 03 02 01 00

10 9 8 7 6 5 4 3 2 1

The paper used in this publication meets the minimum requirements
of ANSI/NISO Z39.48-1992 (R 1997) (*Permanence of Paper*).

051001-3520X6

In memoriam
Gerson D. Cohen

Contents

Preface

The Hebrew narratives that depict Jewish suffering and heroism during the early months of the First Crusade initially captivated me more than three decades ago, in a graduate seminar given by the late Gerson Cohen, to whose memory this book is dedicated. The seminar dealt with medieval Jewish historiography, and it was taught with all of Gerson Cohen's customary enthusiasm and brilliance. Many of the texts evoked my interest, but none so thoroughly as the Hebrew First Crusade narratives. I devoted my seminar paper to those texts and have been fascinated by them ever since.

In the late 1970s I embarked on a study of Jewish fate during the First Crusade, based heavily although not exclusively on the Hebrew narratives. With the appearance of *European Jewry and the First Crusade* in 1987, I assumed that my involvement with the Hebrew First Crusade narratives had come to a close. Such might well have been the case, were it not for the nine-hundredth anniversary of the events of 1096. By mid 1994, I had already received a number of invitations to conferences marking that anniversary. These invitations led me to conclude that, for this important occasion, there should be a popularly oriented account of the events of 1096 and their place in Jewish history. That conviction led me to write *In the Year 1096 . . . : The First Crusade and the Jews.*

As I reimmersed myself in 1096, what most caught my interest was the narratives upon which so much of the historical reconstruction has been based. I thus wrote a study of the *Mainz Anonymous* for a *Festschrift* in honor of Yosef Haim Yerushalmi and an essay on the Trier unit of the so-called *Solomon bar Simson Chronicle* for a *Festschrift* in honor of Isaac Barzilay. Slowly, the notion of putting these materials together in the form of a book-length study of the narratives took shape. I began to sense that some of the conclusions to which I felt myself drawn might be useful in addressing old and unresolved technical issues associated with the narratives. More important, concerns more recently raised regarding, for example, the facticity of the narratives and their theological perspectives might benefit from a new and focused examination of the narratives.

What has resulted has—not surprisingly—exceeded my initial intentions. The present study breaks fairly neatly into two parts. The first is focused on the three Hebrew narratives—the *Mainz Anonymous,* the *Solomon bar Simson Chronicle,* and the *Eliezer bar Nathan Chronicle.* Close scrutiny of the three narratives has led to a number of conclusions: more than three Jewish voices are manifest in these compositions; the Jewish survivors responsible for the materials that have been preserved were animated by divergent objectives; some of these objectives were rigorously time-bound, reflecting a concern with the immediate post-1096 needs of Jewish readers; and, some of these objectives were timeless, a quest for meaning in the aftermath of tragedy.

In the second half of the study, the focus shifts from the three narratives and their components to a series of broad issues, including careful specification of both the time-bound and timeless objectives of the narrative pieces, the implications of the time-bound objectives for an assessment of the reliability of the data preserved and communicated in the narratives, and the implications of the timeless objectives for Jewish understanding of the complex relationship of God, humanity, and history. By the end of the second half of the study, the audacious new sense of this complex relationship that is evident in the Jewish narratives is identified. This sense, dating from the late eleventh and early twelfth centuries, is compared and contrasted with classical and earlier medieval Jewish perceptions of God, humanity, and history and then with the vision projected in contemporary Christian accounts of the First Crusade. These comparisons and contrasts suggest that, just as the Jewish martyrs of 1096 were profoundly influenced by the spirituality of the crusading milieu, so too did the Jewish memorializers of what they perceived to be the remarkable heroism of 1096 imbibe much of their overall outlook from the creative impulses of their environment, impulses often loosely identified as the "twelfth-century renaissance."

It remains for me to acknowledge the impact of a number of friends and colleagues on this endeavor. I should properly begin with mention of the mentor to whose memory the book is dedicated. Gerson Cohen was a remarkable scholar and teacher, taken from his students and colleagues first by the responsibilities of administrative office and then by an untimely death. In class and in conversation, he fairly exploded with knowledge, with excitement, and with creative insight. I have no doubt that he would have contested vigorously many of the conclusions of this study. I likewise have no doubt that our debate would have been illuminating, invigorating, and just plain fun. I, like so many others, sorely miss him.

A number of friends and colleagues have read all or part of the manuscript. Jeremy Cohen read the text in its entirety and offered many illuminating suggestions, enriched by his own extensive work on the 1096 narratives. James Young and David Engel likewise read the manuscript from beginning to end and provided much helpful assistance. Teaching in the Skirball Department of Hebrew and Judaic Studies has enabled me over the years to enjoy the learning of a variety of colleagues. This project has benefited from the input of a number of these colleagues and friends. Let me note in particular the broad assistance of David Engel, cited already, a modernist who has been intrigued by the events of 1096 ever since graduate school; the help of Baruch Levine with the translation of the difficult Hebrew poems (we had a wonderful time tracking down allusions); the suggestions of Jeffrey Rubenstein with regard to chapter 11; and the insights of Elliot Wolfson with respect to the epilogue.

Finally, as always, I acknowledge the loving support of a remarkable family. Our children are now completely grown, fully launched on their own family and professional trajectories. Daniel, Michael, and Rachel—and now their spouses as well—continue to be interested in and supportive of their parents' professional endeavors, as their parents are profoundly interested in and supportive of their undertakings. *Aharon aharon haviv,* my wife Saralea, after more than forty years of marriage, continues to provide the warmth and encouragement that make my work meaningful, indeed that make my work possible.

The Time-Bound and the Timeless in Medieval Ashkenazic Narrative

Medieval Ashkenazic (northern European) Jews were relatively recent immigrants. Beginning in the late tenth century, southern European Jews moved northward, settling in the towns that were at the heart of the remarkable efflorescence of northern European civilization. These immigrant Jews made their way into an environment that was simultaneously supportive of and resistant to their settlement. The support came largely from far-sighted political leaders, who were convinced that the Jewish immigrants would provide useful stimulation to the economy of their domains. The resistance was widespread, rooted in both the realities of Jewish life and the legacy of Christian tradition. The Jews were newcomers and had to endure the hostility and suspicion that is the normal lot of immigrants. They were, moreover, newcomers to an area in which they constituted the only dissenting religious minority and were hence viewed with special concern and animosity. The fact that the immigrants were Jewish and the host society was Christian added further complications. The Jewish immigrants were seen as the descendants of ancestors who had rejected Jesus, the promised Messiah, and had indeed done him to death. This negative legacy much intensified the normal societal distaste for newcomers and dissidents so widely attested in all eras. The resistance to Jewish immigration, based on both tenth- and eleventh-century realities and preexistent tradition, erected barriers to socialization, imposed limits on economic activity, and created the potential for occasional violence.[1]

The Christian environment of northern Europe limited and challenged its Jewish immigrants on the material plane, and it posed a profound spiritual challenge as well. Christianity represented an assault on
the basic belief structure of these Jews (just as Judaism represented a
parallel challenge to the basic belief structure of the Christian majority).
Particularly troubling were the obvious signs of Christian ascendancy
and Jewish degradation. For Christians living in a rapidly developing
and increasingly powerful society, the indices of Jewish weakness—exile, minority status, and difficult circumstances—constituted decisive
proof of the truth of Christianity and the nullity of Judaism.[2] A potent
and proud northern European Christendom at once attracted adven-
turesome Jews, limited them, and raised troubling questions for Jewish
faith. The immigrant Jews had, at one and the same time, to remain
vigilant in the protection of their material interests and creative in their
response to the spiritual challenge posed by the Christian environment.

Since the social, economic, and political circumstances of early Ashkenazic Jewry coupled with the powerful anti-Jewish themes of traditional
Christian teaching exposed the Jewish newcomers to considerable hostility and danger, these immigrants could hardly afford to remain oblivious to developments in majority society and to their potential impact
on Jewish life. Of necessity, the early Ashkenazic Jews had to communicate regularly among themselves with respect to these developments.
Not surprisingly, these time-bound communications have only rarely
survived. Given their association with evanescent circumstances, such
communications were not intended to be preserved and in fact rarely
were. They were written for the present and quickly relegated to the
scrap heap. Occasionally—but only occasionally—happenstance has resulted in the preservation of such materials.

Let us look briefly at one set of such time-bound communications,
three letters composed in the wake of the Blois tragedy of 1171. The
incident was connected to one of a series of late-twelfth-century accu-
sations that Jews groundlessly murder their Christian neighbors.[3] Events
were set in motion by an allegation that a Jew had been seen disposing
of the body of a Christian youngster in the Loire River. This claim was
quickly picked up by a number of Christians profoundly resentful of the
amorous relationship between their ruler and a Blois Jewess. Although
the accusation that Jews murder Christian youngsters had been circulating for a number of decades by 1171, events in Blois diverged from

the normal pattern, deeply threatening northern European Jewry in its entirety. While the authorities regularly repudiated the groundless murder charge, the special constellation of circumstances in Blois resulted in comital support for the murder allegation, eventuating in the death of more than thirty Jewish residents of the town. Given the stature of Count Theobald of Blois, his decision to execute these Jews by burning represented a potentially disastrous blow to northern European Jewry: it was a powerful reinforcement for the growing popular perception that the Jews were internal enemies, lodged within Christian society.[4]

The Blois incident was sufficiently significant to leave numerous traces in both the Christian and Jewish literature of the time.[5] The most significant of these sources was an epistle written in the neighboring Jewish community of Orléans that was intended to depict the Blois tragedy in some detail, to honor the memory of the Jewish martyrs, and to offer a compelling message with respect to the tragedy—all of which it did most effectively. It was written for both the moment and posterity.[6] While its contents were in many ways time-bound, there was enough of the timeless in it to insure its preservation and, simultaneously, the preservation of three other time-bound letters that on their own would not have survived the vicissitudes of time.[7]

For the moment, let us focus on the three time-bound letters. These three communications—a letter by the leadership of Paris Jewry, a letter by the leadership of Troyes Jewry, and a private letter by Nathan ben Meshullam—all transmit information that was critical in the post-Blois ambiance.[8] Let us note the most striking of the three letters, the communal letter composed by the leaders of the Jewish community of Paris.

> Today is a day of glad tidings, to be broadcast to his people Israel by the Great King, who has inclined the heart of flesh and blood in our favor. We journeyed to the king at Poissy to fall before his feet concerning this matter. When we saw that he extended greetings, we indicated that we would like to speak to him privately. He responded: "To the contrary, speak openly!" Then he himself called forth all his ministers stationed in the fortress and said to them: "Listen all of you to what Count Theobald has done—may he and his descendants be uprooted for the entire year! If he has acted properly, then well and good; but if he has behaved improperly, may he be punished. For I too am frightened over what he has done. Now then, you Jews of my land, you have no cause for alarm over what that oppressor has done in his domain. For the folk have alleged against those [Jews] in the town of Pontoise and those in the town of Janville that they did this thing [murder a Christian youngster]. However, when the matter was brought before me, it [the allegation] was found utterly false. . . ."[9] Therefore be assured, all you Jews in

my land, that I harbor no such suspicions in this regard. Even if Christians find a slain Christian in the city or in the countryside, I shall say nothing to the Jews as a result. Therefore be not frightened over this matter."[10]

This letter reports a major development in the post-Blois effort of northern French Jewry to protect itself. The letter is suffused with a strong sense of the importance of the meeting with King Louis VII. Yet despite this sense of significance and despite the vividness of the portrayal, there remains here a failure to project this event onto the broader canvas of Jewish history, a failure to make this an occasion for rumination on the historic fate of the Jewish people. Significant, intense, and vivid though it clearly is, this letter remains in the domain of time-bound dissemination of valuable information. Without its connection to the elegy written by the Jewish community of Orléans over the martyrs of Blois, which is a different kind of composition, the Paris letter—along with those of Troyes Jewry and Nathan ben Meshullam—would surely have been consigned to oblivion.[11]

It seems perfectly obvious that we have at our disposal only the merest fraction of the informational narratives composed by medieval Ashkenazic Jews.[12] While in all medieval cultures the survival of such time-bound communications was minimal, the recurring upheavals in Jewish life and the attendant uprooting of large segments of medieval Ashkenazic Jewry diminished the already limited likelihood that such materials would be preserved.[13] The lack of such written narratives should certainly not be read as indicative of Jewish estrangement from historical circumstances, as a sign of Jewish denigration of the immediate and the worldly.[14] Jews were profoundly immersed in the real world in which they lived. As an endangered minority community, the Jews would not have been able to survive without exquisite sensitivity to that real world, its economic opportunities, and its political entanglements. The immersion of the Jews in their constantly shifting environment means that communication of important information, largely in prose narrative, had to be a staple of Jewish existence.[15]

The Paris letter of 1171, the Troyes letter of 1171, and the personal letter of Nathan bar Meshullam all provide indispensable information on Jewish negotiations in the wake of the Blois episode. As already noted, however, Christian society did more than threaten its Jewish minority in physical terms: it profoundly challenged its Jews spiritually as well. One of the central thrusts of Christian doctrine concerning the Jews involved the hoary conviction that Jewish behavior toward Jesus had constituted a breathtaking historic sin and that divine punishment was swift. Defeat in the war against Rome, loss of political independence, destruction of the Second Temple, and exile to the four corners of the world were all viewed by Christians as elements of the punishment that the Jews richly deserved. Indeed, Christians explained all subsequent persecutions suffered by Jews as further marks of divine opprobrium.[16] For the Jews themselves, this Christian doctrine heightened significantly the challenge normally presented by catastrophe. While human communities are regularly moved by tragedy to intense self-scrutiny, Jews in the Christian orbit were particularly sensitive to disaster since their neighbors were so certain of the meaning of such events. Jews thus had to wrestle incessantly with persecution and suffering, so as to erect strong barriers against absorbing the negative conclusions of their Christian neighbors. Little wonder then that Jews recurrently struggled with the meaning of setbacks both large and small.

Since we have begun this discussion with the Blois incident of 1171 and have seen post-Blois materials that address only time-bound aspects of the event, let us note that the destruction of much of Blois Jewry gave rise also to a number of poems that are utterly timeless in their concerns. Were these the only materials available, we would be unable to reconstruct accurately the events of 1171, since the Jewish poets were hardly interested in the immediate outlines of the happenings that so badly shook twelfth-century Ashkenazic Jewry. Their eyes were focused rather on the timeless meaning of the Blois incident—on the import of the death of thirty-some Jews, not on its details. Let us note a portion of one of these poetic dirges.[17]

> Woe unto us, for we have been despoiled!
> The comeliest and most delicate—the lovely community of Blois,
>   destined for prominence in both Torah and authority—has been
>   delivered to the flames.
> How has burning conferred distinction—and destruction![18]
> Enemies disseminated calumnies deceitfully.
> "You have killed a Christian in the river and drowned him."
> They [the Christians] brought them [the Jews] into confinement and
>   chains to torture them.
> They tormented them and beat them, that they might surrender their
>   faith and their deity.
> They [the Jews], however, withstood the trial, the test, and the
>   burning flames.
> This is the ritual for the burnt offering, the burnt offering on the site
>   of immolation.

Woe unto the wicked one, may his memory be effaced.

He schemed evilly, his plot was the plot of the wicked, by immersing a
man in water in order to clarify the matter.

Thus they exonerated the wicked and convicted the innocent, in order
to uproot him.

Then the ruler Theobald—may his soul rot and his curse render him
accursed[19]—heeding the lie, refused ransom, prohibiting any
mention of it.

No amount of wealth could annul the day of wrath.

He ordered that the children of the bound one [Isaac] be brought for
binding.

This is the ritual of the burnt offering, the burnt offering on the site of
immolation.

Woe unto me for my tragedy! My wound is fatal!

When the wicked one—may his name be blotted out from the earth—
ordered the burning of the pious of the Lord, so full of wisdom,

He brought them to the place of burning, to be burned there.

They [the Christians] said: "Exchange the Divine Glory for one who
effects nothing!"

The righteous spoke out in defiance, to put dust in their [the
Christians'] mouths:

"Burning and boiling are not convincing argument against
proclaiming the unity of the Awesome and Pure."

They sang out the prayer 'Alenu le-shabeah,[20] in order to declare the
unity of the one Lord.

This is the ritual of the burnt offering, the burnt offering on the site of
immolation.

Woe unto me, mother, that you bore me for such pain.

It's as though the people of Sodom were gathered about the place to
encompass it,

Those poisonous serpents with their bundles of twigs to fan [the blaze].

Thirty-two burnt offerings were consumed as a sacrificial gift.

New mothers ran about, exceeding one another in defiance.

They offered up their children as a free-will burnt offering,

As a suckling lamb intended as a free-will burnt offering,

Denoted on the fourth day of the week, on the twentieth of Sivan.

Profound was the shame of that day, to be recalled eternally as a day
of fast and shock by a suffering people.

O God! Recall it on my behalf as a blessing,

For death does separate me from you.

This is the ritual of the burnt offering, the burnt offering on the site of
immolation.[21]

The differences between this poem and the informational letters cited
above are patent. Perhaps the most important is the contrasting audiences to which these pieces were directed. In the three Blois letters, the

audience was contemporary Jews for whom the data included in the missives were critical. These contemporary Jews needed to know, for example, that the king of France had repudiated the allegation of malicious murder and that such a charge would not be accepted in a royal court. In the poem, the audience was God, the present generation of Jews, and future generations of Jews as well. Crucial to this poem and others like it was its meaning, not the relatively irrelevant details of the event in question. This event was one more link in the chain of persecution suffered by the Jewish people; it represented the willingness of this martyred people to offer themselves up voluntarily to the God of Israel: "This is the ritual of the burnt offering, the very burnt offering on the site of immolation."

The time-bound letters addressed themselves to the immediate problems of the 1170s, to the physical challenge posed by Christian society; the timeless poems addressed themselves to the spiritual challenge posed by the Christian majority. The timeless poems rebutted the notion that such persecutions as that of 1171 represented yet one more manifestation of divine wrath with the errant people of Israel; to the contrary, the poets argued, such persecutions represented Israel's heroic reaction to the divine demand for sacrifice.

That the vehicle for time-bound messages would be prose while the vehicle for the timeless would be poetry is hardly surprising. There is of course something inherently prosaic about prose, just as the medium of poetry has its intrinsic appropriateness for the timeless. On occasion, however, the time-bound and the timeless could be fused in prose narrative, so that both sets of audiences were simultaneously addressed and both sets of objectives were simultaneously pursued. I have already noted the Orléans letter that provided the occasion for the preservation of the three post-Blois informational communications. This Orléans letter provides a superb example of the time-bound and the timeless integrated into one composition.[22]

The Orléans letter is a complex composition that in effect moves from the exalted to the increasingly mundane. It begins with a prologue that spells out the reluctance of Orléans Jewry to shoulder the burden of memorializing the heroic martyrs of neighboring Blois. As painful as the task is, there can be no avoiding it, for it has been enjoined upon Orléans Jewry by the king and the distinguished leader of northern French Jewry, Rabbi Jacob Tam.[23] The epistle opens with a focus on the death of the Blois martyrs. This depiction is, at one and the same time, poetic in tone and rich in detail. Midway through the letter, the focus shifts strikingly to the background of the catastrophe. Here the tone becomes thoroughly prosaic, with an emphasis on the precise details of the allegation, the trial, and the complex circumstances in the town of Blois, thus providing the requisite background for understanding the strange and distressing events that transpired there.

We have noted already the emergence of the accusation of malicious and baseless murder leveled against the Jews of northern Europe during the middle decades of the twelfth century and the importance of the post-Blois negotiations in combating the potentially disastrous impact of the Blois executions on that burgeoning allegation. That a political figure of the stature of Count Theobald of Blois would dignify the slander by bringing Jews to trial and then by executing so many of them represented a shattering precedent. We have seen the effort of the leadership of Paris Jewry to counteract the danger by approaching the king of France and the success of this effort, of which all northern European Jews had to be made aware. Beyond this, of course, northern European Jews had to be informed of the details of the events in Blois, so that they might effectively counter any suggestion that the Blois incident proved the truth of the new calumny. It is for this reason that the Orléans letter had to be so thorough, detailed, and trustworthy.

The first objective of much of the detail in the Orléans letter was to provide Jewish readers with requisite information for refuting the groundless murder allegation. Thus, for example, it was important for Jews to know that the witness who set in motion the whole chain of events really saw nothing: it was merely his horse that had bolted at the sight and smell of a Jew washing animal pelts in the Loire River. Similarly, it was important to know that the witness's nonevidence was brought into an environment seething with anti-Jewish hostility brought on by the romantic liaison between the count and a Jewess named Polcelina.[24] It was the cooling of this relationship that encouraged many of the townsmen to strike at the overbearing Jewess—and her coreligionists. Moreover, it was useful for Jews to be aware that an Augustinian canon had played a harmful role in proposing the strange trial method utilized by Count Theobald of Blois, a trial method based on long-outdated notions of ferreting out the truth by ordeal.[25] Finally, the Jews of Blois made a fatal miscalculation, offering the count far too small a bribe. Yet one further factor played a role in the complex chain of events that led to the execution of utterly innocent Jews, and that was an incident in neighboring Loches, where a marriage dispute led to denunciation of the Jews by a distressed coreligionist. Precisely what the denunciation was we do not know, only that it may have further fanned the flames of the count's antipathy. Thus, the Orléans letter amassed considerable detail to show that thoroughly innocent Jews were declared guilty of murder through a concatenation of unfortunate circumstances. Almost incredibly, thirty-some Jews were burned alive as a result of this unhappy chain of events. Anyone provided with the details of this set of developments, however, could clearly see that the execution of these Jews could by no means be taken to prove the new allegation of murder.

Beyond the very important objective of providing requisite data for rebutting the malicious-murder allegation, the Orléans epistle set itself a second task—giving its Jewish readers a sense of the complications of the incident. Among the factors that led to the Blois tragedy were the amorous liaison between Polcelina and Count Theobald, dangerously offensive in its own right; the arrogant behavior of the Jewess, which further embittered many Christians in the town; the incitement of the Augustinian canon; the harshness of Count Theobald; and the misassessment of the level of danger by the Jews of Blois. Clarification of these elements in the tragedy was intended to provide Jewish readers with an understanding that would enable them to behave more intelligently in the future. While some of these factors—like the incitement of the Augustinian canon and the harshness of Count Theobald—could hardly be controlled by the Jews, a better grasp of circumstances could result in earlier and more effective defensive steps.

In addition to providing enough information to rebut the groundless murder accusation and to guide Jewish readers in their behavior, the Orléans letter was intended to memorialize properly a group of Jews that its author (or authors) viewed as martyrs. The key element in this Jewish martyrdom involved the Christian effort to exploit the threat of death as a vehicle for bringing the convicted Jews to baptism and the resolute refusal of these Jews to submit. The letter's depiction of Jewish resoluteness proceeds through a number of stages. Early on, Count Theobald is portrayed as urging conversion, which the convicted Jews unanimously reject. The Christians are then depicted as hoping that a few Jewish victims might weaken on the way to execution, but this hope quickly evaporates. The Jews of Blois are portrayed as greeting the flames with joyous chanting of the 'Alenu prayer, a prayer that highlights the distinction between Jews and others and between Judaism and other faiths. This prayer calls upon Jews to "bend the knee, bow, and offer thanks to the King who reigns over all kings, who spread forth the heavens and established the earth. . . . It is he who is God; there is none other. Our King is the true one; there is none other beside him."[26] Armed with that conviction, the Jews of Blois meet their death as a group, with enthusiasm. Indeed, after the description of group martyrdom, the author provides a more personalized sense of heroism by focusing on three individual Jews who escaped the blaze and might have yet saved themselves through conversion, but who rejected that option and chose—a second time, as it were—death as martyrs.

While the crown of martyrdom was often awarded rather haphazardly, the Orléans letter is highly detailed in its depiction so as to convince all readers that these particular Jews truly deserved the title of martyr, for they had steadfastly chosen death over conversion. The author is anxious to provide the sources of his evidence in order to quell all doubts. Thus, in depicting the joyous acceptance of death with the chanting of the ʿAlenu, he tells us:

> The gentiles came and told us, saying to us: "What is that song of yours, which was so sweet? We have never heard anything so sweet." For at the outset the sound was low, but at the conclusion they [the Jewish martyrs] raised their voices mightily and called out together " ʿAlenu le-shabeaḥ." Then the fire raged.[27]

The concern of the author to cite his sources is yet more strikingly repeated shortly thereafter, at the close of his extensive description of the martyrdom of Blois Jewry.

> Our fellow townsmen and acquaintances [Christian burghers from Orléans], who were there at the event, told us these things. But we are not dependent upon them for verification of all these things.[28] For Baruch ben R. David ha-cohen was there at the time of the conflagration. With his own eyes he saw and with his own ears he heard. Only the conflagration itself he did not see, lest he be swallowed up by the mob that gathered there, outside the town, at the place of the fire. Subsequently, when the folk had calmed from its excitement,[29] when the fire had been quelled, on that day he immediately fled to Orléans.[30]

The Jews of Blois were true martyrs, as proven by the evidence of both Christian and Jewish observers of their execution.

There was yet a further proof of their martyrdom, the fact that their bodies remained intact, with only their souls expiring. Once more, this assertion is grounded in firm testimony.

They wickedly burned the pious of the Almighty by scorching the soul, leaving the body intact. Indeed, all the uncircumcised testify that their bodies were not consumed. Only their detractors said that their bodies were burned, and it seems that they said this only out of their hostility.[31]

Multiple accounts evidenced the genuine martyrdom of the thirty-some Jews of Blois.

The three objectives upon which we have focused are all in the realm of the time-bound, although the establishment of the martyrdom of the Jews of Blois in and of itself offered elements of meaning and consolation to Jewish readers. In a striking way, however, the Orléans letter managed to provide both time-bound information and a timeless perspective on the events it depicted.

How was this timelessness achieved? What was the meaning of the Blois tragedy to the author of the Orléans letter? The Orléans letter clearly projects the Jewish martyrs of Blois onto the stage of "real" Jewish history, that set of great events that mark the distinctive trajectory of Jewish experience. The author of the Orléans letter, so caught up in the historical realities of Count Theobald, the Jewess Polcelina, and the witness and his horse by the river's edge, proclaims at the same time that the event he must depict extends far beyond the town or principality of Blois, far beyond the immediacy of Count Theobald or Polcelina. The martyrs of Blois are elevated to the level of the historic, associated with the great events and institutions of the Jewish past. A timeline is created that stretches back from Blois in 1171 through peak moments of the Jewish past, indeed back into critical junctures of pre-Israelite universal human history.

Immediately at the outset of the narrative, the burning at Blois is linked to the destruction of the Second Temple: "From the time he [the Lord] gave over his people to destruction and set fire to our Temple, holy ones such as these have not been offered up on the pyre."[32] The Blois incident is thus linked to the destruction of the Second Temple; indeed, since that conflagration (over a thousand years earlier), there have been no greater martyrs at the pyre than the thirty-one (or thirty-two) Jews of Blois.

At the end of the passage noted, a second decisive event from the past, this one linked to the destruction of the First Temple, is introduced: "The significance of this fast will exceed that of the fast of Gedaliah ben Ahikam."[33] Now, Gedaliah ben Ahikam's murder represents, as it were, the last death throes of the First Commonwealth, the final act in the drama that saw the end of the Judean polity, the exile of the people from their land, and the destruction of the First Temple.[34] Indeed, the fast instituted in memory of this otherwise obscure figure was one of the four minor fast days specified in rabbinic law.[35] For the author of the Orléans letter, the new fast on the twentieth of Sivan, proclaimed in recollection of the Blois martyrs, exceeds in religious significance the earlier fast, which had been observed by Jews for a millennium or more. This is a rather audacious claim, but one that reinforces the historic significance of the Blois event.[36]

Continuing to move backward through the Jewish past, we note the following potent words at the outset of the Orléans letter: "The Lord is sanctified by those near to him."[37] For readers of the Hebrew text, this brief sentence is highly evocative. It calls to mind a tragic and opaque incident that befell the Israelites, or more precisely the Aaronide family, during the wilderness sojourn. The sons of Aaron, Nadav and Avihu, "offered before the Lord alien fire, which he had not enjoined upon them" and, as a result, were themselves consumed by fire. The basis for the tragic deaths is not at all clear. The uncertainty is compounded by the effort of Moses to console his grieving brother with the following:

> "This is what the Lord meant when he said:
> 'Through those near to me I shall be sanctified,
> And gain glory before all the people.' "

Now, the straightforward meaning of the three cryptic verses (Lev. 10: 1–3) seems to be that the sons of Aaron erred grievously and were accordingly punished.[38]

While this straightforward reading makes sense of the entire three-verse unit, it left some expositors, both early and late, uncomfortable, seemingly because of the note of approbation for the deceased young priests in Moses's consolation of his brother Aaron. This led some to read the consolation in a radically different way:

> Moses came to him [Aaron] and consoled him. He said to him: "Aaron my brother, at Sinai it was said to me: 'I [God] shall in the future sanctify this sanctuary; I shall sanctify it through a great man.' I thought that the sanctuary would be sanctified either through me or through you. Now your sons have been shown to be greater than I or than you, for through them the sanctuary has been sanctified."[39]

The fiery death of the Jews of Blois, then, is presented in a positive sense as a recapitulation of the fiery death of the sons of Aaron, who were chosen for their fate, according to some interpreters, because of a greatness that exceeded even that of Aaron and Moses. One could hardly imagine a more distinguished niche on the plane of historic Jewish experience.

The connection of the Blois martyrs with the sons of Aaron—seen in highly positive terms—is in fact pushed yet one step further. As noted, toward the end of the Orléans letter the author insists on an important point with respect to the physical remains of the Blois martyrs: their souls were extinguished by the flames of the fire, but their bodies remained intact.[40] While the imagery of the burning of the soul but not the body is not confined to Nadav and Avihu, such special circumstances of death are highlighted with respect to the sons of Aaron.[41] It is clear that the author of the Orléans letter saw in this claim a continuation of the connection between the martyrs of his own day and the positively construed victims of an earlier divine fire.

Finally, in one more step backward in time, a decisive figure in pre-Israelite human history is invoked. Maintaining the imagery of sacrifice, the authors absorb and embellish the language of Genesis 8, the narrative that shows Noah, in many senses the progenitor of all humanity, descending from the ark. Upon emerging from the ark,

> Noah built an altar to the Lord and, taking of every clean animal and of every clean bird, he offered burnt offerings on the altar. The Lord smelled the pleasing odor, and the Lord said to himself: "Never again will I doom the earth because of man, since the devisings of man's mind are evil from his youth; nor will I ever again destroy every human being, as I have done."[42]

The language used in the Orléans letter—"and the Lord smelled the pleasing odor"—points unmistakably to the Noah scene. In a sense, then, the martyrs play a role in the drama of humanity in its totality, recapitulating the pure sacrifices offered by Noah and assuring all humanity of protection from divine wrath.

The martyrs of Blois, then, are projected onto the great canvas of Jewish and world history. While there is, on the one hand, full immersion in the immediate realities of the 1170s, there is, at the same time, a powerful sense of Blois as a link in a historic chain that stretches backward through the destruction of the two temples and the wilderness wandering all the way to the near destruction of all humanity during the days of Noah.

Indeed, the author projects the Blois incident, with its tragic and heroic elements, onto a plane beyond the historic plane of Jewish experience; it is in fact projected onto a cosmic plane as well. The author portrays the Blois incident as more than simply a continuation of the great moments of Jewish history. The martyrs are more than simply related to the destruction of the First and Second Temples; they are an innovative continuation of the cosmically significant ritual of those two sanctuaries. The martyrs are portrayed throughout the passage cited as sacrifices offered on the altar, as the sin offerings of the Jewish people. This theme is powerfully stated and restated throughout the Orléans letter.[43] It is in fact for this reason that the fast of the twentieth of Sivan exceeds in importance the fast instituted in memory of Gedaliah ben Ahikam. The fast instituted on the twentieth of Sivan is projected by the author of the Orléans letter as "a veritable Day of Atonement."[44] Just as in days of yore, when Jews found acceptance in divine eyes through the sacrificial offerings brought at the sanctuary, Jews henceforth would find their atonement on the twentieth of Sivan through the sacrifice on the field outside the town of Blois.

More than a historic linkage is achieved with the institution of the new fast: the Jews of Blois take their place of importance on the celestial plane as well.[45] In yet one further set of images, the Blois martyrs are projected into the celestial realms—they actually join the heavenly hosts. These Jews are angels, thirty-one angels. In a striking turn of phrase, the victims of the Blois pyre are identified as those *serafim* who are seen by Isaiah in his great vision as standing in service of the Divine. The *serufim* of Blois, those who were burned for their faith, are transformed into *serafim*, the heavenly figures who proclaim the sanctity of the Lord. Their proclamation shakes the foundation of the universe and fills the divine chamber with smoke, reminding us once again of their death by flames.[46]

What must be emphasized at this point is that the temporal and the atemporal are in no way detached from each other. To put the matter differently, the claims for historic, cosmic, and celestial significance are firmly grounded in the detailed depictions of the terrestrial behavior of the Blois martyrs. The greatness of these martyrs (or sacrifices, or angels), their historic and metahistoric significance, lies in their earthly steadfastness in the face of a potent combination of threat and blandishment.

In the process of tracking the author's projection of the Blois martyrs onto the planes of historic, cosmic, and celestial significance, we have in fact uncovered the letter's construction of the meaning of the Blois episode. We have noted repeated reference to the sacrificial and expiatory functions of the Blois martyrs, the sense that they have taken upon themselves the sins of the world and have offered themselves to the Lord in expiation of those sins. The letter is replete with references to the Jerusalem temples and their sacrificial system, and the suggestion that the twentieth of Sivan constitutes "a veritable Day of Atonement" is highly revealing. Thus, to the Christian challenge that Jewish suffering is a reflection of Jewish sin and divine rejection, the Jewish author of the Orléans missive replied that such was by no means the case. Rather, the Jews of Blois were a blameless group (in both the terrestrial and spiritual sense) that had been singled out to bear the sins of the world and to appease divine anger with others, and thus to redeem those others, by offering themselves in sacrifice. Clearly, in a Christian environment, all these themes resonated strongly. Early Jewish themes appropriated by nascent Christianity were reappropriated by northern European Jewry in the face of the medieval Christian challenge.

The Orléans letter is thus revealed as a complex composition, addressing simultaneously a number of audiences and a number of objectives. It achieves its multiple purposes through an artful combination of prosaic information and poetic hyperbole. It provided immediate information for the Jews of 1171 as they faced the aftermath of Count Theobald's harrowing and precedent-setting espousal of new anti-Jewish stereotypes. At the same time, this complex composition addressed perennial issues and spun out a picture of Blois and its Jews that transcended Count Theobald and the year 1171 and that addressed unremitting Christian challenges to Jewish faith.

The fortuitous combination of sources deriving from the Blois incident has enabled us to discern a spectrum of Jewish accounts of an important event in the history of early Ashkenazic Jewry, ranging from the rigorously time-bound to the free-floating and timeless. Special attention has been accorded to the possibility that some prose narratives could effectively combine time-bound and timeless concerns, eventuating in compositions that were important and meaningful for the moment, yet retained interest and impact for future generations of readers.

Three-quarters of a century before the Blois crisis of 1171, early Ashkenazic Jewry had been wracked by a more spontaneous, more wide-ranging, and deadlier persecution. The call of Pope Urban II in 1095 for Christians to retake the Holy Land had unleashed enthusiastic responses all across western Christendom, responses that far exceeded narrow papal expectations. One of the unanticipated spinoffs of the papal call was the coalescing of a wide variety of military forces, all pointed toward the reconquest of Jerusalem. A further unanticipated byproduct of the papal call was the emergence of an anti-Jewish ideology in limited segments of these diversified military bands. During the spring months of 1096, a number of major Jewish communities across northern Europe were threatened by violence. In most instances, the anti-Jewish hostility proved fairly weak and the forces of law and order strong. In a few cases, the anti-Jewish animus among allied burghers as well as crusaders was potent, and the forces committed to law and order proved ineffective. In such cases, the result was a stunning bloodbath, with a few of the most important Rhineland Jewish communities destroyed almost in their entirety.[47]

The 1096 calamity surely attracted the kinds of attention we have discerned in the wake of the Blois episode. Unfortunately, wholly time-bound Jewish responses have not been preserved, although clearly there were such. In the earliest of the extant Hebrew First Crusade narratives, we are told (quite accurately, as we shall see) of the eruption of the crusade in France, of perceptions of danger on the part of French Jews, and of letters forwarded to the great Jewish communities of the Rhineland.

> When the Jewish communities in northern France heard [of the development of crusading ardor], they were seized by consternation, fear, and trembling, and they reacted in time-honored ways.[48] They wrote letters and sent emissaries to all the Jewish communities along the Rhine River, [asking] that they fast and seek mercy for them from him who dwells on high, so that they [the Jews] might be saved from their [the crusaders'] hands.[49]

There is only cursory reference to the reply that Rhineland Jewish leaders gave this request. A similar reference occurs in a report on a wealthy Jew named Shmarya, who was successful in escaping with his wife and three of his sons from the refuge of Moers, where a group of Cologne Jews had ultimately been converted under duress. This Jewish family and their Christian protector wandered about until effective communication could be established with two of Shmarya's older sons in Speyer. Eventually such communication was established, money was sent from Speyer to the Christian protector, and then Shmarya, his wife, and his young sons were abandoned by the scheming agent.[50] Unfortunately, but not surprisingly, rigorously time-bound materials have not survived from 1096.

By contrast, a substantial number of poems, with poetry's usual timeless quality, have survived. These poems wrestle with the meaning of the tragedy, paying scant attention to the details of the events of 1096. The poems, for example, tell us very little of the attackers or the circumstances of the attacks. They highlight, rather, the martyrological Jewish behaviors of 1096, the symbols current among the martyrs, and the meaning of the sanguinary events. Indeed, there is little interest in aspects of Jewish behavior beyond martyrdom.[51]

The focus of this study is on three Hebrew prose narratives that attempt, like the Orléans letter of 1171, to fuse the time-bound and the timeless. These three narratives—in differing proportions—portray a variety of Christian attitudes and behaviors and diverse Jewish responses and symbols. Like the Orléans letter, the authors of these narratives addressed pressing immediate needs within the post-1096 Jewish communities of northern Europe and, at the same time, addressed the meta-historic meaning of the events depicted. Further, like the Orléans letter, they projected an audience of contemporary readers, of Jewish readers over the ages, and of God himself. It is this combination of the time-bound and the timeless—I would argue—that has made these narratives so compelling to such a wide range of readers and has produced conflicting views of their objectives and techniques. Examining these prose narratives as simultaneously time-bound and timeless will, I believe, open up new perspectives on these fascinating compositions.

CHAPTER ONE

The Hebrew First Crusade Narratives

In 1892, the Historische Commission für Geschichte der Juden in Deutschland, committed *inter alia* to providing documentation illuminating Jewish life in Germany, published its second volume of medieval Hebrew sources, consisting of five narratives describing the fate of German Jewry during the great crusades of the late eleventh and twelfth centuries.[1] While each of these five narrative sources is interesting in its own right, the first three—which depict the events of late spring and early summer 1096—have attracted by far the greatest attention.[2] The three narratives, in the order published in 1892,[3] are: (1) the so-called *Solomon bar Simson Chronicle;*[4] (2) the so-called *Eliezer bar Nathan Chronicle;*[5] (3) the so-called *Mainz Anonymous.*[6]

Prior to the 1892 publication, little of the information provided in these three narratives was widely disseminated. The three texts do not seem to have been extensively copied during the Middle Ages, and very few exemplars have survived.[7] The most important vehicle for knowledge of the events depicted in the Hebrew First Crusade narratives was the sixteenth-century '*Emek ha-Bakha*', composed by Joseph *ha-cohen* of Avignon. Joseph copied from the *Eliezer bar Nathan Chronicle*, thus providing some dissemination of the data contained therein, especially throughout the Sephardic Diaspora.[8] Subsequently, the material in '*Emek ha-Bakha*' was absorbed into the Ashkenazic *Zemah David*, thereby ensuring that the 1096 crisis, at least in the terms described by Eliezer bar Nathan, would be known by German and Polish Jewry.[9]

Subsequent to the publication in 1892 of the three narratives, the events of 1096 have been widely cited in histories of both the crusades and the Jews. For crusade historiography, the assaults of 1096 have illuminated the popular fervor associated with the First Crusade and the misguided directions in which some of that fervor expressed itself.[10] For historians of the Jews, the Rhineland attacks have had far greater significance. They have been projected as a significant marker in the long and complex history of antisemitism.[11] For many, 1096 has emerged as a major turning point in the history of the Jewish people.[12] At the same time, the extreme Jewish responses to these attacks have been seen as unusual manifestations of Jewish martyrological behavior, influenced in no small measure by the fevered atmosphere of late-eleventh-century western Christendom.[13] Obviously, without the three key texts made available in 1892, the Rhineland attacks and the unusual Jewish responses would have remained relatively unknown.[14]

To be sure, the historical reconstructions based on these three important texts necessitate some sense of the reliability of the narratives, involving such matters as their provenance and objectives. In addition, interest has developed in these three narratives as important historical artifacts in their own right. Vigorously written and deeply moving, these accounts have been deemed deserving of careful investigation and analysis. As a result, a considerable literature on the narratives themselves has evolved; this literature addresses a web of complex issues associated with these important and somewhat problematic records.

As already noted, the manuscript foundation for these texts is limited in quantity and, in fact, in quality as well. Multiple manuscripts are available for only one of the three texts: the *Eliezer bar Nathan Chronicle* was published in 1892 on the basis of four manuscripts, one from the fourteenth century, one from the seventeenth century, and two from the eighteenth century.[15] Both the *Solomon bar Simson Chronicle* and the *Mainz Anonymous* were published from single manuscripts, the former from a manuscript of the fifteenth century and the latter from a manuscript of the fourteenth century.[16] Clearly, these texts could hardly be called popular. Moreover, none of the manuscripts is particularly reliable; obvious scribal errors abound.[17] Ironically, the availability of three different accounts of the events of 1096 has created an additional set of problems. The three narratives are obviously related to one another in some fashion, because identical passages can be found in all three texts.[18] More wide-ranging sharing is found in the *Solomon bar Simson Chronicle* and the *Eliezer bar Nathan Chronicle*.[19] These shared passages have given rise to considerable speculation as to the relationships among the three narratives. Some scholars have suggested independent sources, largely letters, absorbed by all three authors; others have suggested an *Urtext,* an earlier historical narrative now lost, from which all three authors drew; yet others have suggested one of the three as the master source, with the others drawn from it. Clarification of the relationship among the three texts is extremely difficult and involves a number of additional issues.[20]

The most important question normally asked of such texts is the date of composition. Only one solid piece of information is available to us on the dating of any of the three narratives. The Cologne unit of the *Solomon bar Simson Chronicle* includes, about half-way through, a curiously worded observation that provides the specific date of 1140 for at least that particular segment of the Cologne unit, or perhaps for the entire Cologne unit, or perhaps for the *Solomon bar Simson Chronicle* in its entirety.[21]

Much more problematic is the dating of the *Eliezer bar Nathan Chronicle* and the *Mainz Anonymous.* Nowhere do these two narratives provide us with the kind of overt evidence found in the *Solomon bar Simson Chronicle.* Since the *Eliezer bar Nathan Chronicle* has generally been attributed to the well-known twelfth-century scholar of that name, the mid to late twelfth century has regularly been assumed as the date of his narrative.[22] The *Mainz Anonymous* has proven the most problematic of all three texts with respect to dating. Suggestions have ranged from the fourteenth century back to the late eleventh century.[23] Obviously, the dating of these two narratives and the relationships among all three texts are intertwined issues. A strong case for the *Solomon bar Simson Chronicle* as the antecedent of the other two would necessitate a late dating for them. Alternatively, a strong case for an early dating for either of the other two narratives would affect the relationship of that narrative to the *Solomon bar Simson Chronicle.*

In order to avoid impeding the flow of discussion, I have opted to survey the major published views of the relationships among the narratives and their dating in an appendix to this study. At the conclusion of this survey, I enunciate a series of methodological conclusions, which are worthy of repetition:

> The precise boundaries of each narrative—exactly where each begins and ends—must be ascertained. Much early argumentation was based on the contention that the opening section of the *Solomon bar*

Simson Chronicle is lost. Rejection of that contention has had an impact on the thinking of a number of the researchers reviewed.

Each of the narratives must be examined to discern whether it is the work of one hand or a composite text. If any of the narratives is a composite text, then its constituent elements must be carefully identified and analyzed.

Allowance must be made for the uniqueness of each narrative. Many researchers have assumed that the three texts are interchangeable, with common objectives and themes. Such an assumption is unwarranted.

The imaginative core of each narrative and primary unit must be identified. Each of the available sources—whether an entire narrative or a discernible unit within a composite narrative—must be examined as a literary and imaginative whole, with major themes and emphases.

Medieval textual borrowing must be properly understood. Much of the discussion of the relationship of the three texts has been carried out without a sufficient sense of precisely how medieval Jewish authors treated sources at their disposal.

The assumption of a uniform relationship among all three narratives—all independent, or two derived from one, or one derived from two—should be rejected. It is perfectly reasonable to find one relationship between two of the narratives and a completely different relationship between two others.

Early studies of the three Hebrew narratives focused on rather technical matters, particularly the relationships among the texts and the dating of the texts. Of late, new concerns have been voiced and new avenues explored. The first of these new concerns involves the facticity of the accounts. To what extent do they reflect the realities of 1096? To be sure, this new concern cannot be divorced from the more technical issues. If in fact some of the material is quite early, then the likelihood of facticity is enhanced; if all the material is quite late, then the likelihood of facticity is diminished. Yet, beyond the question of dating, there is a further and independent matter of reliability that has come to the fore.

Discussion of the facticity of the Hebrew First Crusade narratives can be conducted on two levels. On the scholarly agenda today are general questions as to the capacity of observers to provide "reliable" evidence for events perceived and the capacity of language to communicate "reliable" data for such events. The discussion of the facticity of the 1096 narratives has not been conducted on this highly philosophic plane. The questioning of the reliability of the data provided in the three narratives has been far more focused, more prosaic, and ultimately more useful.

The most radical position has been enunciated by Ivan G. Marcus. Marcus has expressed a number of views on the facticity of the narratives; for the sake of this overview I would like to focus on his most extreme formulations, since they lay out the issues with clarity and force.[24] Marcus has argued in a number of publications that the search for "facts" in medieval Jewish historical narratives is misguided, that the genre simply cannot provide such "facts." In Marcus's own words:

> What appear to be facts in a medieval chronological narrative, then, should be considered a highly edited version of the "deeds" (*gesta*) which the narrator learned from traditional accounts, hearsay or eye-witness reports. The events actually reported qualify for inclusion only when they fit the narrator's pre-conceived religious-literary schema. Medieval chronicles are, in this sense, fictions: imaginative reorderings of experience within a cultural framework and system of symbols.[25]

It seems important to place this rather skeptical view in its proper setting. For a long time now, skepticism as to the historicity of the biblical records has been widespread. While the issue remains to an extent unresolved, no one is any longer discomfited by the suggestion that biblical materials may not accurately reflect the realities they purport to describe. Over the past few decades, however, there has been something of a revolution in stance toward the data supplied in the talmudic corpus. Once treated as utterly reliable and the firm basis for reconstructing the history of Palestinian and Babylonian Jewry in late antiquity, talmudic materials have come under increasing scrutiny and have been subjected to increasing skepticism. The bases for this skepticism are, again, not philosophic. They involve the normal historiographic issues of conflicting sources, distance of sources from the events depicted, and the objectives animating authors of narrative accounts.[26] It is in this context that the skepticism expressed by Marcus should be seen. Given this set of concerns, the 1096 narratives and their facticity should be examined in precisely the same terms—congruence among sources, dating of evidence, and analysis of the objectives motivating authors.[27]

A less extreme skepticism has more recently been proposed by Jeremy Cohen. His questions as to the facticity of the 1096 narratives are somewhat more limited: they are focused on the motivations ascribed to the 1096 martyrs and the symbols that animated them. More specifically, he wishes to distinguish between the broad depiction of events in the

Hebrew narratives, which is relatively trustworthy, and the ascription of motivations and symbols, which he believes to have been heavily influenced by Christian spirituality in the first half of the twelfth century. Since Cohen posits that all the narratives were composed during the mid twelfth century or later, he suggests that the authors introduced into their accounts meaningful Jewish symbols intended to counter twelfth-century Christian imagery.[28]

Cohen's suggestions too must be seen in the context of broader historical currents. One of the new perspectives that has emerged in crusading historiography of late is a strong sense of the First Crusade as a rapidly developing movement, with new themes and symbols evolving during the course of the four-year undertaking. It has been argued, for example, that martyrdom was not present as an early concern of the crusaders, but that it emerged during the course of the arduous and deadly campaign.[29] Cohen's suggestion that mid-twelfth-century themes were introduced into the narratives is reasonable if all the narratives indeed stem from the mid twelfth century or later. Thus, dating of the narratives is critical to an assessment of Cohen's interesting suggestions. In addition, the previously noted issues of congruence of sources and auctorial objectives must once more be taken into consideration.

Moving beyond the issue of facticity, a number of scholars have begun to probe the 1096 narratives as works of historical writing and/or theology. There has been growing interest in Jewish historical perspectives over the ages and in Jewish responses to crisis and tragedy. In both contexts, the 1096 narratives have figured prominently.

In a probing examination of Jewish historical memory, thinking, and writing, Yosef Haim Yerushalmi devotes brief but valuable attention to the Hebrew First Crusade narratives. The context of this attention is Yerushalmi's broad sense that historical writing did not flourish among medieval Jews because they thought that the essential patterns of history had been spelled out in Scriptures and that later Jewish history, at least in its preredemptive stage, was of minimal importance and interest.[30] According to Yerushalmi, "only in two instances in medieval Jewish historical writing can one detect a full awareness that something genuinely new has happened and that there is a special significance to the events themselves." These two instances are the Hebrew crusade narratives and the twelfth-century Sefer ha-Kabbalah of Abraham ibn Daud. According to Yerushalmi, however, "Ibn Daud and the Crusade chronicles are, in this respect, exceptional rather than exemplary, and ultimately even they show a marked tendency to pour new wine into old vessels."[31] For our purposes, Yerushalmi alerts us to the important issues of the innovativeness of the Hebrew First Crusade narratives and the interplay of old and new in them.

In the wake of the catastrophe that struck world Jewry during the middle decades of the twentieth century, recent scholarly attention has fastened on historic patterns of Jewish response to tragedy. Among the broadest investigations of this important theme is Alan Mintz's *Hurban: Responses to Catastrophe in Hebrew Literature*. Mintz begins with biblical, rabbinic, and medieval literary reactions to catastrophe, moves to the literature occasioned by the late-nineteenth- and early-twentieth-century outbreaks of violence in eastern Europe, and concludes with recent literary responses to the Holocaust.[32]

In his analysis of medieval Jewish literary reactions to tragedy, Mintz highlights the reactions to the violence of 1096. Unfortunately for our purposes, he chooses to focus on the poetry evoked by the events of 1096, rather than the prose narratives that are our concern. He does, however, dwell on the innovativeness of the Jewish literary responses to 1096 and makes a brief but interesting observation on the prose narratives. After noting the existence of both prose and poetic materials occasioned by the events of 1096, Mintz distinguishes between the stances of social historians and his own interests.

> Social historians have been chiefly interested in the chronicles because they constitute the first sustained examples of the genre of contemporary historical writing in Hebrew—it is no coincidence that the nature of the events warranted a new form of writing—and because as historians they are concerned with removing the layers of literary and mythic molding to get at "historical reality." My concern here proceeds in the opposite direction: from the events as they happened toward their symbolization and stylization. The focus will therefore be on the poems, for it is there that the processes of image-making are most intensely at work.[33]

Interesting for our purposes is Mintz's reinforcement, from a different perspective, of Yerushalmi's sense of the innovativeness of the Hebrew First Crusade narratives. Clarification of this innovativeness will constitute another major concern of the present study.

I would venture one slight disagreement with Mintz on these matters. While I agree that the 1096 poetry offers a more clear-cut opportunity to study "the processes of image-making," I would urge that, because image-making in the 1096 Hebrew narratives is less clear-cut, these narratives are ultimately more interesting for the study of symbolization and stylization. To put the matter slightly differently, it is precisely the interaction of time-bound and timeless concerns that makes the narratives ultimately more fascinating—even for studying post-1096 image-making—than the simpler poems.

This brief survey of prior work on the Hebrew First Crusade narratives serves as a useful backdrop for identifying the main thrusts of the present investigation. This study begins with a close scrutiny of the three 1096 narratives. The boundaries of each is clearly delineated, and each is carefully examined in its entirety in an effort to ascertain, first of all, its literary integrity. I conclude that the *Mainz Anonymous* is the work of a single historical imagination; the *Solomon bar Simson Chronicle* a compilation of prior compositions, each of which must be carefully identified and analyzed; and the *Eliezer bar Nathan Chronicle* a reworking of the *Solomon bar Simson Chronicle,* highlighted by the addition of poetic dirges over the destroyed Jewish communities of the Rhineland. Among the compositions absorbed by the editor of the *Solomon bar Simson Chronicle*—in addition to the *Mainz Anonymous*—are a striking depiction of events in Trier and a radically different account of the destruction of Cologne Jewry. Thus, the three narratives actually provide us with five distinct perspectives on the events of 1096.

After the five available post-1096 voices are scrupulously identified, the next items addressed are the dating and the objectives of each independent literary unit, two interrelated issues. Dating will help clarify objectives, and objectives will help clarify dating. In a general way, the earlier compositions—the *Mainz Anonymous* and the Trier unit of the *Solomon bar Simson Chronicle*—reflect the fullest time-bound orientation. Those voices at the greatest distance from the events tend, not surprisingly, to lose the time-bound focus and highlight the timeless. I argue that the *Mainz Anonymous*—like the Orléans letter noted earlier—is unique in its effort to integrate the time-bound and the timeless. These matters, all involving close analysis of the three 1096 narratives, occupy the first half of the study.

The second half of the book is organized in terms of issues, rather than sources. In the light of the analysis of the discrete literary units in the first half of the book, I clarify the time-bound and the timeless objectives of the diverse voices available to us. Close examination of the varied time-bound objectives of our authors leads readily to consideration of the facticity of the data provided in the narratives. If time-bound objectives did indeed animate our authors, what implications does this have for the reliability of the data transmitted in the narratives? Did the time-bound objectives necessitate an effort to transmit verifiable and reliable information?

Careful consideration of the timeless messages of the narrators leads in an alternative direction—the identification of an innovative sense of the complex relationship between the divine and the human in shaping the course of history. At the close of this study, the innovativeness of this seemingly new style of historical narrative and this seemingly new conceptualization of God, humanity, and history—an innovativeness suggested, for example, in the Yerushalmi and Mintz studies—is rigorously examined. Is it possible to discover precedents in either the classical or the medieval literature of the Jews? If not, are there alternative models for this innovative style of historical writing and these innovative formulations of the interaction of the divine and the human? Again, these far-reaching considerations are ultimately rooted in a close reading of each of the literary units discernible in our three narratives. From the particular to the more general is the broad organizing principle of this study.

CHAPTER TWO

The *Mainz Anonymous*

Structure, Authorship, Dating,
and Objectives

Of the three Hebrew First Crusade narratives, the *Eliezer bar Nathan Chronicle* has been the most widely copied and read; more recently, scholarly attention has focused on the so-called *Solomon bar Simson Chronicle.*[1] However, it has been my sense for some time now that the most interesting, impressive, and valuable of the three compositions is the *Mainz Anonymous.*[2] The *Eliezer bar Nathan Chronicle*—I shall argue—is but an epitome of the lengthier *Solomon bar Simson Chronicle,* with poetic additions;[3] the *Solomon bar Simson Chronicle* is a rich but often maladroit compilation of a variety of independent sources;[4] the *Mainz Anonymous* is a tightly organized, carefully conceptualized narrative, written by one person quite close in time to the events themselves. The burden of this chapter is to lay bare the tight organization and careful conceptualization of the *Mainz Anonymous,* to argue for unitary authorship, to make the case for early composition, and to identify the diverse objectives of the gifted author.

The *Mainz Anonymous,* as we now have it, is a truncated text. It begins: "It came to pass in the year 1028 after the destruction of the [Second] Temple." It ends: "All these things have been done by those whom we have specified by name. The rest of the community [of Mainz] and the leaders of the congregation—what they did and how they acted for the unity of the Name of the King of kings, the Holy One, may he be blessed, like R. Akiba and his associates."[5] The text we now have is preceded by the copyist's remark: "I shall begin the account of the per-

secution of yore. May God protect us and all Israel from persecution."
It concludes with a further comment by the copyist: "There is missing
here I know not how much. May God save us from this exile. The
[account of] the persecution of yore is completed."[6] In the manuscript
these comments are identified as the copyist's by dots over both the
introductory and concluding observations. We thus obviously have the
opening of the original text and lack some portion of the close.[7]

What has survived of the *Mainz Anonymous* is presented in a smooth
and uninterrupted third-person narrative; unlike the *Solomon bar Simson Chronicle*, it contains no first-person interjections.[8] The *Mainz
Anonymous*, as we now have it, does not aspire to recount the entire
story of Christian violence and Jewish suffering in 1096. It focuses
closely on three great Rhineland communities—Speyer, Worms, and
Mainz—and includes requisite background information. The narrative
divides neatly into four consecutive segments: the early development of
the crusade and its attendant anti-Jewish hostilities, the abortive assault
on Speyer Jewry, the two costly attacks on the Jewish community of
Worms, and the deadly anti-Jewish violence in Mainz.[9] The progression
of the narrative is seamless; the story moves effortlessly along a chron-
ological continuum that stretches from the first announcement of the
crusade, which took place in late 1095, through the destruction of
Mainz Jewry in late May 1096.[10]

While the *Solomon bar Simson Chronicle* begins with a broad and
theologically oriented prologue to the events of spring 1096, the *Mainz
Anonymous* whisks the reader immediately into a careful sequential report on the events of late 1095 and early 1096. This chain of events was
initiated by the sudden eruption of the First Crusade in northern France
and was propelled by the enthusiasm of both the nobility and the broad
populace in France for the crusading enterprise.[11] The goals of this totally unanticipated new effort were to conquer Jerusalem and to reclaim
the Holy Sepulcher. The exhilaration produced by these twin objectives
evoked powerful anti-Jewish sentiment among some of the French crusading forces. The reportage of these related developments is crisp, to
the point, and corresponds precisely to information provided in other
sources, both Christian and Jewish.[12]

Having described the crusade and its attendant anti-Jewish hostility,
the author of the *Mainz Anonymous* next turns to the reactions of
French Jewry. Given their proximity to the point of earliest development
of the crusade, the Jews of northern France sensed immediately the destructive potential of the new venture. In their fright, they turned to the

revered Jewish communities of the Rhineland, seeking the prayers of these distinguished brethren on their behalf. Allowing himself to indulge in a bit of tragic irony, the author of the *Mainz Anonymous*—almost certainly a Rhineland Jew—reports a response by the leaders of Mainz Jewry that highlights the utter ignorance of the new danger among his confreres. To be sure, they were not to remain oblivious for very long.

Immediately after depicting the insulation of Rhineland Jewry from awareness of the crusade and its dangers, the *Mainz Anonymous* portrays the early movement of French crusading bands eastward into areas of western Germany. The author describes these crusading bands as seeking provisions and indicates that the German Jews acceded quickly to these requests (perhaps demands might be more accurate). These observations are thoroughly corroborated by the Trier unit of the *Solomon bar Simson Chronicle,* which depicts the arrival of the crusading band that coalesced around Peter the Hermit. The Trier unit describes in fuller detail the crusaders' demand for provisions and Jewish acquiescence. Indeed, the Trier unit and the opening segment of the *Mainz Anonymous* agree further in noting that, although Jewish contributions to the provisioning of the French crusaders successfully obviated any anti-Jewish violence by these French crusaders, their movement through western Germany occasioned the arousal of the heretofore peaceful Rhineland burghers.[13]

The passage of the French crusaders set in motion yet another dangerous development. A number of German barons were attracted to the crusading ideal, moved by promises of otherworldly reward for participation in the sacred mission.[14] As had already happened in France, the response of the nobility was accompanied by broader enthusiasm on the part of the lower classes. All this is, once more, well attested in the Christian sources.[15] We might note in particular that Peter the Hermit left the Rhineland fairly rapidly, thus eliminating any possibility that the new crusading recruits might be brought under his direct control. The German bands stirred up by the passage of the French and by the preaching of their leaders were yet more radical in their thinking and behavior than the French forces of Peter.[16]

Just as had happened in France, German crusading ardor was quickly refracted into hostility against the Jews. Once again, the *Mainz Anonymous* highlights the leadership of Mainz Jewry. Now, these leaders undertook prayers and fasts on behalf of Rhineland Jewry itself. What had earlier been a distant danger—the problem of others—had come far closer to home. Indeed, this rich segment of our narrative ends with an indication that the entreaties of the Rhineland Jews went unanswered, that hostility was transformed into overt—although as yet random—acts of violence: "For the crusaders came wearing their signs [i.e., their crosses], with their standards planted before our houses. When they saw one of us, they ran after him and pierced him with their spears, to the point that we were fearful of stepping beyond our thresholds."[17]

What we have seen thus far is careful reconstruction of early anti-Jewish violence in the Rhineland. Our author is anxious to provide accurate information on the broad development of the crusade, on the elements in the Christian population that became hostile to the Jews, on the thinking that animated these hostile groupings, and on the diverse forms of anti-Jewish behavior to which this thinking led. In all this there is no significant theological speculation; this portrayal is the work of an observer committed, for a variety of reasons, to an accurate reconstruction of a set of events. Other sources, both Christian and Jewish, provide recurrent confirmation of the reliability of the *Mainz Anonymous* account.

These same interests and tendencies are apparent in the Speyer segment of the *Mainz Anonymous*. The author is concerned to portray intensifying danger and does so effectively. By the end of the opening section of his account, he has reached the point of random violence, with Jews fearful of stepping outside their homes. Events in Speyer take this incipient violence yet a step further. The narrative indicates that the persecution in Speyer was the work of a coalition of crusaders and burghers (*to'im ve-'ironim*), a combination of anti-Jewish forces that was to recur elsewhere. In fact, the *Mainz Anonymous* had already noted that German burghers and German crusaders had both been aroused by the passage of the French forces. Now these two groups began to collaborate with each other, although only in the most rudimentary way.

The violence in Speyer is depicted as relatively casual. At no point in the account of events that took place on the Sabbath of 3 May 1096 does an organized crusading force make an appearance. Rather, the narrative relates that a loose combination of crusaders and burghers planned to seize the Jews at their morning prayers in the synagogue. Forewarned, the Jews of Speyer prayed earlier than usual and regained the safety of their homes. All this suggests a relatively low level of danger. This changes a few weeks later: the Jews of Worms and Mainz would hardly be slipping into the synagogue a bit early and then heading home. At this slightly later juncture, only the strongest fortifications offered the possibility of safety. Clearly, the coalition of crusaders and burghers that threatened the Jews of Speyer was as yet somewhat weak. Nonetheless, eleven Jews lost their lives in this ill-conceived and ill-prepared anti-Jewish assault.

The relative weakness of the attack is reflected in the successful countermeasures taken by Bishop John of Speyer. While there is no reason to suspect the sincerity of John's desire to save his Jews, there is similarly no real doubt as to the parallel commitment of the bishop of Worms and the archbishop of Mainz to save their Jews.[18] The critical difference, it seems, lay in the strength of the anti-Jewish forces at work. Our author is concerned to specify the precise actions taken by Bishop John. They were three: he gathered the Jews into his fortified chambers for immediate protection; he punished a number of the burgher malefactors by chopping off their hands;[19] and he subsequently removed the Jews of Speyer into rural fortifications, in which they managed to survive the dangerous weeks of May 1096.

The *Mainz Anonymous* is lavish in its praise of Bishop John of Speyer. Two more figures are also noted positively. The first is the emperor. According to our narrative, Bishop John's sequestering of the Jews of Speyer was achieved through some kind of imperial assistance, although the precise nature of this intervention is not spelled out. Mentioned more clearly is the energetic *parnas* of Speyer Jewry, Moses ben Yekutiel. This highly placed Jew is cited as having influenced the bishop toward his protection of the Jews of Speyer; he is also praised for his subsequent activities on behalf of those forcibly converted, activities that eventuated in their return to Judaism.[20]

The *Mainz Anonymous* makes a passing but important observation with respect to the Jews of Speyer and their circumstances in the rural fortifications to which they were removed: "They remained there, fasting, weeping, and mourning; they were deeply despairing of their lives. For every day, there gathered against them crusaders, gentiles, Emicho—may his bones be ground up!—and the populace, in order to seize them and to destroy them."[21] Thus, our author, in telling the story of Speyer Jewry, was well aware of Count Emicho and his followers. The decision not to accord Emicho a role in the abortive assault on Speyer Jewry was conscious on his part. Emicho was in the vicinity, but he was not part of the disorganized Sabbath attack on the Jews of Speyer.

Indeed, it is yet more striking that the author of the *Mainz Anonymous* did not make Count Emicho part of his tale of Worms Jewry. Again, this was not a casual oversight. The assault on Worms Jewry is portrayed as an intermediary stage between the random violence inflicted by the German crusaders in general and, more specifically, by a loose coalition of crusaders and burghers in Speyer on the one hand and the thoroughly militarized crusading attack launched by Count Emicho and his band in Mainz on the other. Worms Jewry was the victim of more organized violence than had taken place heretofore, but these Jews had not yet been exposed to the most organized and intensive effort to destroy a Rhineland Jewish community.

Worms Jewry is presented as learning quickly of the loss of life in Speyer and recognizing—although hardly fully—the extent of the threat it now faced. Seemingly alerted as none of their peers had yet been, the Jews of Worms were still uncertain as to how profound the threat was and how best to meet it. The community divided into two groups. The more confident chose to remain at home, whereas the more anxious opted for safety in the bishop's palace.[22]

According to the *Mainz Anonymous,* a loose coalition of crusaders and burghers was once more set in motion, this time through a ruse.[23] A Christian corpse was paraded through town by conspirators, who claimed that the Jews had boiled this recently buried corpse and had poured the resultant fluids into the town water supply in an effort to poison the populace of Worms.[24] In the supercharged atmosphere of 1096, this allegation was sufficient to spark a riot against those Jews who had elected to remain in their homes. It is at this juncture that our author, for the first time, depicts acts of Jewish martyrdom and introduces a dirge of sorts in honor of these martyrs. This is the first point at which the relatively spare historical account is broken. Interestingly, at precisely this point, the *Mainz Anonymous* also speaks for the first time of Jews who chose to convert. It goes to considerable lengths to present the honorable motives that led to this decision, the obvious insincerity of the conversion, and the support the converts received from their brethren who had more wisely sought safety in the bishop's palace.

While the decision to seek safety in the bishop's palace was surely the saner course, the intensifying animosities of May 1096 made this seeming haven ultimately unavailing. Even here, at the point of the most fully orchestrated assault thus far depicted, no organized crusader army had yet made its appearance. The narrator is once more quite concerned to specify the anti-Jewish elements involved. They included the two groups recurrently noted, crusaders and burghers, augmented by a new group—villagers from the surrounding countryside. For the first time, the author portrays full-scale battle. The bishop's palace represented a formidable challenge to the anti-Jewish coalition. The kind of random violence heretofore described was no longer possible, since the remaining Worms Jews were ensconced in a defensible refuge. What was required now was military siege by the coalition of crusaders, burghers, and villagers. "They [the members of this coalition] besieged them [the Jews ensconced in the palace] and battled them. There took place a very great battle, one force against the other, until they [the crusaders, burghers, and villagers] seized the chambers where the children of the sacred covenant were."[25] The author of the *Mainz Anonymous* has carefully and explicitly identified a new level of hostility.

Not surprisingly, at precisely this juncture the narrative also portrays a new level of Jewish martyrdom. In the account of the events in Speyer, there is only the briefest mention of eleven Jews losing their lives. For the first assault in Worms, the *Mainz Anonymous* describes more fully and more feelingly the killing of larger numbers of Jews, accompanied by a first dirge in honor of the martyrs. The second assault on Worms Jewry, which constituted a new stage in the anti-Jewish violence, called forth a new form of Jewish response. Here, for the first time, we encounter Jews killing themselves and their kin, a far more radical martyrdom than the submission to death at the hands of the crusaders depicted thus far.[26]

At this point, the *Mainz Anonymous* introduces an effective literary pattern (utilized in the Mainz segment as well), consisting of generalized statements that provide an overview of Jewish martyrological responses, followed by highly moving depictions of individual martyrs and their actions. Thus, after a broad statement on the willingness of Worms Jews to offer themselves as sacrifices and to slaughter their children out of devotion to the God of Israel, the author proceeds to reconstruct the unusual act of a Jew named Meshullam ben Isaac, who put himself into an Abraham-like posture and prepared to emulate the patriarch's readiness to sacrifice his son Isaac. After a spirited interchange with his wife and after securing the assent of the boy to the sacrifice, Meshullam ben Isaac moved beyond the patriarch Abraham, actually taking the life of the lad before rushing forth with his wife to encounter death at the hands of the enemy. Striking in this account is the portrayal of the Jewish martyrs' need to make their radical acts willful by articulating their allegiance to God. Although the articulations of the martyrs were, in all likelihood, uttered in the vernacular, the narrator artfully presents them in a Hebrew version that highlights intertextual references to the biblical story in Genesis 22, thereby reinforcing Meshullam ben Isaac's emulation of Abraham.[27]

The *Mainz Anonymous* provides three more discrete episodes, intended to flesh out the broad portrait of Jewish martyrdom and to emphasize some of its salient features. The story of Isaac ben Daniel focuses the reader's attention on the bestiality of the enemy in its effort to bring Jews to conversion and, in the process, affords an opportunity to reiterate the unflagging devotion of the Jewish martyrs, all pain notwithstanding.

The story of Simhah *ha-cohen* introduces for the first time the Christian argument that the catastrophe itself was overwhelming evidence of divine abandonment, rendering absurd any Jewish behavior other than conversion. The same episode also introduces the theme of Jewish aggression, with Simhah feigning willingness for conversion in order to be brought into the presence of the bishop, where he takes vengeance for the episcopal failure. Simhah is portrayed as killing three Christians and utterly terrifying others, until the breaking of his knife turns him into a defenseless target.

The last of the four specific episodes involves a Jewess who had been successful in escaping the two rounds of slaughter in Worms proper by hiding with sympathetic Christians outside town. The story has its puzzling aspects. After protecting her through the periods of actual assault, her Christian friends turned upon her, seemingly moved by the notion that the carnage in Worms served as irrefutable proof of divine rejection and that the surviving Jews thus had no reasonable option other than baptism. These strangely sympathetic protectors implored her to convert. Precisely why such friends should then be moved to put her to death is not altogether clear. What the author seems to be trying to convey is a broad message of the ultimate unreliability of Christian associates, no matter how well-disposed they might seem: the chaos spawned by the crusade turned once trustworthy allies into unpredictable enemies. Again, the individual episodes allow for the substantiation of the general pattern, as well as for the introduction of diversified and nuanced Jewish behaviors.

The portrayal of the martyrdom of Worms Jewry ends with a return to generalization, concluding with praise of the martyrs and prayerful conviction of their eternal reward. The combination of detailed information and mournful praise is by no means surprising. We regularly encounter the same combination in the Christian crusade narratives.[28]

The Mainz unit of the *Mainz Anonymous* is the fullest of its four component segments. The broad tendencies already noted in the depiction of both Christian and Jewish behaviors remain very much in evidence. The sense of the progressive deepening of hostility and danger established throughout the previous three sections of the narrative is carefully maintained. The fate of Mainz Jewry shows, on the one hand, direct continuity with foregoing developments; at the same time, the Mainz story introduces new elements into the picture. The Mainz unit represents in effect the culmination of tendencies so precisely plotted by our author.

Events in Mainz are presented as the next stage in the escalation of the anti-Jewish violence that began sporadically and then spiraled into the Speyer and Worms episodes. The Mainz segment begins by indicating that Jewry's awareness of the events in Speyer and Worms, which prompt the Jews of Mainz to address prayers to the divine authority and to initiate negotiations with the local terrestrial powers.[29] Depiction of the negotiations is particularly striking. Writing in the wake of the near-total destruction of Mainz Jewry, the author vacillates in his portrait of the local archbishop and his associates, accusing them first of harmful intentions and then reversing himself by describing a genuine desire to assist that turned out badly.[30]

While the narrator describes the Mainz episode as a culmination of the tensions that had expressed themselves in random violence and in the assaults on Speyer and Worms, he at the same time acknowledges that Mainz Jewry did not need the evidence from neighboring communities to become unsettled by the dangers threatening it. We recall that the French Jews had written to their Rhineland brethren in the closing months of 1095, which had elicited a tragically insouciant response from the Jewish leadership in Mainz. The subsequent passage of French crusaders through the Rhineland and the animosities they stirred up had already occasioned intense fasting and prayer in Mainz.

Indeed, the narrator deftly informs us that there had been warning signs in the town of Mainz itself. He depicts a fascinating incident in which an allegedly wondrous goose and its mistress aroused some of the Mainz burghers with the argument, already encountered, that divine favor for the crusaders was an indication of the rupture of God's covenant with the Jews.[31] Jewish straits were once more projected as evidence of Jewish error and divine repudiation. This claim divided a group of Christians, with crusaders and their burgher allies railing against the Jews and a separate group of burghers stepping forth to protect their endangered Jewish neighbors. This incident frightened the Jews of Mainz profoundly, moving them to abandon their homes and their synagogue.

A second incident deepened Jewish fears. A pair of Jews who lived near the synagogue allegedly heard the sounds of weeping emanating from the abandoned sanctuary. Assuming that some of the Jews sequestered in the archbishop's palace had made their way surreptitiously to the synagogue, these two Jews—who had curiously enough elected to remain in their homes—hastened there.[32] Finding the building locked, these two Jews perceived the weeping to be a divine sign of impending disaster and informed their brethren in the archbishop's palace and in the burgrave's palace of their experience. These Jews also interpreted the event as a divine portent of catastrophe.

At this juncture, with most of Mainz Jewry holed up in fortified buildings and profoundly shaken, a new stage in the anti-Jewish violence is introduced, with the appearance for the first time of an organized crusader band, the band that had coalesced around the central figure of Count Emicho.[33] Our author relates that, because of the precautionary closing of the town gates, Emicho and his troops were forced to camp for two days outside Mainz. The Jews utilized this period to attempt negotiations with the count. In effect, the Jews of Mainz sought—unsuccessfully—to emulate the tactics of their French brethren, offering both immediate support and letters addressed to other Jewish communities urging similar assistance to the crusaders. What had worked in France, at an earlier and different stage of the development of anti-Jewish hostility, failed utterly outside Mainz.

Emicho's army did not have to storm the gates of Mainz. According to the *Mainz Anonymous,* easy access into the town was effected through the collaboration of sympathetic burghers, who simply opened the gates in defiance of the authorities. Emicho and his crusaders made their way directly to the palace of the archbishop, besieging it in formal military fashion. The militia of the archbishop—as well as the archbishop himself—beat a hasty retreat. The Jews organized their own protective force and attempted to carry on the battle against Emicho's army, but their efforts were unavailing. The crusaders fought their way into the palace, and the fate of the Jews gathered therein was sealed.

The martyrdom of the Jews sequestered in the archbishop's palace in Mainz is described in somewhat more detail than is any prior martyrdom. Even here, however, while arguing the uniqueness of this martyrdom and portraying it in broad—even cosmic—terms, the author of the *Mainz Anonymous* remains sensitive to terrestrial specifics. Thus, he begins with the efforts of those Jews who fought to keep the crusaders at bay and notes the escape of some of these armed Jews, under the leadership of Kalonymous ben Meshullam, into the recesses of the arch-bishop's palace. The first unarmed victims of crusader fury were Isaac bar Moses and a group of followers, who chose to submit passively to the blows of Count Emicho's troops as they made their way into the courtyard.

Still proceeding sequentially, the narrator focuses on the activist mar-tyrdom of most of the Jews now exposed to the crusaders' wrath. The radical pattern of Jews dying at their own hands, noted first in Worms, predominates in the courtyard of the archbishop of Mainz.[34] These Jews are made to proclaim in the most moving terms their absolute devotion to the God of Israel and their willingness to die on his behalf. Imagery of the Temple and its cultic practice abounds in these exhortations, as does conviction of immediate otherworldly reward. Special notice is made of the role of the Jewish women in the courtyard. "The pure women threw money outside [that is to say, out of the courtyard], in order to distract them [the crusaders] a bit, until they [the Jews in the courtyard] might slaughter their children. Moreover, the hands of mer-ciful women strangled their children, in order to do the will of their Creator."[35]

Ever focused on the detailed picture, the author next describes the crusaders moving from the courtyard up into the chambers of the palace. Breaking down the doors to these chambers, the crusaders found Jews in the throes of self-inflicted death. The narrator highlights one room that held out longer than the others. He depicts general behaviors on the part of the Jews in that room, including the reviling of the crusaders, the killing of children by the adult Jews, and then their own suicide. At this point, the narrator once more fills out the broad picture by focusing on one specific Jewess and her children. The story of Rachel the daughter of Isaac is the fullest and most moving of the specific martyrological accounts in the *Mainz Anonymous*.

From the archbishop's palace, the exhilarated crusaders proceeded to the second major refuge of Mainz Jewry, the palace of the local bur-grave. There too battle took place, with the crusaders victorious. Once more, a set of Jews lost their protection and lay exposed to death. Again, the author fills out the general depiction by describing in some detail the behaviors of specific Jews. The end result was the thorough destruc-tion of this second large enclave of Mainz Jews.

According to the *Mainz Anonymous*, Count Emicho and his follow-ers were determined to hunt down every last Jewish refuge. Although the bulk of Mainz Jewry had already perished, the crusaders continued to seek out Jews who had hidden themselves elsewhere. The story of David *ha-gabbai,* who had sought safety with a friendly priest, is told in some detail. More sketchily drawn is the portrait of Samuel ben Naaman, a Jew who had elected to remain in his home.[36] It is at this point that our narrative's account of the fate of Mainz Jewry is abruptly terminated. It is impossible to determine what might be missing from the original text.[37]

Having completed a close look at the structure of the *Mainz Anonymous,* what have we learned? I would argue, first of all, that our scrutiny of the narrative indicates decisively the hand of one author. The seamless flow of the narrative and the consistent interests and themes all point to one historical imagination underlying the account. To be sure, no single Jew could have witnessed firsthand the successive stages of crusader violence portrayed in the *Mainz Anonymous.* Clearly, our author absorbed evidence from a variety of oral and—perhaps—written sources. Nonetheless, the anonymous narrator spun his materials into a well-organized and coherent record that moves from the incipient violence of late 1095 in France down through the near-total destruction of Mainz Jewry in May 1096. As noted, the *Mainz Anonymous* was surely not intended as an overall portrait of Jewish fate during the First Crusade. Its focus was obviously the fate of the three great Rhineland Jewish communities of Speyer, Worms, and Mainz, with fullest attention lavished on the last and arguably greatest of the three. These three Jewish communities were at least fortunate in having a gifted narrator tell their tale.

Let us proceed to identify the objectives of our author, utilizing the categories of the time-bound and the timeless already established. Clearly, much of the *Mainz Anonymous* was addressed to time-bound concerns. Our author was committed to providing maximal information on the genesis and development of the First Crusade, on the groupings in Christian society that responded to the exciting new initiative, on the diverse Christian reactions to crusading and crusaders, on the refraction of crusading ardor into hostility against the Jews, on the stances of different elements in Rhineland society toward the endangered Jews, and on the varied Jewish responses to the utterly unanticipated danger. Depiction of these multifaceted realities is highlighted by the author's insistence that the developments of late 1095 and early 1096 were stunning and disorienting in their rapidity and by his conviction that Christian and Jewish thinking and behavior were, as a result, chaotic and highly diversified.

As we have seen, the leitmotif of the *Mainz Anonymous*'s presentation is the breathless pace at which events developed. Early on, when French Jewry experienced the emergence of the crusade, it addressed petitions to its Rhineland brethren, who knew nothing of the new threat. The French crusaders, whose arrival in the Rhineland was unanticipated by both Christians and Jews, stirred up the local barony and the lower classes in utterly unpredictable ways. Despite instances of random violence and the first clumsy assault in Speyer, Worms Jewry was uncertain as to how to proceed, with the community divided in its responses. Even in Mainz, by far the best forewarned of the three communities depicted, there was a measure of uncertainty, with Jews opting for safety in the archbishop's palace, in the burgrave's palace, or in private homes.

Not surprisingly, the unanticipated enthusiasm for the crusade and the rapidly escalating violence produced chaos, uncertainty, and the widest possible spectrum of responses among Christians and Jews. Our narrator highlights this diversity of action and reaction. The *Mainz Anonymous* transmitted to its Jewish readers a precise sense of wide-ranging Christian attitudes and behaviors. As we have seen, it depicts carefully the mix of Christians who participated in the anti-Jewish assaults, the varied responses of other Christians at this crucial juncture, in some instances the contradictory behaviors of specific groups of Christians (e.g., the burghers of Worms who first protected and then persecuted the Jewess Minna, and the archbishop of Mainz who confidently promised protection and then utterly failed to provide it), the steady deepening of anti-Jewish sentiment, and the increasingly intense violence to which these feelings led.

Our author shows considerable commitment to informing his Jewish readers as fully as possible about their Christian contemporaries. His assumption rather clearly is that Jews would go on living among these Christian neighbors and that accurate information on patterns of Christian thinking and behavior would be extremely useful for this future coexistence. To be sure, there had been no way to predict the explosion of 1096, and future developments might of course take similarly unanticipated forms. Nonetheless, the fullest possible knowledge of the complexities of 1096 would provide useful guidance for further eruptions.[38]

The *Mainz Anonymous*'s time-bound interest in a variety of Jewish responses is similarly manifest. While martyrdom is certainly at the center of the author's interest, for reasons we shall examine shortly, the narrative by no means focuses exclusively on Jewish martyrdom. Diverse

Jewish attempts to forestall violence through the increasingly turbulent months of late 1095 and early 1096 are identified. These efforts were on occasion successful and on occasion unsuccessful.[39] The Worms segment of the narrative introduces, along with the first significant martyrdoms, the initial instances of Jewish conversion. To be sure, the most stirring of the Jewish responses recounted involve Jewish willingness to sacrifice life for the God of Israel.

Interestingly, even in depicting the Jewish martyrs, our author maintains his commitment to portraying rapid developments in thinking and behavior and the widest possible range of martyrological responses. Clearly, Jewish martyrological fervor intensifies as we proceed from Speyer to Worms to Mainz. Jewish martyrdom is portrayed in the *Mainz Anonymous* in all its specificity and diversity. Jews fought and died; Jews were slaughtered by their enemies; Jews provoked their foes by words and deeds of opposition, thus hastening their death at the hands of these aggressors; Jews took their own lives in a number of ways; Jews took the lives of their family members, most strikingly the lives of their children, again in a variety of ways. The Jewish martyrs do not fall into simple categories: they include men and women, the aged and the young, high born and lowly. The commitment to accurate portrayal of complex realities on the Christian side is paralleled by a similar commitment to nuanced depiction of diversified Jewish thinking and behavior.

Time-bound concern with the variety of Jewish responses to the crisis of 1096 is both didactic and apologetic. The centrality of martyrdom in the *Mainz Anonymous* was surely intended to urge such a course of action upon Jewish readers, at least when no other alternatives were available.[40]

While the didactic objectives of the *Mainz Anonymous* are fairly obvious, the apologetic thrusts should not be ignored. Our narrator argues in effect that his fellow Jews were hardly obtuse in their failure to appreciate the depths of the danger confronting them. Early on, in depicting the letter of the French Jews and the insouciant Rhineland response, the author imputes Jewish ignorance to divine decree. In a broader way, his portrait suggests repeatedly that the Rhineland Jews are hardly to be condemned for their failure to understand that this new and utterly unanticipated phenomenon—the First Crusade—might pose a potent threat to their well-being.

Equally apologetic is the thoroughly sympathetic portrait of the Jewish converts in Worms. Given the heavy focus on martyrdom, we might well have anticipated a condemnation of conversion or at least an obscuring of this reality. Not so in the *Mainz Anonymous*. The motivations for conversion are presented positively and the response of fellow Jews is portrayed as accepting and understanding.

Finally, some of the martyrs who are the heroes of the *Mainz Anonymous* also required apologetic justification. As noted, the martyrdoms of 1096 were carried out in a variety of ways. When Jews allowed themselves to be slain by their enemies rather than accept conversion, their behaviors were fully within the established legal norms of Jewish tradition and were consonant with the precedents established by earlier Jewish martyrs.[41] Suicide was far more problematic, although at least one major talmudic precedent could be cited and in fact was.[42] Murder of others was both unprecedented and highly problematic.[43] In effect, the author of the *Mainz Anonymous* made a case for the rectitude of the extreme forms of Jewish martyrdom through his lavish and laudatory depiction of such martyrs.

The Rhineland Jews of 1096 were hardly fools; the converts from Judaism were not to be condemned; the martyrs who behaved in unprecedented ways were not aberrant. More positive is the author's assertion that the Rhineland martyrs—all of them—were extraordinary heroes. As we shall see shortly, the Jewish martyrs played a key role in the understanding of the meaning of the tragedy presented in the *Mainz Anonymous;* there was a metahistorical, timeless quality to their actions. On a more terrestrial level, the reality of great Jewish heroism required adequate memorialization on the part of our author, which he furnished brilliantly. There is a palpable sense of responsibility to the deceased to enshrine properly the grandeur of their actions.

The heavy focus on the time-bound in the *Mainz Anonymous* constitutes the most compelling argument for its early dating. As noted already, initial readings of the narrative suggested a fourteenth-century provenance; more recently a mid-twelfth-century dating has been proposed. I have argued of late for a much earlier dating, indeed a dating close to the events themselves.[44]

A close look at two specific passages in the *Mainz Anonymous* serves to introduce the argument for early composition. An interesting digression during its portrait of the fate of Speyer Jewry provides two useful pieces of evidence with respect to the date of composition. While lauding Bishop John of Speyer for his energetic and effective protection of Speyer Jewry, our author praises Moses *ha-parnas* of Speyer for his role also: "R. Moses ben Yekutiel *ha-parnas* stood in the breach as well and dedicated himself to them [the Jews of Speyer]. Through him, all those forcibly converted who remained throughout the empire of Henry returned [to the Jewish faith]."[45] This brief digression provides us, first of all, with a clear *terminus a quo* for the composition of the *Mainz Anonymous*. Since the return to Judaism of those forcibly converted took place in June 1097, the *Mainz Anonymous* cannot have been written prior to that date.[46] At the same time, reference to "the empire of Henry" suggests a fairly early date, at least before the death of Henry IV in 1106. It seems highly unlikely that a much later Jewish author would designate the empire as Henry's long after his demise.[47]

A second reference in the text is more ambiguous. In depicting the passage of the French crusaders through German territory, the narrative describes them as "battalion after battalion, like the army of Sennacherib."[48] The image of the army of Sennacherib was seemingly introduced to imply failure to conquer Jerusalem.[49] This image might conceivably be taken to refer to the crusaders in their entirety and to suggest a Jewish hope expressed before the stunning victory of 1099. Given the narrative's excellent information and precision, however, it seems likelier that the image was introduced to highlight the failure of the French bands that crossed Germany to reach their destination and to participate in the achievement of 1099. This likelier reading of "the army of Sennacherib" thus shows Jewish awareness of the disasters that befell the popular French crusading forces that coalesced around Peter the Hermit during the late spring and summer of 1096, reinforcing our *terminus a quo*, rather than our *terminus ad quem*. The overall sense with which we are left is of a narrative that was composed no sooner than a year after the events depicted, but surely not decades later.

While these two specific items are useful, the most telling evidence for the early composition of the *Mainz Anonymous* is its strong time-bound orientation. A Jewish author writing in the middle decades of the twelfth century would have been most unlikely to have shown the same concern for the details of Christian and Jewish thinking and behavior. As we shall see, the Cologne segment of the *Solomon bar Simson Chronicle*, surely dated toward the middle of the twelfth century, is utterly devoid of this time-bound orientation.[50] Moreover, the accuracy of the *Mainz Anonymous* information on the development of the crusade and the early behavior and thinking of the lay crusaders reinforces the sense of an account composed while accurate recollections were still fresh.[51] The author's interest and the accuracy of his information combine to provide a sense of early provenance, with all the implications that early provenance provides.

One of the most striking aspects of the time-bound message of the *Mainz Anonymous* is the careful spatial and temporal plotting the author furnishes. His story moves precisely from France through Speyer through Worms through Mainz; dating is likewise painstakingly plotted, beginning in late 1095 and moving the reader rapidly but sequentially through the bloody days of May 1096.[52] At the same time, however, the author establishes another set of spatial and temporal dimensions to his account. On a different plane, the *Mainz Anonymous* takes us from the Rhineland to Jerusalem to hell and/or paradise and moves us temporally from the precreation void through the immortality of afterlife.

These alternative planes are invoked with the opening words of the *Mainz Anonymous:* "It came to pass in the year 1028 after the destruction of the [Second] Temple."[53] Immediately, we as readers are transported to another time and place. On the spatial plane, the precise focus on the Rhineland towns of Speyer, Worms, and Mainz is counterpointed with heavy emphasis on Jerusalem.[54] The Holy City was, after all, the goal of the Christian undertaking, an enterprise that the Jewish narrator went to considerable lengths to demean. Thus, our author depicts the crusaders as moved by the yearning to travel to "Jerusalem the Holy City and to reach the sepulcher of the crucified, a trampled corpse that can neither profit nor aid."[55] In response to and rebuttal of the crusaders' emphasis on Christian Jerusalem, the Rhineland Jews and their memorializer constantly evoke recollections of the Jewish Jerusalem and its sacred Temple. In the course of lamenting the pious Jews of Mainz, poised on the brink of destruction, our narrator concludes: "Alas for them! For, from the day on which the Second Temple was destroyed, there have been none like them. Subsequently, there will be none like them."[56] The crusaders may have thought that they were setting out to recapture the glory of Jerusalem; in the eyes of the *Mainz Anonymous,* however, it was the Jewish victims of the crusaders' excesses who were truly linking themselves to the sanctity of the Holy City.

The Rhineland martyrs and the Jerusalem Temple are regularly associated by our narrator. Twice he interrupts his generally spare account to introduce brief outbursts—one from Isaiah and the second from Lamentations—that introduce imagery of the destruction of the First Temple.[57] More striking yet, our narrator recurrently portrays the martyrs as offering themselves as sacrifices on the Temple altar. Thus, he depicts the martyrs of Worms gathered in the bishop's palace, upon seeing their battle lost, in the following terms: "They accepted the divine judgment and put their trust in their Creator and offered up true sacrifices."[58]

Likewise, in his description of the slaughter of her four children by Rachel in Mainz, our author recurrently uses the verb *z-v-ḥ,* indicating her slaughter of these youngsters as a sacrificial offering.[59]

Related to the Temple imagery is the recurring figure of the patriarch Abraham preparing to offer his son Isaac in response to divine command, an act seen by later Jewish tradition as a precursor of the subsequent Temple ritual. We recall the actions of the Jew Meshullam ben Isaac in Worms, who re-created the Abraham-Isaac paradigm with his own son Isaac. Noting the parallel of the biblical Isaac and the Worms Isaac, both born to aged mothers, he pursues the parallel by suggesting that he too would "offer him up as did Abraham our father with his son Isaac."[60] He then went beyond the act of his ancestor, actually slaughtering the lad, since no divine stay of execution intervened. The image of the *ʿakedah*—of Abraham's binding of his son Isaac—recurs regularly. "Ask and see! Was there ever such a multiple *ʿakedah* as this, from the days of the first Adam?"[61]

The spatial dimensions of the tale are drastically expanded from the narrow confines of the Rhineland eastward to the Holy Land and the Holy City. In fact, these spatial dimensions are expanded yet farther, to the cosmos in its entirety. Upon depicting the victorious entry of Count Emicho's crusading force into the archbishop's courtyard in Mainz, a prelude to the slaughter of the Jews gathered therein, the *Mainz Anonymous* breaks forth into a dirge: "Sun and moon, why did you not hide your light? You stars, to whom Israel had been compared, and you twelve planets, like the number of the tribes of Israel, the sons of Jacob, how is it that your light was not hidden, so that it not shine on the enemy intending to blot out the name of Israel?"[62]

Indeed, the boundaries of the tale extended even beyond the physical universe. In describing the destruction of the group of Jews who had sought safety in the palace of the Mainz burgrave, the *Mainz Anonymous* quickly tells the story of a Jew named Moses bar Helbo, who addressed his two sons with the following: "My sons Helbo and Simon, at this moment hell beckons and paradise beckons. Into which do you wish to enter?"[63]

The sense of contrasting outcomes—eternal punishment on the one hand and eternal reward on the other—abounds throughout the narrative. Let us note the aggressive challenge flung out by the Jew David *ha-gabbai* of Mainz to the crowd that had gathered to witness his insincerely promised conversion: "If you kill me,[64] my soul will repose in paradise, in the light of life; you, however, will descend to the pit of destruction, to everlasting infamy, where you will be judged with your deity, who was born of lust and who was crucified."[65] Like the more restricted distinction between the crusaders' vain imagery of Jerusalem and the Jewish commitment to the truly sacred Jerusalem, when contemplating life after death the author of the *Mainz Anonymous* and his protagonists regularly contrast the hellish end designed for Christians and the glorious rewards intended for the Jewish martyrs of 1096.

Just as there is an extended spatial plane reflected in the *Mainz Anonymous,* so too is there an extended temporal dimension. The Jewish heroes of 1096 are regularly compared to great figures from the Jewish past. The closest in time are the postdestruction victims of the Hadrianic decrees, such giant figures as Rabbi Akiba and his fellow martyrs. The timeline is pushed backward to the destruction of the Second Temple, which—as we have seen—is highlighted throughout the narrative. From the period prior to the destruction of the Second Temple, we encounter reference, in the lengthy and moving Rachel of Mainz episode, to the female martyr—the mother of the seven sons—of the Antiochene persecution.[66] The Abraham figure, which played such a striking role in the martyrological thought of 1096, hearkens to an even earlier time.

As noted, the first break in the spare *Mainz Anonymous* account comes in the depiction of the initial attack in Worms, the assault on those Jews who had chosen to remain in their homes under the protection of friendly burghers. After describing a ruse that moved the mob to anti-Jewish violence, our author recounts the slaughter of almost all those Jews who had elected to remain in their homes. He depicts them as having died for the sanctification of God's Name,

> which is awesome and exalted for all ages. He rules above and below. He was and will be, the Lord of hosts is his Name. He is crowned through the designation of seventy-two appellations. He created the Torah nine hundred seventy-four generations prior to the creation of the world. There were twenty-six generations from the creation [of the world] down to Moses the progenitor of the prophets. Through him [Moses] the holy Torah was given. Moses came and wrote in it: "You have affirmed this day that the Lord [is your God, that you will walk in his ways, that you will observe his laws and commandments and rules, and that you will obey him. And the Lord has affirmed this day that you are, as he promised you, his treasured people, who will observe all his commandments, and that he will set you, in fame and renown and glory, high above all the nations he has made and that you shall be, as he promised, a holy people to the Lord your God]."[67]

The Torah that the Jewish martyrs were observing with their dying breath stretches back into the precreation void; it is the true Torah, dwarfing in its duration and truth the recent and deviant beliefs of the Christian world.

Projection of the events associated with the First Crusade from the carefully plotted space and time of France and the Rhineland and of late 1095 and early 1096 onto a far larger canvas was hardly accidental; such a projection was crucial to the timeless message that the *Mainz Anonymous* sought to convey. Alongside the time-bound message concerning the Christian world and its diverse responses to the eruption of the crusade and concerning the chaotic but heroic Jewish reactions to this unanticipated threat, our author addresses a profound and timeless set of issues—the meaning of the tragedy. In the abstract, every tragedy provokes questioning in a monotheistic community. What is the meaning of such tragedy? Why has the God who controls history allowed such a catastrophe to beset his people? Since the violence and death of 1096 hardly constituted the first such disaster in Jewish history, a set of responses was readily available. Not all of these responses could in fact be advanced, however, for the *Mainz Anonymous* indicates that the crusading adventure posed a special spiritual challenge to traditional Jewish thinking.[68]

Christian neighbors, even some highly sympathetic to the Jewish plight, concluded from the Jewish suffering of 1096 that God had in fact abandoned the Jews and that the only reasonable option for Jewish behavior in the face of such divine rejection was conversion. This argument recurs throughout the *Mainz Anonymous,* expressed in episodes from both Worms and Mainz.[69] The martyrs of 1096 are portrayed as rejecting this assertion, convinced that the covenant between God and the Jews remained in force. A major objective of the *Mainz Anonymous* was to make this case as explicitly as possible, to explain Jewish suffering in a way that would reinforce Jewish commitment rather than diminish it.

In making his brief for the ongoing covenant between the Jews and their God, the author of the *Mainz Anonymous* intrudes himself minimally into the rapidly unfolding tale. There are of course occasional auctorial interventions. We have noted the first of these: his lament over the Jewish victims of the first of the two violent assaults in Worms. By and large, however, the author's technique is to let the events and the protagonists speak for themselves. It is through the language the author uses and the speeches he places in the mouths of the Jewish martyrs that the timeless messages of 1096 are principally conveyed.

Strikingly, the author of the *Mainz Anonymous* manages to project

much the same sense of development on the timeless plane that he introduces into his description of the time-bound sequence of events.
There is a palpable sense of an unfolding theology, of a deepening perception of the meaning of the events that parallels the ever-intensifying
violence of the events themselves.

Early on, our author makes a passing reference to the traditional
scheme of sin and punishment. After describing the passage of French
crusaders through the Rhineland, the demand for funds from the Jews,
and Jewish acquiescence, he notes: "But all this was unavailing. Our sins
brought it about that the burghers in every town through which the
crusaders passed harassed us."[70] This invocation of the sin-punishment
paradigm was clearly not intended in a serious manner; it disappears
entirely from the narrative after this brief and superficial appearance.
The disappearance of this most traditional line of postdisaster rumination is not difficult to comprehend. Given the Christian argument that
the suffering of 1096 reflects divine condemnation of the Jews, any explanation of the tragedy in terms of Jewish shortcomings would ultimately prove problematic, seemingly reinforcing the Christian case.

More neutral is the notion of a divine decree, with its sense of in-
scrutability. Imagery of a divine decree recurs a number of times in the
first half of the narrative, with the suggestion that such decrees can never
be understood—they can only be accepted. This line of explanation does
not in any way suggest Jewish shortcomings and culpability; at the same
time, it hardly offers much in the way of positive explanation for the
calamity. It is a useful prelude to the author's profoundly positive portrayal of the catastrophe.

As the narrative progresses, the emphasis on the positive intensifies.
The Jews are increasingly depicted as fulfilling a divine mandate. To be
sure, this divine mandate remains by and large beyond human comprehension; what is clear and intelligible, however, is that God ordained
this suffering, that the Jews were reacting in a manner dictated by God
himself, that Jewish behavior reflected the highest level of fulfillment of
the divine-human covenant, and that the result of this remarkable adherence to the covenant could only be the highest form of reward. Here
we have a strong and positive Jewish response to the Christian argument
that Jewish suffering proved an abrogation of the relationship between
God and the Jews. To the contrary, according to the *Mainz Anonymous,*
Jewish suffering reflected radical fulfillment of the divine-human pact
from the human side, which had to entail eventual fulfillment of the
divine side of the agreement. All this is captured nicely in the reference

to Deuteronomy 26:17–19, noted above.[71] At the very first instance of major calamity, the *Mainz Anonymous* cites this important biblical statement of the covenant, arguing that the Jewish martyrs were fulfilling the human side of the pact, indeed were radically complying with God's laws and commandments and rules. This could only mean in turn activation of the divine side of the agreement. Whereas Christian observers may have misinterpreted the Worms losses as evidence of God's abandonment of the Jewish people, the *Mainz Anonymous* presents powerfully what it sees as the correct reading of these events: the Jewish martyrs of Worms had fulfilled God's mandate; in turn, God was surely bound to set the Jews, "in fame and renown and glory, high above all the nations that he has made."

The extended spatial and temporal parameters of the 1096 crisis were introduced in order to buttress the case for Jewish fulfillment of the covenant. The 1096 martyrs were simply part of the chain of Jewish heroes who had chosen to answer God's demand for adherence under even the most trying of circumstances. They were eleventh-century compatriots of Rabbi Akiba and his associates of the second century and of the Jewess and her seven sons of the second pre-Christian century. This chain represented unswerving devotion to the God of Israel.

The radical reinterpretation of the Temple cult was similarly introduced to buttress the case for fulfillment of divine injunction. The Jerusalem cult represented the highest form of Jewish worship of God, and the martyrs of 1096 were reviving this cult in the most striking manner possible. They were answering the divine call for sacrifice in a manner that was shocking but, at the same time, shockingly impressive. They were the bulls and rams and lambs of Jerusalem of yore; they were the offerings presented before the Lord.

In the process of advancing these positive assertions, the author of the *Mainz Anonymous* was making at the same time a bold polemical anti-Christian assertion, very much related to the crusade itself and its focus on Jerusalem. Christians claimed to be setting forth to redeem the sacred precincts of Jerusalem, but it was their Jewish victims who were making the true pilgrimage. Christianity claimed that Jesus was the true sacrifice offered before God and that the crusaders, in offering their lives to the venture, were emulating him; in fact it was the Jewish martyrs of 1096 who were the authentic revivers of the Temple cult, who were the genuine sacrifices offered on the altar of holiness.

The *'akedah* imagery that is so central to the *Mainz Anonymous* was the linchpin of the author's argument. On the one hand, the Abraham-

Isaac imagery extended backward to the origins of the Jewish people the
chain of heroes so devoted to God that they made the most painful of
human sacrifices, the sacrifice of life and the lives of loved ones. More
important, the ʿ*akedah* imagery reinforces the central notion of Jewish
fulfillment of divine mandate, with the attendant, divinely lavished reward. Abraham's willingness to offer his beloved son was the direct
response to a divine command: "Take your son, your favored one, Isaac,
whom you love, and go to the land of Moriah, and offer him there as a
burnt offering on one of the heights that I will point out to you." The
episode ends with God's recognition of the strength of commitment required for Abraham's assent and a divine promise of recompense.

> Because you have done this and have not withheld your son, your favored
> one, I will bestow my blessing upon you and make your descendants as
> numerous as the stars of heaven and the sands on the seashore; and your
> descendants shall seize the gates of their foes. All the nations of the earth
> shall bless themselves by your descendants, because you have obeyed my
> command.[72]

The message is again clear: if such was the divine response to Abraham's
willingness to sacrifice his beloved son, the divine reward for the Jewish
martyrs' actual sacrifice of sons and daughters had to be yet grander, if
such were possible.

The ʿ*akedah* image deepened significantly the case presented in the
Mainz Anonymous for Jewish martyrdom as a response to divine command. At the same time, it offered a more specific rationale for the divine
mandate. In the biblical account itself and, even more prominently, in
subsequent Jewish lore, God's command to sacrifice the beloved son
Isaac is portrayed as a test, as a means utilized by God to plumb the
depth of Abraham's commitment and thereby to assure Abraham's folk
the promised eventual reward. Through the ʿ*akedah* imagery, the problematic notion of a divine command to suffer takes on some semblance
of fuller meaning.

As was true for the Temple imagery, invocation of the Abraham-Isaac
figure has its polemical edge as well. Once again it reflects Jewish reap-
propriation of a key biblical theme. Christian tradition had seized upon
the Abraham-Isaac figure for its own purposes, for buttressing its own
central notions of Jesus as prefigured sacrifice. Now, under the pressure
of the events of 1096 and stimulated by the invigorated spiritual imag-
eries of their environment, the Jewish martyrs and their memorializer
and explicator reappropriated the ʿ*akedah*. Abraham's willingness to

sacrifice his beloved son was not truly reprised among the Christians; it was genuinely relived by the Rhineland martyrs.

Thus, the carefully plotted time-bound tale was paralleled and supplemented by a timeless story. While the time-bound tale bore a set of important political and apologetic messages to the survivors, the timeless story was addressed in a different manner to the survivors, beyond them to the generations, and ultimately to God himself. A violent and unanticipated physical challenge was met in a variety of ways by the Rhineland Jews of 1096; an equally audacious and threatening spiritual challenge was similarly countered by these Jews and by their gifted if nameless memorializer and rationalizer.

CHAPTER THREE

The *Solomon bar Simson* *Chronicle*

The Editorial Prologue and Epilogue

The *Solomon bar Simson Chronicle,* unlike the *Mainz Anonymous,* has reached us in its entirety.[1] It opens with a specification of the date of the catastrophe visited on Rhineland Jewry and closes with a series of verses calling down vengeance upon the Christians responsible for the assaults and beseeching salvation for the Jewish victims of those assaults.[2] This complete narrative was introduced *in toto* into a later composite account of the fate of Speyer Jewry.[3] The compiler of the composite account begins with material now lost,[4] recounts the full story of 1096 by means of the *Solomon bar Simson Chronicle,* tells of recent persecution in Blois,[5] and concludes with some final remarks on Speyer Jewry.[6] For our purposes, the most important point is that the *Solomon bar Simson Chronicle,* as available to us, is a complete text.

As we move from the *Mainz Anonymous* to the *Solomon bar Simson Chronicle,* we find immediately a number of striking differences. Most striking of all is the shift from a seamless and coherent narrative with little auctorial intervention to a rather episodic and disjointed narrative, in which the presence of the editor regularly intrudes. In lieu of the smooth flow from place to place and time to time in the *Mainz Anonymous,* we find such recurrent transitional phrases as: "Now I shall tell and recount great wonders done that day by these saintly ones";[7] "Now I shall recount and relate to all how this occurred";[8] "Now I shall tell of the killing of R. Kalonymous the saintly *parnas* and his band";[9] "Now I shall tell how it took place that these saintly ones were killed";[10] "Now

I shall tell what the community of Cologne did";[11] "The Trier incident has been told to me";[12] "Now I shall tell of those in Metz";[13] "Now it is fitting for me to speak in praise of those forcibly converted."[14] These artificial transitions are only the most obvious indices of a narrative that is choppy and disjointed.

Indeed, we can readily analyze the *Solomon bar Simson Chronicle* into a series of component elements: (1) an editorial prologue;[15] (2) a lengthy unit devoted to events in Speyer, Worms, and Mainz, derived—I shall argue—from the *Mainz Anonymous,* although altered and expanded considerably;[16] (3) an extended account of events in Cologne;[17] (4) a potpourri of reports, involving the Jewish communities of Trier, Metz, Regensburg, and Sh-l-ʾ, with the tale of Trier Jewry being by far the longest and most interesting;[18] (5) a statement in praise of those forcibly converted;[19] and (6) an editorial epilogue, which reports with great relish the disaster that befell the German crusading bands in Hungary, a disaster which the editor presents as the beginning of the anticipated process of divine revenge.[20] All these elements are presented episodically. Although the events depicted take place during the spring and summer months of 1096 (the *Solomon bar Simson Chronicle* makes no real reference to the early development of the crusade in France), the narrative conveys none of the gripping sense of the developing movement, the accelerating anti-Jewish violence, and the intensifying Jewish commitment to martyrdom that is one of the glories of the *Mainz Anonymous.*

Most important to our purposes is recognition that the *Solomon bar Simson Chronicle* is an edited work, that its editor took a number of disparate accounts and wove them into a comprehensive report on Jewish suffering in 1096. In terms of its scope, the *Solomon bar Simson Chronicle* exceeds by far the bounds of the *Mainz Anonymous,* which focuses strictly on the three Rhineland communities. The commitment of our editor to creating this broader picture of 1096 is impressive. It is critical, however, to acknowledge his role as that of editor, rather than author.[21]

That the *Solomon bar Simson Chronicle* is an edited work is proven by the disparity of the various segments of which it is composed. Such disparate units could hardly have been written by one and the same person. The simplest way to highlight this disparity is to contrast the Speyer-Worms-Mainz unit with the Cologne unit. Given that the origin of the Speyer-Worms-Mainz unit was the *Mainz Anonymous* (a case I shall make in the next chapter), our editor necessarily takes over the

elements that convey a concern with the time-bound that is evident in
the *Mainz Anonymous,* including the diversity of the Christians who
were involved in the anti-Jewish violence, the varied responses of the
Christians who were not part of the anti-Jewish violence, and the frantic
efforts of Jews to secure safety for themselves and their families. When
we move from the Speyer-Worms-Mainz unit to the Cologne unit, it is
clear that the latter is utterly insensitive to the time-bound, reflecting a
totally different set of objectives and a wholly different historical imagination. Gone is the concern with Christian attackers, Christian onlookers, and Jewish behaviors other than martyrdom. The narrative is concerned almost exclusively with the martyrological responses of the Jews
of Cologne. It is unthinkable that the same historical imagination produced both the Speyer-Worms-Mainz and the Cologne units of the *Solomon bar Simson Chronicle.*

Let us note one specific reflection of the difference between these two
units of the *Solomon bar Simson Chronicle.* As we have seen, the *Mainz
Anonymous* highlights the figure of Count Emicho as chief persecutor
of the Rhineland Jews; it notes his presence in the area into which Speyer
Jews had been dispersed and the fear he occasioned; it focuses on his
role in the destruction of Mainz Jewry. Close reading of the Cologne
unit makes it obvious that the troops of Count Emicho must have been
responsible for hunting down most of the seven enclaves into which the
Jews of Cologne had been dispersed for their safety.[22] To be sure, the
Cologne unit's account of the fate of these Jewish enclaves indicates in
passing, but nonetheless quite clearly, that a crusader band was responsible for the destruction of almost all of them.[23] At no point, however,
does the Cologne unit take the trouble to identify Count Emicho's co-
hort as the specific band responsible for the destruction, which it surely
was. The striking disparity between the Speyer-Worms-Mainz unit's
careful identification of Count Emicho and his followers and the Cologne unit's inattention to the identity of the rampaging crusaders responsible for the obliteration of Cologne Jewry points to the profound
disparity between these two component elements in the *Solomon bar
Simson Chronicle,* demonstrating convincingly that it is an edited work,
with diverse segments compiled into a running record of the tragic 1096
drama.

Beyond the shift from authored work to edited work, close scrutiny
of the *Solomon bar Simson Chronicle* shows also the intrusiveness of
the editor, as opposed to the reticence of the author of the *Mainz Anonymous.* We have noted already the artificial transitions that highlight

the editorial voice. More significant by far are the interpretive interpolations by the editor, as he recurrently lays bare the meaning of the events depicted. The author of the *Mainz Anonymous* intruded himself in this fashion only rarely, but the editor of the *Solomon bar Simson Chronicle* does so regularly and at considerable length. Our editor was deeply concerned with theological issues and with the timeless dimensions of the events of 1096, and he aired his views assertively and obtrusively.

Is it possible to say anything conclusive with regard to the date at which the narrative was compiled? A *terminus a quo* is readily available and has been noted from the earliest research on it. The Cologne unit of the *Solomon bar Simson Chronicle* includes, about half-way through, the only specific observation on dating in any of the three narratives. This unit in fact tells us little of events in Cologne itself. Its focus is upon the fate of the Cologne Jews who for their safety were dispersed by the well-intentioned archbishop among seven fortified outlying towns. The Cologne unit is an orderly record of the destruction of five of these seven groups of Jews. Toward the end of the doleful tale of the Jews gathered in Altenahr, the narrator mentions a Jewess who was found alive among the corpses left by the crusaders. The converts occupied with the burial of the dead nursed this woman back to health, and she lived for many years thereafter. To be sure, the harrowing events of 1096 stayed with her. According to the narrator, "from that day forth she fasted every day, eating only once per day, except for Sabbaths, festivals, and new moons, down till now, the year 4900 [=1140]."[24] The 1140 date specified here actually provides only a *terminus a quo*, since it need not reflect the date of the compilation as a whole. The compilation cannot precede 1140; it may well postdate it.

The *terminus ad quem* is less certain, but perhaps not too difficult to reconstruct. It is almost impossible to imagine that the *Solomon bar Simson Chronicle* could have been written after the debacle of the Second Crusade.[25] Given the glee with which the far less significant downfall of the German crusading bands is described, it is inconceivable that our editor knew of the events of the late 1140s and did not include them. It thus seems likely that the composite narrative was edited between 1140 and 1148–49. The goad to the composition was almost certainly the impending Second Crusade, with the editor determined to provide extensive recollection of the events of 1096 and recurrent petitions for the downfall of the newly developing crusading enterprise.[26] Some evidence of this dating and purpose is reflected in the closing comments of the editor. After depicting with delight the destruction of the German crusading bands, he continues: "But the enemy have still not desisted from their wicked designs. Every day they depart for Jerusalem. But the Lord has delivered them to slaughter like sheep to slaughter and has designated them for a day of killing."[27]

The same passage that provides us with the 1140 *terminus a quo* for the composition also gives the compilation its widely used designation. The passage just now cited continues: "And I Solomon bar Simson copied this occurrence in Mainz. There I asked the elders about the entire incident. From their mouths I arranged everything properly. They recounted to me this instance of martyrdom."[28] Precisely what this unknown Solomon bar Simson was responsible for has never been clear. He may have been the author of the Altenahr piece only; he may have written the entire Cologne unit; he may have been the editor of the entire narrative.[29]

Given that the *Solomon bar Simson Chronicle* is an edited work, compiled in the 1140s, probably with news of the impending Second Crusade in the air, we might well anticipate a number of editorial interests, ranging from the time-bound to the timeless. To be sure, identifying the objectives of a composite work presents serious difficulties. To what extent are we dealing with preexistent units and their inclinations? To what extent were these preexistent units altered by the editor in pursuit of his objectives? In some measure these problems are insuperable, although considerable clarity can be achieved through careful analysis.

For the purpose of this analysis, I propose the following procedure. In this chapter, I shall treat the two units in which the hand of the editor is most obvious, namely the prologue and the epilogue. In the following chapter, I shall attempt to show how the editor treated the earlier *Mainz Anonymous,* making it the basis for his report on events in Speyer, Worms, and Mainz, but adapting the earlier account to his purposes. In the third of the chapters on the *Solomon bar Simson Chronicle,* I shall analyze the characteristics and objectives of two further independent units, the reports on events in Trier and Cologne. I shall also once again attempt to discern the hand of the editor in his introductions and conclusions to these independent narratives.

THE PROLOGUE

The opening of the *Solomon bar Simson Chronicle* differs markedly from that of the *Mainz Anonymous.*[30] The latter, we recall, plunges us immediately into the time-bound realities of late 1095 and early 1096, tracking carefully and precisely the origins of the crusade in France, crusade-related anti-Jewish hostility, the fearful reactions on the part of French Jewry, the ignorance of the enterprise on the part of the Rhineland Jews, the movement of French crusaders into western Germany, the recruitment of new crusaders in the Rhineland, further evocation of crusade-related anti-Jewish hostility, the parallel arousal of the burghers against their Jewish neighbors, early Jewish fright, and sporadic anti-Jewish violence. I suggested, in the previous chapter, that the author of the *Mainz Anonymous* was clearly committed to providing his readers with full information on the emergence and development of the crusade.

In contrast, the *Solomon bar Simson Chronicle* opens with precious little information about the development of the crusade and its anti-Jewish thrust. The bare historical bones embedded in the prologue involve the arousal of the crusaders, the refraction of crusading fervor into hostility against the Jews, Jewish fears and supplication, and divine rejection of these prayers. The carefully constructed spatial and temporal sequencing of events in the *Mainz Anonymous* disappears in the *Solomon bar Simson Chronicle*. For example, the latter speaks of the emergence of the crusade in the following terms: "There arose initially the ruthless, the barbarians, the fierce and impetuous people, French and German, and committed themselves to journeying to the Holy City." Notable here is the absence of differentiation between the French and the Germans that is so painstakingly plotted in the *Mainz Anonymous*. Clearly, our editor's time-bound concerns are extremely limited, to the point of near nonexistence. While the stimulus to composing the narrative was, in all likelihood, the impending Second Crusade, and while the editor may well have wanted to provide some guidance to his fellow Jews in the face of the potential for renewed violence, time-bound information was hardly a serious priority.

Our editor's central concern, at this opening point of his composite narrative, lay with the theological issues raised by Jewish suffering. Thus, in this brief prologue, the real focus of attention lies with the closing theme—divine rejection of the supplications of the Jews in 1096. The narrative lavishly depicts the Jews and their traditional responses of repentance, prayer, and charity. "They afflicted themselves with hunger and thirst for three consecutive days, both night and day, above and beyond daily fasting, until their skin shriveled on their bones and became dry as wood. They called out, emitting a great and bitter cry." This remarkable outpouring of petition failed, however, to move the God to whom it was addressed. "But their Father did not answer them. He closed off their prayer; he enveloped himself in a cloud, so that their prayer would not pass through; he despised their tent; he removed them from his presence." The Jews took the requisite and proper steps; God failed to respond.

Why this absence of divine response? We should begin by recalling once more the primary concern of the author of the *Mainz Anonymous:* to explain God's rejection of the Jews in terms that would nullify the Christian assertion that Jewish sins had brought about the divine rejection. The range of explanations that the *Solomon bar Simson Chronicle* might advance to explain divine silence was therefore circumscribed. Again, the traditional sin-punishment paradigm would have proven dangerously counterproductive.

Instead, our editor advances a complex explanation that absolves the Jews of 1096 and many generations of their ancestors of any hint of guilt:

> For there existed a decree from "the day of my accounting." Now, this generation [the generation of 1096] was chosen before him [God] to be his portion, for they had the strength and the valor to stand in his sanctuary and do his bidding and to sanctify his great Name in his world. Concerning them David said: "Bless the Lord, o you his messengers, you great heroes, those who do his bidding."

The first element in this complex explanation for the catastrophe of 1096 goes back to what Jews perceived to be the great historic sin of their ancestors, the sin of the golden calf. What was most striking about this communal failure in the desert was, above all else, its proximity to the high point in Israelite and human history. Immediately after the only moment on record of direct divine communication with the totality of a people, after being exposed to God's awesome majesty, the Israelites of yore pressed for an image to reassure themselves in the face of Moses's absence. Moses, returning to the camp, responded with outrage and a number of harsh steps, including the slaughter of three thousand sinning brethren. On the morrow, Moses took a different leadership tack, stepping forth to win divine forgiveness for the breathtaking sin. He acknowledged the shortcomings of his people and asked for either divine forgiveness or for total destruction, himself included. God's response was as follows: "He who has sinned against me, him only will I erase from my record. Go now, lead the people where I told you. See, my angel will go before you. But when I make an accounting, I will bring them to account for their sins."[31] This appears, then, to presage a de-

lay—seemingly temporary—for any retribution beyond that enacted immediately by Moses. The sin remained, but retribution was to be exacted
at a later time. According to the editor of the *Solomon bar Simson
Chronicle,* that time arrived in 1096. The punishment promised by God
in the wilderness was inflicted upon the descendants of the early Israelites. This seems at first blush a rather strange claim, but its logic is not
all that difficult to fathom.

Although this rather unusual explanation for the catastrophe roots
the tragedy of 1096 in Jewish sinfulness, it hardly reinforces the Christian case encountered repeatedly in the *Mainz Anonymous,* the argument that the historic Jewish sin of deicide brought about divine punishment, up to and including the tragedy of 1096. According to the
editor of the *Solomon bar Simson Chronicle,* there was indeed an overwhelming sin in the Jewish past, a shortcoming for which the divine
decree was imposed in 1096, but that iniquity had nothing whatsoever
to do with the Jerusalem of the Second Temple period. The Christian
claim simply represented a misreading of the historical record of sin and
punishment. The sin for which punishment was meted out in 1096
stretched back to the days of Moses in the wilderness; the Jerusalem of
Jesus played no role in the divine retribution exacted in 1096.

In the process of rooting the tragedy of 1096 in the sin of the golden
calf, the editor of the *Solomon bar Simson Chronicle* does more than
refute the Christian reading of Jewish sinfulness: he also highlights what
he perceives to be Christianity's fatal flaw. The shortcoming over which
the wrath of God was kindled against his people in the wilderness was
the request for a surrogate deity during Moses's absence, that is, the failure to be satisfied with the awesome presence of the one true and incor-
poreal God. For Jews over the ages, the need for a surrogate God was in
fact the defining characteristic and failing of Christianity. Thus, the sin
for which the Jews of 1096 had been chosen to bear divine punishment
was the sin that Christians continued to perpetrate on a regular basis.

Now, why then were the Jews of 1096 singled out to bear the burden
of the sin of the golden calf? It was surely not because they were guilty
in any sense of recapitulation of that sin. To the contrary, they were
chosen to bear the punishment, because "they had the strength and the
valor to stand in his sanctuary and do his bidding and to sanctify his
great Name in his world." The selection of the 1096 generation was the
result of strength, not weakness—virtue, not shortcoming. Reflected in
this is the same kind of thinking encountered in the *Mainz Anonymous,*
the sense of a uniquely gifted generation singled out because of its

remarkable capacity to answer the divine call for self-sacrifice. There is, in this opening statement of the *Solomon bar Simson Chronicle,* the same echo of the sacrificial cult we encountered in the *Mainz Anonymous:* the Jews of 1096 were "chosen before him [God] to be his portion," a phrase redolent of the sacrificial system, "for they had the strength and the valor to stand in his sanctuary and do his bidding and to sanctify his great Name in his world."

Thus, our editor opens his composite narrative by focusing on the problem of Jewish suffering in 1096 and by providing a Jewish alternative to the Christian reading of these events. The generation of 1096 was singled out to bear the long-deferred punishment decreed by God for the sin of the golden calf; that sin had nothing whatsoever to do with Jesus and his fate; these Jews were selected for their virtue and their heroism, not for their failings.

While neglecting the concern with the time-bound that is so evident in the *Mainz Anonymous,* the editor of the *Solomon bar Simson Chronicle* certainly shared the former's commitment to the timeless realm. In his prologue and elsewhere, he reinforces his overall theological message with frequent allusions to major biblical institutions and figures. To be sure, medieval Hebrew poetry and prose tended strongly toward citation and intertextual reference; nonetheless, this prologue is unusually rich in such intertextual references.[32]

The language employed to describe the martyr-heroes of the narrative recurrently evokes recollections of prominent biblical episodes and personalities. We have already seen that Temple imagery is advanced in the depiction of the Jewish heroes of 1096 in the *Mainz Anonymous* and the prologue to the *Solomon bar Simson Chronicle.* Not surprisingly, the language of the prologue regularly evokes Lamentations, the biblical dirge over the destruction of the First Temple. The depiction of divine indifference to the prayers of the endangered Rhineland Jews includes three obvious references to Lamentations. In the description of Jewish appeals to God, the Jews of the Rhineland are portrayed as fasting intensely, to the point that "their skin shriveled on their bones and became dry as wood," a direct citation from Lamentations 4:8. Similarly, the striking images of God shutting out the prayers of the Jews and screening himself off with a cloud, so that no prayer might pass through, are both taken from Lamentations 3. Invocation of this terminology reinforces the link between the Jewish martyrs and the destroyed Temple, imparting the sense that the martyrs possessed the strength to stand in God's sanctuary and hallow his Name.

Let us note a number of further allusions to revered figures of the Jewish past. In describing the Jewish reaction to the news of the crusading venture and its anti-Jewish implications, our editor describes the following: "They afflicted themselves with hunger and thirst for three consecutive days, night and day, above and beyond fasting daily." Embedded here are a number of interesting intertextual allusions. In the first place, the notion of fasting three consecutive nights and days takes us back to the biblical book of Esther, specifically the fourth chapter, where Esther, willing to endanger herself on behalf of her fellow Jews, enjoins them to fast—along with her—in this unusual way.

Included in the editor's picture of Jewish fasting is reference to similar behavior on the part of another group of distinguished Jews. In depicting the daily fasting, above and beyond the extreme three-consecutive-day total, the term used is *hit'anu*, a somewhat unusual usage that takes us back to the biblical book of Ezra. Chapters 7 and 8 depict the return of a group of Babylonian Jews to Jerusalem under the leadership of Ezra. After listing the constituents of his camp, Ezra says: "I proclaimed a fast there by the Ahava River, to afflict ourselves [*le-hit'anot*] before our God to beseech him for a smooth journey for us and for our children and for all our possessions."[33] There is an interesting irony here, in that the appeal invokes an image of Jews making their way *peacefully* to the Holy City.

The same sentence upon which we have been focused includes yet another highly evocative term—*'inu nafsham,* "they afflicted themselves." This important expression recurs repeatedly in the descriptions of the Day of Atonement ritual in Leviticus and Numbers.[34] Now, this ritual of affliction is a critical element in the process of purification and atonement. The intertextual implication of this term dovetails perfectly with the overt argument that the events of 1096 represent an atonement for the unpunished guilt associated with the sin of the golden calf. As already noted, for our editor the Rhineland Jews had been singled out for slaughter because "they had the strength and valor to stand in his sanctuary and to do his bidding and to sanctify his great Name in his world." Thus the self-affliction alludes to the atonement ritual, and the innovative twist imposed by our editor is that the atonement ritual would eventually go far beyond fasting, that the remarkable behavior of the martyrs of 1096 came to constitute an innovative and radical atonement ritual rooted in human self-sacrifice.

Our editor concludes his prologue with verse 20 of Psalm 103. This psalm begins and ends with a call in a variety of directions to praise the

Lord, of whose goodness the psalmist sings. Its opening call is to the
human soul: "Bless the Lord, O my soul, all my being, his holy Name.
Bless the Lord, O my soul and do not forget all his bounties." The
closing call to praise the Lord is addressed to the heavenly hosts and
then to the totality of creation, thus uniting all levels, from the human
through the celestial. The call to the heavenly hosts to praise the Lord
is interpreted by our editor as a reference to the Rhineland martyrs:
"Bless the Lord, O his angels, mighty creatures who do his bidding, ever
obedient to his bidding." Here the innovative theodicy is expressed
sharply. The Rhineland martyrs did not in fact suffer for their inade-
quacies; they were singled out for their superhuman—taken literally—
devotion to God. They were "angels . . . , ever obedient to his bidding."

In referring Psalm 103:20 to these Rhineland martyrs, our editor ends
his prologue by reevoking the imagery of Exodus 32. The tangible sign
of God's reconciliation to the Israelites after the sin of the golden calf
was to be the angel that would lead them. Now, as the Jews of the
Rhineland prepare to shoulder the burden of that sin—because of their
unique capacity to do so—they are compared by the author to angelic
figures. They are the symbol, as it were, of divine reacceptance of the
people of Israel.

The prologue to the *Solomon bar Simson Chronicle* focuses on the
Jewish hero figures; secondary are the villains of the piece, the crusaders
who in their misguided zeal attacked the children of the true Israel.
While much more will be said of these villains in the epilogue—as we
shall shortly see—there are a number of rich allusions that already ad-
umbrate a message that will be articulated directly in the closing segment
of the narrative: the crusaders are no more or no less than another link
in the historic chain of oppressors of God's people; their fate will surely
be the fate of all those persecutors who have gone before.

The very first descriptors used by our editor to designate the crusaders
portray them as *'azey fanim,* "the ruthless." This is a particularly evocative term, as it sends the auditor-reader back to one of the most striking
warnings in the Pentateuch. In chapter 28 of Deuteronomy, there is a
contrasting set of predictions, a set of positive outcomes that were to
eventuate from the observance of the laws transmitted by Moses, followed by a chilling set of catastrophes that would flow from the failure
to observe those laws. The latter predictions open with natural calamity,
which is then succeeded by the appearance of powerful and merciless
enemies. An excerpt from this section of the Mosaic prediction is worth
noting for our purposes.

The Lord will bring a nation against you from afar, from the end of the earth, which will swoop down like an eagle—a nation whose language you do not understand, a ruthless nation, that will show the old no regard and the young no mercy.[35]

The expression *'azey fanim* thus serves as a striking evocation of this Deuteronomic prophecy, affording the sense that the crusaders are precisely the ruthless people that the Lord had threatened to bring upon Israel. Given the emphasis throughout the middle sections of the narrative upon the utter lack of pity that the crusaders showed to the young and the old, this imagery of a ruthless enemy rings very true in view of the actual behavior of the crusading hordes.

The sense of the crusaders as yet another link in the chain of historic enemies of the Jewish people is reinforced by a phrase taken from the prophecy of Habbakuk. The book of Habbakuk opens with a Psalm-like plea to God to undo the injustice of Israel's suffering at the hands of its enemies, with a focus in this case on the Babylonian destroyers of the Temple. This Babylonian enemy is designated as *ha-goy ha-mar ve-ha-nimhar,* "a fierce and impetuous people." Utilization of this phrase in the early depiction of the crusaders conjures up once more the sense of a historic chain of persecutors and reinforces the connection between the martyrs of 1096 and the Temple.

Particularly noteworthy in this tendency toward intertextual reference is the heavy utilization of Psalms, with their designation of enemies and their prayers for divine vengeance upon these enemies. Thus, the anti-Jewish slogan of the crusaders includes the following: "Let us take vengeance first upon them. Let us wipe them out as a nation; Israel's name will be mentioned no more." This extended phrase is a quotation from Psalms 83:5, the setting of which is a plea for divine punishment of Israel's historic enemies. Let us note the opening verses of this plea:

O God, do not be silent;
    do not hold aloof;
    do not be quiet, O God!
For your enemies rage,
    your foes assert themselves.
They plot craftily against your people,
    take counsel against your treasured ones.
They say, "Let us wipe them out as a nation;
    Israel's name will be mentioned no more."
Unanimous in their counsel,
    they have made an alliance against you—
    the clans of Edom and the Ishmaelites,

> Moab and the Hagrites,
> Gebal, Ammon, and Amalek,
> Philistia with the inhabitants of Tyre;
> Assyria too joins forces with them;
> they give support to the sons of Lot.

By referring to this Psalm, the editor places the crusaders in a long line of persecutors of the Jewish people and pleads that God avenge his folk upon these most recent oppressors.

The specific language used with respect to the crusaders echoes yet another passage from Psalms, a passage that once again beseeches divine retribution against the enemies of the Jewish people. In our editor's depiction of the crusaders, there is a curious expression—*ve-samu'ototam 'otot,* meaning "they put on their insignia." This unusual usage is a direct quotation from Psalms 74:4, a description of the enemies who pillaged the Temple. In terms reminiscent of Psalm 83, the psalmist laments the arrogance and audacity of this enemy:

> They made your sanctuary go up in flames;
>   they brought low in dishonor the dwelling place of your presence.
> They resolved, "Let us destroy them altogether!"
>   They burned all of God's tabernacles to the ground.

Once again, through citation of biblical terminology, imagery of the crusaders as synonymous with the historic enemies of the Jewish people is reinforced, at the same time that the recurrent linkage of the Jews of 1096 and the Temple is buttressed yet once more as well.

To cite a third reference to Israel's traditional enemies that is based on Psalms, the crusaders are designated early on as *'am lo'ez,* a barbarian people. The reference conjured up from Psalms 114:1 is that of the Egyptian enemy: "When Israel went forth from Egypt, the house of Jacob from a people of strange speech [*me-'am lo'ez*]." Thus, for a third time, the specific usage echoes the language of Psalms and reinforces the sense of the crusaders as yet one more link in the historic chain of enemy peoples. Just as the earlier enemies of Israel have met their doom, so too shall the crusaders. As we shall see shortly, the plea for divine vengeance is one of the central thrusts of the *Solomon bar Simson Chronicle,* a thrust implicit in the recurrent allusions to the crusaders as a continuation of the chain of persecutors of the Jewish people.

Thus, the editor of the *Solomon bar Simson Chronicle* begins to reveal himself to us in the prologue to his compilation. His time-bound interests are minimal. Warning Jews in the 1140s of what might happen by portraying the specific realities of 1096 might have been a useful undertaking, but it does not seem to have lain at the center of our editor's interests. To be sure, one could argue that simply by incorporating such earlier compositions as the *Mainz Anonymous* in his compilation, our editor was achieving that goal, and such is surely the case. Nonetheless, the editor's own direct concern lay much more with the theological and the timeless. He was personally far more involved with the significance of the events of 1096 than with their details. The obvious focus of attention in his prologue was Jewish suffering and its meaning; the groundwork he laid for an understanding of the Christian enemy and its ultimate fate was secondary.

THE EPILOGUE

The epilogue shifts focus from the Jews of 1096, who dominate the prologue, to their persecutors. More precisely, it reverses the priorities of the prologue, in which the Jewish martyrs are primary and the Christian oppressors secondary. The editor introduces this epilogue by indicating that "after all these things [the anti-Jewish violence depicted through the sources collected], after they had done their desires and will [upon the Jews], they turned to journey on their pilgrimage to Jerusalem." The story he tells is rooted in the oral testimony of survivors of the debacle that struck the popular crusading forces—both French and German—as they attempted to make their way eastward. "The remnant returned and reported [all this] and our hearts were gladdened."[36]

The debacle is described in two stages. The first involves the French crusading forces that coalesced around Peter the Hermit and the second focuses on the German forces, preeminently those of Count Emicho. Although our editor was not interested in this distinction in his prologue, he was aware of the difference and highlighted it in his epilogue.

The story of Peter the Hermit follows Peter and his troops eastward into the Christian kingdom of Hungary, where Peter established a kind of treaty with the king.[37] Peter asked for and received permission to pass peacefully through the kingdom. However, the dire circumstances of this large and ill-provisioned crusading horde made peaceful passage difficult, if not impossible. Our editor depicts an incident in an unidentified fortified town, in which a minor dispute escalated into major violence, with the French crusaders eventually killing the entire civilian population of the town. Notice of this incident reached the king and alerted him to the dangers attendant upon the passage of the anarchic French crusading force.

Faced with the difficulty of crossing the Danube, the French crusaders once more turned violent, sacking an unnamed village and utilizing the wood from its looted homes to build a bridge over the river. By this time, a thoroughly aroused king of Hungary had warned his fortified towns not to admit the unruly crusading host. Facing a closed fortification just beyond the Danube, Peter pleaded for the sale of provisions outside the walls of the town, but was denied. A second petition, promising to pay outrageous prices for the necessary provisions, was similarly repulsed. This rejection led to full-scale assault upon the fortified town, its capture, and three days of sacking.

This series of assaults moved the king of Hungary to call together his vassals and to initiate a new set of protective steps. Key to these protective steps was the closing of the borders of Hungary against any further crusader incursion. In addition, measures were taken against those crusaders who remained on Hungarian soil.

> As to those who had already entered [Hungary], they [the Hungarians] began to ambush the laggards. When they found a hundred crusaders in a group, they would kill them. On the morrow they did the same, and likewise on the next day, until they killed all of them, all those traveling with Peter the priest. The Holy One blessed be he avenged the blood of his servants upon them. Not one man was left of them.

Now, the stories of skirmish in Hungary dovetail more or less with evidence supplied by a number of Christian chronicles concerning the fate of Peter and his followers in Hungary. The closing note of this account, however—the assertion of total destruction of the French crusading band—is surely inaccurate. Considerable evidence indicates the passage of the bulk of the French crusading force through Hungary, its arrival and safe sojourn in Constantinople, and its eventual destruction at the hands of the Muslims at Civetot. Even there the destruction was not total. It is known that Peter and other leaders managed to survive the massacre at Civetot, and they reappeared at later stages of the crusade. Thus, our editor's account is surely embellished. The point of this account is clear: what allegedly happened in Hungary—the annihilation of the French crusading force—was an act of divine vengeance. The revenge that our editor had hinted at in his prologue is asserted overtly in his epilogue. God was indeed incensed with the crusaders for their persecution of his loyal Jewish followers and wasted no time in visiting punishment upon these malefactors.

This reading of the fate of the French crusading forces is reiterated with yet greater relish in our editor's report on the German bands, with Count Emicho at the center of attention. With regard to the German bands, we can distinguish less confidently between relatively reliable narrative and editorial embellishment, since there are far fewer Christian sources available for reconstructing the fate of the German popular bands.[38] Our editor's tale begins with the German crusaders finding the borders of Hungary closed to them, because of the tensions stirred up by their French predecessors. The first major problem was encountered at the border town of Innsbruck, where a siege of the closed fortification was mounted by the German invaders. In the face of the difficulty of the siege, the German bands sent a four-man delegation to plead with the king of Hungary for safe passage. After three days of incarceration, the four emissaries supposedly promised to deliver to the king the head of Count Emicho. Forewarned of this treachery, Emicho supposedly fled, breaking the discipline of the ranks. What resulted was a fearful slaughter, with the German crusaders finding their death either by the swords of the Hungarian troops or by drowning in the bogs of the area. According to our editor, those fortunate enough to escape the Hungarians and the bogs made their way to the Danube, where they attempted to cross over the bridges erected through the violence of the French crusaders. In the process, the bridges broke and innumerable German crusaders met their death in the waters of the Danube, "to the point that they [the German crusaders in flight] crossed on their backs [the backs of the drowned] as though they were crossing on dry land." Many of the details of this story are highly implausible. The point of all this is clear, however. God did in fact avenge the deaths of his steadfast followers, the Jewish martyrs of 1096.

Our editor ends with a coda, describing an eclipse of the sun at that time in 1096 as presaging a great defeat for the crusaders.[39] Nonetheless, "the enemy have still not desisted from their wicked designs. Every day they depart for Jerusalem." For our editor, the fate of this new wave of crusaders will be the same as that decreed for their French and German predecessors—utter annihilation. The narrative in its entirety ends with a revealing series of biblical verses that call down God's wrath on the enemies of Israel, in the process reevoking the imagery of the pious and faithful Jewish martyrs of the First Crusade and begging vindication.

At the heart of this series of biblical verses are three from the book
of Lamentations:

> Give them, O Lord, their deserts
> According to their deeds.
> Give them anguish of heart;
> Your curse be upon them!
> Oh, pursue them in wrath and destroy them
> From under the heavens of the Lord![40]

The overt message with respect to the crusaders is clear: the wickedness
of the crusaders and the sanctity of their victims require the harshest
divine reprisal. At the same time, by featuring so prominently these
verses from Lamentations, our editor once more reinforces the connection of the Jewish martyrs with the Jerusalem Temple and reinforces the
message of his prologue. The Jewish martyrs of 1096 were chosen by
God to expiate an earlier Israelite sin because of their strength and devotion.

The amended verse from Psalms that opens this sequence introduces
the twin elements noted in the Lamentations verses. On the most obvious level, it too is a plea for divine recompense: "Pay back our neighbors
sevenfold"[41] for the measure of their deeds. The verse in its original
setting speaks of punishment for abusing God; the editor amends this
to make the reprisal commensurate with the deeds of the crusading enemy. Once again, the setting of the psalm involves the historic enemy
that destroyed the Jerusalem Temple, reintroducing at the beginning of
this sequence of verses the theme of the martyrs' relation to the destroyed
sanctuary. In addition, this opening verse also introduces the positive
emphasis on the redemption of Israel as taking place simultaneously
with the punishment of its enemies. Thus, the closing verse of the psalm,
which immediately succeeds the verse cited by our editor, concludes:
"Then we, your people, the flock you shepherd, shall glorify you forever;
for all time we shall tell your praises." Punishment of the wicked and
reward for the righteous will go hand in hand.

The closing two verses of the sequence, both taken from Isaiah, reiterate seriatim each of these two themes—punishment and reward. The
first, from Isaiah 34, a general prophecy against the nations, speaks
overtly of divine vengeance: "For it is the Lord's day of retribution, the
year of vindication for Zion's cause." The second of the closing verses
focuses on the rewards in store for Israel. Taken from Isaiah 45, a section
devoted to visions of redemption, the verse concludes the entire narrative
on a thoroughly positive note: "Israel has won through the Lord triumph

everlasting. You shall not be shamed or disgraced in all the ages to come."

While the prologue and the epilogue each focus on one of the two sides of the coin, the combination is coherent and consistent. The crusaders in their wickedness are but another link in the chain of historical oppression of the Jewish people. Their fate will be that of all prior enemies; God will ultimately inflict requisite punishment. Writing in the 1140s, with agitation for the new crusade in the air, our editor is convinced—or at least hopeful—that this new undertaking will set in motion the revenge so richly deserved for the violence of 1096. He vacillates between his certainty of impending divine vengeance and his petitions for this requisite revenge. What befell Peter the Hermit and Count Emicho constitutes a mere foretaste of the more wide-ranging retribution in store for the new crusading movement; the editor and his fellow Jews will see with their own eyes the onset of divine punishment for the atrocities of 1096.

At the same time, our editor reinforces his case for requisite divine revenge by highlighting the greatness of the Jewish victims of crusader bestiality. The true heroes of the First Crusade were not the Christian conquerors of Jerusalem; the true heroes of the First Crusade were its Jewish victims. Seemingly shamed by their suffering, they were in fact singled out for this persecution by their great strength and courage. Their vindication is inevitable. So great is their merit that they and their successors "will not be shamed or disgraced in all the ages to come."

CHAPTER FOUR

The *Solomon bar Simson Chronicle*

The Speyer-Worms-Mainz Unit

The lengthiest unit in the composite *Solomon bar Simson Chronicle* describes the fate of three major Rhineland Jewish communities, those of Speyer, Worms, and Mainz. The parallels between this unit and the *Mainz Anonymous* have given rise to much speculation as to the relationship between these two compositions. Two broad positions have been taken on this relationship—either that the texts are independent of each other or that one is the source of the other.[1] The view that the *Mainz Anonymous* and the *Solomon bar Simson Chronicle* are independent of each other comes in two distinct forms. The first suggests that both narratives are independently derived from communal letters, that is, that the parallel passages stem from these earlier communal missives.[2] Our analysis of the *Mainz Anonymous* makes this suggestion implausible. One of our most important findings is the evidence of a consistent and controlling historical imagination behind the *Mainz Anonymous*. Although written sources may well have been utilized by its author, the end result is a composition that shows unmistakable auctorial skill and adaptation. The second case for independence suggests that earlier written materials were absorbed into an *Urtext,* a brilliant original narrative from which both of our extant texts were derived.[3] While not impossible, it is hard to see the advantage of positing an early *Urtext* and two subsequent spinoffs. It seems much easier and more economical to suggest that the *Mainz Anonymous*—in its own right an early and brilliant narrative—simply served as the basis for the later *Solomon bar Simson Chronicle.*

A second position projects a relationship of dependency, with one narrative the source of the other. To be sure, scholars have disagreed as to which is the primary and which the derivative account.[4] However, in the light of our analysis thus far of both narratives, the relationship between the *Mainz Anonymous* and the *Solomon bar Simson Chronicle* becomes transparent. Given the early dating for the former, the mid-twelfth-century dating for the latter, and its composite nature, it seems perfectly obvious that the editor of the later narrative utilized the earlier as a key element in his composition.[5]

Utilization of prior materials by medieval Jewish narrators is an issue of considerable interest. Only rarely are we in a position to identify an original and a subsequent reworking. One such instance involves the Orléans letter depicting the Blois tragedy of 1171, a letter discussed extensively in the prologue of this volume.[6] This letter circulated widely across northern Europe, reaching Ephraim ben Jacob of Bonn somewhere in Germany. Ephraim, involved with the composition of a record of anti-Jewish incidents during the closing three decades of the twelfth century, used the information provided in the Orléans letter to open his collection, a reflection of his sense of the importance of the incident and—in all likelihood—his respect for the formulation provided by Orléans Jewry. Despite this respect, Ephraim permitted himself great freedom in reproducing the account emanating from Orléans. He felt comfortable adding a few details, and—most strikingly—he allowed himself to reorganize completely the sequence of the narrative, a reorganization that to modern sensibilities strips the gripping Orléans presentation of much of its impact. To judge from Ephraim's adaptation of the Orléans missive, medieval authors felt considerable latitude in the way they handled the narrative materials at their disposal.[7]

This same sense of editorial latitude is reinforced by the reworking of the *Mainz Anonymous* in the *Solomon bar Simson Chronicle.* Our editor felt no compunction about freely altering the material available to him for telling the tale of Speyer, Worms, and Mainz. Once more, to the modern eye, the changes introduced seem by and large deleterious. The unit, as we find it in the composite narrative, has lost much of its coherence and the driving force associated with its rapid movement from moment to moment and place to place. My tasks in this chapter are two: to identify—to the extent possible—the changes introduced by the

editor of the *Solomon bar Simson Chronicle* and to analyze the interpretation imposed on the entire segment by the editorial glosses.

DELETIONS AND ADDITIONS

There is little reduction of the *Mainz Anonymous* by our editor. Most
striking in this regard is the considerable diminution of the reports on
Speyer and Worms. Since the *Solomon bar Simson Chronicle* has been
preserved as an element in an extended compilation on Speyer Jewry
and was seemingly preceded by a far more extensive depiction of 1096
events in Speyer and Worms, it might be suggested that the compression
of the *Mainz Anonymous* reports on Speyer and Worms was effected by
the later compiler, who shortened the account of these first two Rhineland communities because he had already told their story in another
segment of his collection.[8] This possibility, however, is highly unlikely,
since Eliezer bar Nathan, when he epitomized the *Solomon bar Simson
Chronicle,* already had the condensed version of the Speyer and Worms
episodes at his disposal.[9] Thus, it was in fact our editor who reworked
these two episodes, for unfathomable reasons.[10]

    What precisely did our editor retain and what did he eliminate? Let
us look first at the Speyer segment. The story, as formulated in the *Solomon bar Simson Chronicle,* is extremely sketchy. It simply tells us that
the enemy—note the lack of precision, which contrasts sharply with the
accuracy of the *Mainz Anonymous* original—"arose against the [Jew-
ish] community of Speyer and killed eleven saintly souls, who were the
first to sanctify their Creator on the sacred day of the Sabbath. They did
not wish to be baptized." The sketchy account then proceeds to mention
one specific Jewess, who "slaughtered herself for the sanctification of
the Name," a specific item not mentioned in the *Mainz Anonymous.*
Finally, our editor notes that "the rest were saved by the bishop without
baptism."[11]

    Missing here is the elaborate and precise tracking of the crusaders'
anti-Jewish sentiment that we see in the *Mainz Anonymous.* The latter's
account of events in Speyer was carefully plotted on a continuum that
began in France, moved into the Rhineland, and then focused on Speyer.
Since the first two stages were omitted by the editor of the *Solomon bar
Simson Chronicle*, it is hardly surprising that the sense of progression
represented by Speyer should have been lost as well. For our editor,
Speyer represented simply another instance of murder by the crusaders,
rather than a stage in escalating anti-Jewish sentiment and violence.

In parallel fashion, the *Mainz Anonymous* conveys a sense of growing Jewish awareness of danger, intensifying Jewish commitment to resistance, and ever more extreme Jewish behaviors. Our editor effaces this aspect of the *Mainz Anonymous* as well. Instead, the account of the incidents at Speyer offers the first instance of self-inflicted death, in this case on the part of a Jewess. Reflecting a general tendency toward homogenization, this Jewess is depicted as "the first of those who were slaughtered and who slaughtered themselves in all the [Jewish] communities."

In a general way, then, the reformulated Speyer incident loses all sense of development and uniqueness. Instead, it becomes part of a broad pattern of anti-Jewish violence and Jewish heroism. What counts for our editor is the typical and the repetitive. Put differently, the time-bound concerns of the *Mainz Anonymous*—the desire to provide as accurate a picture as possible of attackers, bystanders, and Jewish victims—are effaced in favor of a more timeless account of attacking crusaders and Jewish hero-victims.

This tendency, manifest in the Speyer segment, is repeated in the Worms segment as well. Once more, all the particularities so elegantly sketched in the *Mainz Anonymous* are eliminated. The story of the first assault in Worms, highly specific in its details, gives way in the *Solomon bar Simson Chronicle* to a stereotyped depiction that could have been introduced almost anywhere in the narrative.

> The wolves of the wild arose against those who remained in their homes and assaulted them—men and women, infants, youngsters, and aged. They dismantled the steps, destroyed the houses, plundered and pillaged. They took the Torah and trampled it in the mud; they ripped it and burned it. They devoured the children of Israel ravenously.[12]

This is a generic portrayal of anti-Jewish violence; there is nothing specific in it at all.

In his account of the assault on the bishop's compound, our editor writes with only slightly more detail. Once again, the attackers are utterly undifferentiated. In describing the Jewish martyrs, our editor does distinguish among those slain directly by the enemy, those who offered themselves to the swords of the crusaders, and those who took their own lives and the lives of family members. None of this is illustrated with the individual portraits that give the *Mainz Anonymous* much of its emotional impact. Our editor does mention a number of Jews forcibly converted, although again his report lacks the specificity encountered in his source. Finally, he adds an overall number of casualties: "Approximately eight hundred was the number of those killed, who were killed on those two days."[13] We have no way of knowing the basis for this assessment of the number of casualties during the two days of assault in Worms, and we thus have no way of evaluating the reliability of this figure.

If for Speyer and Worms our editor chose to reduce the length of his account and to diminish the specificity of his source, for Mainz his account is much lengthier than that found in the *Mainz Anonymous,* as we now have it. To be sure, we cannot be certain whether large portions of the supplementary material represent editorial additions or whether they were part and parcel of the original and lengthier version of the *Mainz Anonymous.*[14]

Recall that the narrative we now have takes us from the assault on the archbishop's compound to the attack on the burgrave's palace to two incidents in which Jews who had sought safety with Christian friends were hunted down and killed. It is at this point that the extant text of the *Mainz Anonymous* suddenly breaks off. The *Solomon bar Simson Chronicle* follows the same sequence and then adds four additional segments:

An account of Isaac ben David *ha-parnas,* who had converted under duress during the slaughter, ostensibly to save his mother and his children. This Isaac, distraught over the tragedy and his own behavior, brought about the death of his mother by burning down his ancestral home and then took his own life and the lives of his two children in the synagogue.[15]

A miscellaneous section that speaks of the demise of the great rabbis of Mainz prior to the catastrophe, the Jewesses of Mainz and their heroism, a certain Samuel ben Isaac and his story, and the death of some of the Jews who initially survived the assaults on the archbishop's palace.[16]

A lengthy account of the fate of Kalonymous ben Meshullam *ha-parnas* and his armed associates, who had found refuge when the archbishop's compound fell, who were transported across the river to safety by the archbishop's men, and who subsequently met their deaths in a variety of ways.[17]

A coda calling for punishment of the enemy and reward for the Jewish martyrs.[18]

It is extremely difficult to know how much of this might have been found in the original *Mainz Anonymous*. I will venture just a few observations. It is inconceivable to me that the entire four-part conglomeration that I have just described was originally found in the *Mainz Anonymous*. The lack of organizational sophistication reflected in this supplementary material simply does not square with the careful sense of structure exhibited in the *Mainz Anonymous* as we now have it. The same historical imagination that so carefully plotted the story line from France in late 1095 to Mainz in mid 1096 could not have been responsible for the loosely constructed, often chaotic jumble of materials that closes the Mainz unit of the *Solomon bar Simson Chronicle*.

What then of the individual elements that have been identified? On stylistic grounds, the story of Isaac ben David *ha-parnas* might well have belonged to the original *Mainz Anonymous*. It is a taut and riveting tale. There is, however, one characteristic of the closing portion of the story that does not accord well with the style of the *Mainz Anonymous*. Toward the end of the tale, our present version expresses some interesting uncertainty:

> There are those who say that the converts heard that they [the Christians] wanted to make of the synagogue a mint and that for this reason the pious one burned it. He himself was burned in the synagogue. Then there are those who say that they heard that the enemy wanted to make of the synagogue a church, and therefore they burned it.[19]

Such a report of alternative versions of a story appears nowhere in the present *Mainz Anonymous;* it does appear yet again in the *Solomon bar Simson Chronicle,* in the account of Kalonymous and his followers.[20] On stylistic grounds, this technique might well indicate a different hand from that responsible for the *Mainz Anonymous*.

The second added element, a miscellany that is actually a hodgepodge, hardly squares with the brevity, accuracy, and organizational excellence of the *Mainz Anonymous*. The unit on Kalonymous and his followers is by and large well written, although again it shows the unusual technique of expressed uncertainty. The coda shows all the characteristics of the closing section of the prologue, which we have already analyzed. In sum, it is very hard to know how much of this additional material can be traced back to the original *Mainz Anonymous;* it would hardly be surprising if little or none of it had its origin there.

Thus, the beginning of the Mainz unit shows compression of his source by the editor, and the ending shows considerable addition, the scope of which is not easy to establish. There is one further set of additional materials, this time introduced into the body of the extant *Mainz Anonymous* account, additions that are interesting for both their content and the light they shed on our editor and his sense of narrative style (or lack thereof).

To recapitulate one more time, the *Mainz Anonymous* depicts the French crusaders as they move from France into the Rhineland, the arousal of crusading ardor among the Rhinelanders, and then the assaults on the Jews at Speyer, Worms, and Mainz. The *Solomon bar Simson Chronicle* begins its story with a brief resume of events in Speyer and Worms and then focuses on Mainz. For Mainz, it initially follows the excellent organizational pattern of its source, opening with the fright of the Mainz Jews over the reports from Speyer and Worms and their appeal to the archbishop. At this point, the *Mainz Anonymous* relates that there were in fact developments in Mainz itself, independent of the reports of violence in Speyer and Worms, that served to alert these Jews. The author cites two incidents, one involving the passage of a popular crusading band seemingly led by an inspired goose and the second involving voices in the abandoned and locked synagogue of Mainz. In the *Mainz Anonymous,* these episodes are effectively placed to heighten the sense of a thoroughly frightened Jewish community. The *Solomon bar Simson Chronicle,* by contrast, breaks the tight story line by introducing two new items that are not present in the Mainz Anonymous.

The first digressive addition involves a major baronial figure, Duke Godfrey, seemingly Godfrey of Bouillon, who eventually emerged as a major figure among the victorious armies that conquered Jerusalem.[21] According to our narrator—the editor of the *Solomon bar Simson Chronicle*—this Godfrey swore that he would not depart without avenging the blood of Jesus upon his crucifiers. This threat aroused the leader of Mainz Jewry, Kalonymous ben Meshullam *ha-parnas,* to undertake negotiations with the absent emperor, negotiations that turned out to be highly successful. The vigilant *parnas* elicited an imperial edict to the authorities in Germany, ordering that they protect their Jewish subjects zealously. As a result of this imperial order, "the wicked duke swore that it had never occurred to him to do them [the Jews] any harm. Nonetheless, they bribed him in Cologne with five hundred silver *zekukim,* and they bribed him similarly in Mainz. He promised them [the Jews], on his staff, that he would behave peaceably."[22] Now, this is an interesting piece of information added by our editor to his original source. It may well be accurate, although it hardly seems as reliable as the data supplied by the earlier *Mainz Anonymous*.

What I should like to focus upon, however, is the sense of narrative cohesion in this addition. The *Mainz Anonymous* in fact tells a somewhat parallel tale, but places it far more appropriately at an earlier point in its account. When describing the movement of French crusaders eastward into the Rhineland, the resultant arousal of nobility and common folk to the crusade, and the stimulation of these new recruits and some of their burgher peers to anti-Jewish animus, the *Mainz Anonymous* speaks of a nobleman named Ditmar, otherwise unknown, who "said that he would not depart this kingdom until he would kill a Jew. Then he would set forth."[23] In the *Mainz Anonymous,* this brief episode makes perfect sense. The much embellished version in the *Solomon bar Simson Chronicle* seems woefully misplaced.

The second interpolation is even more interesting and even more obviously misplaced. A fascinating aspect of the *Mainz Anonymous* is its omission of any reference to papal initiative in the calling of the crusade. In all likelihood, this absence reflects an early Rhineland perception that the movement sweeping into the area was essentially a lay French movement.[24] Indeed, the prologue to the *Solomon bar Simson Chronicle,* while losing some of the specificity of the *Mainz Anonymous* portrait, still speaks of the arousal of the French and Germans. Inexplicably, after describing the fears of the Mainz Jews evoked by the reports from Speyer and Worms and before telling the story of the crusading band and the inspired goose, our editor in effect interjects an alternative opening to the entire 1096 story. Once again, this interpolation betrays a considerable lack of narrative sensibility.

This alternative opening to the entire tale begins with a version of the crusaders' anti-Jewish sloganeering that is far lengthier than that found either in the *Mainz Anonymous* or in our editor's prologue. This more complex justification for anti-Jewish action begins with the notion of vengeance for the crucifixion, adding that "he himself [Jesus] said: 'A day will arrive when my children will come and avenge my blood.' " To this the crusaders purportedly added: "We are his children, and it is our responsibility to exact his vengeance upon you." This then opens the way to fuller castigation of the Jews for their alleged rebelliousness toward God and fuller explication of divine abandonment of the Jews, a theme we encountered in the *Mainz Anonymous:* "Your God was never pleased with you, even when he promised to do well by you, for you have behaved wickedly before him. For this reason, he has forgotten you and no longer desires you, for you have been a stiff-necked people. He has set himself off from you and has shone his light upon us and has taken us as his portion."[25]

After this lengthy justification of anti-Jewish action, our editor proceeds to introduce the pope as the instigator of the crusade. The papal call is depicted, along with the enthusiastic response it elicited. This leads our editor to offer yet another version of crusader sloganeering. Jewish fears are elaborately described, leading to extensive supplication. Our editor reports divine rejection of these Jewish pleas and closes with a series of petitions for divine mercy. Once more, the interpolation is most interesting, but betrays a considerable lack of narrative sophistication.

Thus, analysis of the *Solomon bar Simson Chronicle*'s use of the *Mainz Anonymous* reveals considerable latitude in the utilization and adaptation of earlier narrative materials. Wherever we have checked closely the deletions and accretions, we have found them deficient in the sense of narrative rhythm and development that so characterized the earlier account. What was a compellingly taut narrative has been cut in places, which results in a loss of narrative development and impact; what was effectively spare storytelling has been bloated considerably by the editor of the *Solomon bar Simson Chronicle*.

EDITORIAL GLOSSES

Even where he follows the *Mainz Anonymous* quite closely, our editor introduces observations intended to highlight the meaning of the events depicted; where he adds to his source, he is yet more expansive in interpreting the catastrophe of 1096. It hardly seems amiss to suggest that our editor is far less a historian of the events of 1096 and far more an interpreter of these events as others depicted them. Given our analysis of the prologue and epilogue to the *Solomon bar Simson Chronicle*, it is interesting to identify the central themes in the recurrent editorial glosses to the Speyer-Worms-Mainz story.

Where the editor of the *Solomon bar Simson Chronicle* more or less reproduces his source, the editorial glosses tend to be restrained, falling into a number of identifiable modes. Simplest is the interpretation of the events through the citation of a biblical verse. Thus, at the conclusion of his foreshortened report on the persecution in Speyer and Worms, our editor concludes: "Concerning them [the Jews of Speyer and Worms], Jeremiah [the purported author of Lamentations] wailed:

'Those who were reared in purple have embraced refuse heaps.'"[26] This particular verse directs the reader's attention to an entire segment of Lamentations, which contrasts the nobility of predestruction Jerusalem and its inhabitants with the utter degradation to which they had been reduced. We have already noted the centrality of citations from Lamentations in the editor's prologue to the compilation, so we are fully aware of the significance of this particular biblical book. Again, the relationship of Rhineland Jewry to the sanctity of the divinely ordained sanctuary is emphasized.

A second style of editorial gloss involves direct rumination on the events depicted. Early on in his description of the events in Mainz, our editor interjects the two additional elements noted above. He concludes each with his own observations, two sets of reflections that are in fact diametrically opposed to each other. After depicting the purported threat announced by Duke Godfrey and the successful intervention of Kalonymous of Mainz with the emperor, our editor indicates that Kalonymous's success did not in fact translate into safety for the beleaguered Rhineland Jews. Despite the warnings of the emperor and despite the personal oath of the duke, safety was not to be. This inspires some reflection on the editor's part. The duke's promise to behave peacefully toward the Jews, highlighting the Hebrew *shalom,* leads the editor of the *Solomon bar Simson Chronicle* to observe ruefully that "he who [truly] makes peace [*shalom,* that is to say, God] turned away from them [the Jews] and hid from them and blinded his eye to his people and delivered them to the sword." This artfully articulated statement of Jewish fate of course raises an obvious question, which our editor does not dodge.

> No prophet or visionary and no person of wisdom and discernment can explain how the sin of the divinely chosen congregation [the Jewish people] could have weighed so heavily that they [the crusaders and their allies] could have so destroyed the saintly communities [of the Rhineland], as though they were simply spilling forth water. However, he [God] is surely a righteous judge, and we bear the shortcomings.[27]

This is a purposely opaque statement, lacking the conviction of the editor's prologue and his closing comments to his next insertion. In this curious statement, the leitmotif is uncertainty as to the basis for the tragedy, uncertainty that is, of course, tempered by the assumption that God is a righteous judge and Israel—as noble as it might be—suffers inevitable human frailty.

The interpolation that immediately follows—in point of fact an alternative introduction to the entire tale—with its embellished crusader slogans and its introduction of the papal presence, ends on a remarkably different note. Here our editor combines biblical citation with straightforward and confident explication of the tragedy. Description of the papal call to the crusade and its attendant outburst of anti-Jewish hostility leads to an anguished and intertextually rich depiction of the tragedy that befell Rhineland Jewry. Our editor concludes once more with a citation from Lamentations: "See, O Lord, and behold to whom you have done this!" This citation leads into a set of laments largely woven out of further verses from Lamentations and other biblical books.[28] The great Jewish community of Mainz is bemoaned. The concluding note, however, rings with confident comprehension: "There was a divine intention in order to test those who fear him in suffering the yoke of his pure awe."[29] Although the previous interpolation ends with the notion that neither prophet nor sage can possibly understand the tragedy, this second addition concludes that the point is abundantly clear: God had ordained this suffering as a means of testing the most loyal of his followers. This latter view dovetails nicely with the central themes identified in both the prologue and the epilogue to the compilation.

The editorial glosses in the body of the text taken over from the *Mainz Anonymous* are significant but relatively restrained; those appended to the editor's concluding additions to the material from the *Mainz Anonymous* are far lengthier and richer. Once more, biblical citations are introduced as a means of highlighting aspects of the events described. Thus, in introducing the Isaac ben David episode, the eventual burning of both ancestral home and synagogue, our editor once more turns to Lamentations: "For these things do I weep, my eyes flow with tears." He then artfully specifies those events over which he weeps and over which his tears flow: "Because the Temple of our God was burned and over the burning of Isaac ben David *ha-parnas,* who was burned in his home."[30] There is here a striking and meaningful double entendre. On one level, the passage retains the original biblical sense of the verse as a lament over the destruction of the First Temple; on another level, the passage refers to the burning of the synagogue of Mainz. For our editor, the two are of course intimately related, one to the other.

One of the additional elements appended by our editor depicts fleetingly the almost fortuitous death of most of the great rabbis of the Rhineland prior to the catastrophe. This brief notice is explained by a portion of a verse from Isaiah: "In the face of evil [or even "prior to evil"] the righteous are taken away."[31] God made special provision for

the righteous rabbis of the Rhineland by removing them from the scene
before the tragedy of 1096. Once again, however, citation of the biblical
verse involves far greater complication. The passage in its entirety reads:

> The righteous man perishes,
> And no one considers;
> Pious men are taken away,
> And no one gives thought
> That because of evil
> The righteous was taken away.
> Yet he shall come to peace,
> He shall have rest on his couch
> Who walked straightforward.[32]

The passage is extremely difficult, yet its overall message is one appropriate to the 1096 tragedy. Ultimately, the righteous find everlasting
peace, a broad message that our editor was certainly anxious to convey.

The lengthiest and most striking glosses of all are those that take the
form of petitions to the divine, petitions rooted in the realities that the
narratives recount and generously sprinkled with appropriate biblical
citations. There are a number of such lengthy petitions. Since the themes
and even the verses cited are highly repetitive, let us note only the fullest
of all, the petition that follows the narrative's depiction of the death of
Kalonymous *ha-parnas* and all his followers.

This fullest of the petitions opens by calling down divine vengeance
on those responsible for the catastrophe: "May he who spoke and the
world was created avenge the blood of his servants that has been
spilled." There follows a set of biblical verses intended to highlight the
arrogance and cruelty of Israel's persecutors. Once again, the clear message is that the oppressors of 1096 formed simply another link in the
chain of Israel's enemies. God had to visit upon these recent enemies all
the punishment that he had inflicted on their predecessors. The verses
shift subtly into lament for the slain of Israel, who likewise take their
place in a historical chain, this time a chain of righteous sufferers.
Quickly the focus shifts back to the persecutors, their wickedness, and
God's avenging fury. The weave of verses is complex and impressive;
they combine into a powerful litany of pain and anger.

This string of verses leads into a prose petition for vengeance that
turns into a scathing indictment of Christianity and its adherents.

> [God] will provide our vengeance tangibly. May vengeance for the spilled
> blood of his servants be made known publicly and speedily, for the sake of
> his great Name, which has been bestowed upon us. So that all creatures might

know and understand their [the Christian attackers'] sin and guilt for what
they did to us. He shall repay upon their heads in measure with what they
inflicted upon us. Then they will comprehend and understand and take to
heart that for vanity have they cast our corpses to the ground, that for inanity
have they killed our righteous, that for a trampled carcass have they spilled
the blood of saintly women, that for the words of an enticer and a subverter
have they spilled the blood of infants and sucklings. Their faith is vanity.
They fail to acknowledge the one who created them.[33] They do not tread on
a path that is good and straight. They fail to understand and to take to heart
the one who fashioned sea and dry land. In all their deeds they have been
foolish and misled. They have lost all wisdom; they have put their trust in
vanity.[34] They fail to recognize and recollect the Name of the living God,
king of the universe, who exists forever and for all ages. May the blood of
our righteous serve us as merit and atonement for the generations that suc-
ceed us and for our progeny forever, like the binding of Isaac our forefather,
when Abraham our forefather bound him on the altar.[35]

This lengthy petition captures once more the double focus we have
discerned in the editor's prologue and epilogue to the entire composition. The castigation of Christianity and its adherents is vigorous and
impassioned: for all its shortcomings—intellectual, spiritual, and
moral—the Christian world fully deserves the dire punishment that God
will undoubtedly inflict. By contrast, the great devotion of the martyrs
of Speyer, Worms, and Mainz will serve coming generations of Jews
with merit and atonement, in precisely the same way that the willingness
of Abraham to sacrifice his beloved son has so long served the Jewish
people.

These lengthier editorial glosses reinforce the impressions gleaned
throughout this chapter. The editor of the *Solomon bar Simson Chronicle* appropriated the efforts of the gifted historian who composed the
Mainz Anonymous, reproduced much of that narrative, distended it
somewhat through his deletions and additions, and incorporated the
Speyer-Worms-Mainz unit to reinforce the general message that he
sought to convey to his readers. As a historian, he is unimpressive; as
an elegist and an interpreter, he shows considerable skills in the artful
use of biblical sources and vigorous independent invective and praise.

CHAPTER FIVE

The *Solomon bar Simson Chronicle*

The Trier and Cologne Units

The editor of the *Solomon bar Simson Chronicle* adapted preexistent reports on the events of 1096 in order to provide a sweeping sense of the tragedy and to impose a certain perspective on the catastrophe in its entirety. In the case of the Speyer-Worms-Mainz unit of the composite narrative, we are in a unique position in that we can assess the editor's adaptation against the original source he utilized. A number of additional sources can be identified, but in no other case are we fortunate enough to have the original from which our editor drew.

Of the remaining units utilized by our editor, the two lengthiest and most interesting are those that describe events in Cologne and Trier.[1] The Cologne unit is by far the fuller of the two. I shall, however, treat the Trier unit first, because it seems to be earlier in date of composition. In the case of both these units, I shall attempt to assess the original composition and then to analyze the ways in which the editor of the *Solomon bar Simson Chronicle* adapted this original work to his purposes.

TRIER

Events in Trier in 1096 took a somewhat different course from those in Speyer, Worms, and Mainz. In Mainz, the Jewish community seems to have been destroyed in its totality at the hands of an organized crusader band led by Count Emicho; in Worms, the Jewish community seems to have met much the same fate, this time at the hands of a potent coalition of crusaders and burghers; in Speyer, the Jewish community emerged relatively unscathed, protected from a weak coalition of crusaders and burghers by a determined bishop. In Trier, the Jewish community was converted almost in its entirety. As a result, the story recounted by the anonymous narrator had to differ in many respects from that told in the *Mainz Anonymous*. As was true for the latter, the narrator of the fate of Trier Jewry was deeply committed to reconstructing in considerable detail the precise unfolding of events. The overall objectives of the two · narratives, however, differ markedly.

The Trier narrative[2] covers a time span of approximately two months, from early April through late May or early June 1096.[3] This two-month period is not depicted in day-by-day fashion; rather, the portrayal is episodic, with a focus on three major developments: the arrival in Trier of the French crusading forces under Peter the Hermit; the subsequent arousal of the Trier burghers against their Jewish neighbors; and the decisive violence that eventuated in the massive forced conversion of the Jews of Trier. By the end of this three-part recital, we as readers are provided with a sense of evolving developments, a portrait of the forces arrayed against the Jews of Trier and their anti-Jewish motivations, and a depiction of the behavior of these Jews.

Let us begin with the first of the three subunits.[4] Unlike the *Mainz Anonymous,* the Trier narrative does not present a broad picture of the crusade and its arousal of anti-Jewish animosity and violence. The account opens rather abruptly, with the intrusion of Peter the Hermit and his followers from France. Our narrator is quite precise in his depiction of the arrival of Peter in Trier. He specifies the date as the first day of Passover, which fell on Thursday, 10 April 1096, and tells us that Peter was accompanied by a multitude of followers.[5] Although the appearance of Peter and his associates was likely to have frightened the Jews of any town through which they might pass, the timing in Trier was particularly distressing. Friday, 11 April 1096, was Good Friday, a time regularly fraught with tension and danger for the Jews of medieval Europe. As Thursday was the first day of Passover, the second day of that festival coincided with Good Friday, which was always a difficult juxtaposition, with Christians commemorating the crucifixion likely to be upset by the coterminous Jewish holiday celebration. Thus, Peter's presence in Trier at this particular time had to make the Jews of Trier especially apprehensive.

Despite the dangerous timing, which might have aroused Peter to take an anti-Jewish posture, our author indicates that nothing of the sort took place. He provides us with the interesting information that Peter carried with him a letter from the Jews of France urging their co-religionists elsewhere to support Peter with the provisions necessary for his expedition. Our author describes the Jews of Trier as profoundly shaken by the arrival of Peter and his hordes, noting that Jewish existence in Trier had heretofore been most peaceful. According to our author, the Jews of Trier heeded the advice of their French brethren and supplied the requested provisions, with the anticipated and happy result that Peter and his followers speedily left Trier without inflicting any harm on its frightened Jewry. This rather detailed account of the passage of Peter the Hermit corroborates nicely the general indication in the *Mainz Anonymous* that the French crusaders passed through western Germany with little damage to the Jews.[6]

At this point, however, when the Jews of Trier might have considered themselves fortunate to have survived a crisis unscathed, it quickly becomes clear that such was not in fact the case. Even while describing the passage of Peter through Trier, our author introduces the burghers of that town, at first in what seems to be a curious aside: "When he [Peter] came here, our souls departed and our hearts were broken; trembling seized us and our holiday [recall the Passover dating] was turned into mourning. For to this point the burghers did not intend to inflict any harm on the [Jewish] community, until these holy ones arrived." Now, the depiction of Jewish fears is certainly understandable, but one would assume that these anxieties involved Peter and his minions. Reference to the burghers at this juncture is strange, reflecting understanding conferred by hindsight. Immediately after noting the provisioning of Peter and his peaceful departure eastward, our author continues: "Then our wicked neighbors, the burghers, came and were envious of all the happenings that had befallen the rest of the [Jewish] communities in the land of Lotharingia. They [the burghers of Trier] heard what had been done to them and what had been decreed for them—great tragedy."[7]

What the Trier narrator seems to be suggesting is that the burghers of Trier—heretofore quite friendly and peaceable—were first aroused against their Jewish neighbors by the arrival and preaching of Peter the Hermit, even though he indicates that Peter and his associates departed without inflicting any harm on the frightened Jews of Trier. We might of course speculate that Peter's preaching in and of itself did some harm.[8] Further, it is possible that the Jewish provisioning of Peter's forces might have suggested to some of the burghers of Trier the precariousness of

Jewish circumstances and the potential for exploitation of that precariousness for financial ends. The narrator notes explicitly that the first impact of the heightened burgher animosity involved Jewish bribery.[9]

To be sure, our narrator tells us that yet another factor influenced the burghers of Trier, and that was reportage of anti-Jewish violence in Lotharingia. Once more, we are reduced to speculation. What was the exact linkage between anti-Jewish violence elsewhere and enhanced anti-Jewish sentiment in Trier? It might simply be the normal contagion of violence, a phenomenon widely noted in all eras; alternatively, the report of anti-Jewish outbreaks may have instilled in the burghers of Trier the conviction that the hopelessness of Jewish circumstances dictated conversion or its alternative, death. Such a conclusion on the part of Christians, sometimes even previously friendly Christians, is well documented, and we have encountered it repeatedly.[10] Now, the major assaults of which we know began in mid and late May 1096, more than a month after Peter's passage through Trier.[11] Thus, in depicting the hardening of burgher attitudes, our author seems to be pointing toward an indeterminate period, stretching from mid April, the time of Peter's departure from Trier, through mid or late May, the point at which reports of the atrocities in the Rhineland began to circulate.

In the middle section of the Trier narrative, the author portrays in some detail one illustrative incident from this period of intensifying anti-Jewish sentiment.[12] The precise date of this incident is not specified; it is only identified as having happened "at that time," that is to say during the indeterminate period between mid April and late May. The author relates that, by the time of this incident, the Jews of Trier had already felt it necessary to seek refuge in the bishop's palace. They had, as part of their plan for safe haven, secreted their Torah scrolls in a "strong house." The storage of the precious and revered Torah scrolls became known to the "enemy," and the knowledge moved these Christians to break into the "strong house" via its roof, to strip away the valuable ornamentation on the Torah scrolls, and to desecrate publicly the scrolls so sacred to the Jews. Some of the Jews in the bishop's palace, accompanied by members of the bishop's militia, went immediately to the site of this sacrilege, wept over the desecrated objects, retrieved them, and brought them back into the safety of the palace.

In a more general way, the Jews of Trier are portrayed as having devoted the period between Passover (which began, as noted, on Thursday, 10 April) and Shavuot (which fell on Friday and Saturday, 30 and 31 May) to fasting, repentance, and charity. At the same time, there was a more worldly thrust to their activities: these Jews also taxed themselves with increasing severity in order to raise the funds needed to bribe those who might assist them.

The heart of the Trier narrative lies in the extensive depiction of the disaster that struck Trier Jewry beginning on the Sunday of Pentecost, 1 June.[13] According to our author, the anti-Jewish agitation, which had in any case been in evidence for some time, was fed by the influx of numerous visitors from the Rhineland, who were attracted by a combination of the religious observance and what seems to have been a fair held at that time. These outsiders reinforced powerfully the anti-Jewish animus that the author had already noted in the local populace. The additional visitors seem to have further frightened the insecure Jews of Trier. Our author has the Jews of Trier retreating to the palace of the bishop in the face of the Pentecost agitation. Recall the incident of the Torah scrolls, which showed the Jews already using the palace as a refuge. Such use seems to have been episodic, with Jews periodically gathering in the face of danger and dispersing when the danger abated. Thus, the Pentecost agitation once more forced the Jews of Trier to leave their homes and seek refuge in the bishop's palace.

At this point, our author introduces crusaders into the picture. "Then the killers came and preened over the slaughter and decimation that they had occasioned against the people of the Lord, the holy communities [of the Rhineland]."[14] It is not at all clear whether these crusaders arrived as an organized military force (à la the arrival of Emicho and his followers in Mainz) or as random groups of crusaders (as had been the case in Speyer and Worms). In any case, added to the existing hostility of the burghers and the influx of visitors from the Rhineland, the arrival of the crusaders created a potent new threat.[15]

One of the critical issues associated with the calamity involves the posture of the Rhineland authorities, preeminently the bishops of the major towns.[16] The Jewish narrators of the events of 1096 were sometimes quite ambivalent, uncertain in the wake of failure as to whether these authorities were genuinely committed to their Jewish clients. The depiction in the *Mainz Anonymous* of Jewish negotiations with the archbishop of Mainz affords us a striking example of such subsequent Jewish uncertainty. As we recall, the author of that report vacillates, initially depicting the advice of the archbishop as wickedly deceiving from the outset and then indicating that in fact the archbishop genuinely intended to assist, but was ultimately incapable of so doing.

The author of the Trier narrative provides us with fascinating information on the vexing question of the stance of the ecclesiastical authorities in the face of crusade-related anti-Jewish agitation and violence. We have already noted the gathering of the Jews in the episcopal palace and the dispatch of episcopal militiamen to recover the despoiled and desecrated Torah scrolls, both suggesting serious commitment on the part of the bishop of Trier. On the Sunday of Pentecost, with the endangered Jews of Trier sequestered in his palace, Bishop Engilbert ascended the lectern in the Church of Saint Simon and preached publicly on the issue of the Jews. In this instance, there can be no real doubt of the bishop's intent. The bishop of Trier was committed on both legal and ecclesiastical grounds to ensuring Jewish safety and was willing to use his pulpit to voice unequivocal opposition to the anti-Jewish agitation. Unfortunately for the bishop of Trier and for its Jews, the message was an intensely unpopular one, so unpopular that the bishop himself had to go into hiding in the face of the crowd's resentment of his pro-Jewish sermon.[17]

The failure of the bishop's sermon left the Jews of Trier and their erstwhile protector exposed to great danger. The enraged mob of locals and outsiders sought to kill the Jews and the bishop as well. The Jews were insulated by the walls of the palace, which our author describes lavishly. The bishop of Trier, a recent newcomer, seems to have been able to use the prestige of his office to avoid death.[18]

At this point, the narrator begins to focus on the efforts of the bishop to convince the Jews of Trier to convert. This effort seems to have begun a full two weeks after Pentecost. The bishop had achieved some kind of respite from his attackers, but he had become convinced that he was incapable of putting down the violence decisively and protecting his Jews indefinitely.

The narrator provides us with an opening dialogue between the bishop and the Jews. The bishop acknowledges that, in theory, anti-Jewish violence and forced conversion were unacceptable; he indicates that he is bowing to cruel necessity. The dialogue is interesting and instructive. The bishop indicates that by rights he should have protected his Jews as he had pledged—until there remained no Jewish community in Lotharingia. Although the destruction of Jewish communities had not yet reached that proportion, he expresses to the Jews his inability to offer further protection, citing as evidence the mortal danger in which he found himself. The Jews respond by asserting a less grandiose and more utilitarian prior pledge on the part of the bishop—that he would ensure their safety until the emperor returned to take up his protective responsibility. The bishop's response is striking: he claims that even the emperor could no longer protect the Jews of Trier from the unruly mobs threatening them. When the bishop tells them that they must either convert or face death, the Jews are portrayed as replying defiantly and heroically: "If each of us had ten lives, we would offer them all for the unity of his [God's] Name, before [we would permit them] to sully us."[19] According to our author, this defiance moved the bishop to allow his Jews four days respite, so that they might observe the oncoming festival of Shavuot.[20]

With the passage of the respite and with the bishop still sensing himself in danger, an emissary was sent to the Jews, demanding their conversion. The Jews responded with one last desperate effort to renew episcopal protection. They offered all their possessions to the bishop in return for his safeguarding their lives and relenting in his demand for conversion. The time for such measures had clearly passed, however, and the offer was rejected out of hand.

We might usefully consider for a moment the circumstances at this desperate juncture, circumstances that our author depicts but does not analyze. It seems, first of all, that the walls of the episcopal palace could have held out; there is no suggestion that they could have been breached by the mob. It seems, rather, that the bishop was under intense pressure as master of this refuge and protector of the Jews gathered therein to end the standoff. It further seems that the bishop was intent on preserving Jewish lives. Simply to force open the palace and lay the Jews open to the fury of the mob does not seem to be an option he was willing to exercise. Caught between the pressures to break the standoff and his commitment to preserving Jewish life, the bishop of Trier seems to have opted for a series of terrifying tactics designed to cow the Jews into conversion. Precisely how the beleaguered bishop conceptualized this conversion—whether it was a genuine conversion to be subsequently enforced or an insincere conversion to be rapidly undone—lies beyond our narrator's interest.[21]

For the rest of his account, the author of the Trier narrative is concerned overwhelmingly with portraying adamant Jewish resistance to the bishop's effort at forced conversion, with the objective of showing that those Jews who did convert did so entirely against their will. The tableau that he creates is a striking one: an enormous mob gathered at the peripheries of the palace while a delegation of episcopal and town notables negotiated with the Jews at the palace gate. A prominent leader of the Jewish community, Asher ben Joseph *ha-gabbai,* was led out,

joined voluntarily by a young lad named Meir ben Samuel. These two
Jews were confronted with an image of Jesus and ordered to bow down
before it. They responded with a blasphemous outburst and met their
deaths. Two additional Jews—an elderly man and a young woman—
were subjected to the same treatment and similarly met their death. This
opening effort at terrorization was not effective, and a new tack was
taken.

Frustrated in their efforts to frighten the Jews of Trier into conversion, episcopal officials next initiated a program of conversion by physical force. "They [the bishop's officials] said to one another: 'All this
[i.e., the Jewish resistance to conversion] the women achieve, by moving
their husbands to firmness in rejecting the crucified.'[22] All the officials
then came and seized the women with great force, beating them and
smiting them, and led them to the church in order to baptize them."[23]
According to our author, the groundwork for such actions had been laid
some days before, when the well inside the palace had been sealed, so
that the Jewish women could not throw their children down it in order
to avoid forcible baptism. Further, during the night prior to this decisive
day of confrontation, episcopal functionaries had forestalled any Jewish
efforts toward self-inflicted death. Again, the bishop's goal was to solve
the impasse through forced conversion without occasioning significant
loss of Jewish lives.

The author of the Trier narrative concludes with four instances of
self-inflicted Jewish martyrdom, all involving women—two natives of
Trier and two visitors from Cologne. The story thus closes with a total
focus on Jewish martyrdom and its rewards. Despite the intense focus
on these relatively few Jewish martyrs, the perceptive reader cannot
avoid the broader reality: obviously, the vast majority of Trier Jews
succumbed to the forced conversion decreed by the bishop of that
town.[24]

Thus, the author of the Trier narrative put together a well-ordered
and gripping account of the fate of the Jews of that town during the
spring months of 1096, an account that is highly detailed and shows a
good feel for the unfolding of events. In his role of historian, our author
is subject to only one major criticism, a lack of care with respect to
dating. His dating for the decisive episode in the Trier drama is hopelessly garbled. The Trier narrative places the onset of this decisive episode on the Sunday of Pentecost, which in 1096 fell on 1 June. The
result of the popular agitation on Pentecost was, as we have seen, mortal

danger to both the Jews and the bishop who sought to protect them. After two weeks of this danger, the bishop approached the Jews and insisted upon their conversion. They requested a four-day respite, during which they would prepare for and celebrate Shavuot. Now, as already noted, Shavuot in 1096 took place on Friday and Saturday, 30 and 31 May, the days that immediately preceded the Sunday of Pentecost. Thus, the chronology of this closing episode is hopelessly and inexplicably confused. I can offer no suggestion as to why a narrator with such a fine sense of historical development should have so badly misdated the critical events in the story he wove.

Let us now attempt to identify the objectives of this Trier narrative. They are rather thoroughly time-bound, with no real rumination on the timeless meaning of the events depicted.[25] As a time-bound description, the Trier narrative shares key concerns with the *Mainz Anonymous*. Both are committed to conveying a sense of intensifying danger and increasingly extreme Jewish response. In the *Mainz Anonymous,* the developments portrayed spread over a period of several months and take place in the broad space of northern France and western Germany; in the Trier narrative, both time and space are more limited. Nonetheless, sensitivity to temporal and spatial issues is a feature of both.

To be sure, the objectives of the two narratives—in their time-bound aspect—differ. As we have seen, the *Mainz Anonymous* seeks to inform its Jewish readers as to the complex realities of the non-Jewish world; to provide guidance for future Jewish behavior; to advance an *apologia* for what might be construed as political obtuseness on the part of the Rhineland Jews, for conversion by some, and for the radical martyrdom of others; and to memorialize the heroism of the Rhineland Jewish martyrs. By contrast, the Trier narrative, while much interested in conveying the complexities of Christian society, was rather more single-mindedly committed to providing an *apologia* for the conversion of Trier Jewry. The factors that led to this conversion, all Jewish heroism notwithstanding, lie at the core of the narrative.

Identification of this core concern on the part of our author leads to a reasonable guess as to the date of composition of the narrative. Elaborate depiction of the events of 1096 in order to clarify the reasons for the conversion of the dedicated and heroic Jews of Trier makes most sense as an activity undertaken not too long after the tragedy itself, while the memory of the events and the special fate of Trier Jewry still made survivors of the ordeal somewhat uncomfortable. While there is no foolproof key to dating, I would argue that the identification of the central thrust of the narrative as a rationalization for the conversion of Trier Jewry strongly suggests a fairly early date of composition.

Identification of the central thrust in the Trier narrative furthers in a number of ways our sense of the *Solomon bar Simson Chronicle* and its editor. Clearly, the Trier narrative hardly fits the central themes emphasized by the organizer of the composite report on 1096. The *Mainz Anonymous* was surely more congenial to the concerns of our editor. In all likelihood, he did not have an extensive choice of materials at his disposal and utilized those that were available. *Faute de mieux,* the Trier unit was integrated into the *Solomon bar Simson Chronicle.*

There was not all that much that our editor could do with the Trier narrative, and thus we find very little in the way of editorial gloss in this portion of the *Solomon bar Simson Chronicle.* It is worth noting, first of all, the lack of editorial introduction to the Trier unit of the composite narrative. The introductory remarks are spare in the extreme: "The tale of Trier has been told to me."[26] This bland opening contrasts sharply with that of the Cologne unit, to be analyzed shortly. Editorial glosses in the Trier account are brief and are limited to the endings of each of the three segments.

The first section of the Trier narrative closes with a description of extensive Jewish attempts to bribe the burghers of Trier. Our editor concludes: "All this was unavailing on the day of the Lord's wrath. For there was an intention on the part of the Lord against all that generation, which was chosen by him as his portion, to fulfill his command."[27] The language here is highly reminiscent of the prologue to the entire *Solomon bar Simson Chronicle.* The second segment of the narrative, which is focused on one incident in the period between Passover and Pentecost, again ends with a recounting of Jewish efforts at bribery—with a similar sense that these efforts ultimately proved unavailing—and a similarly brief editorial observation: "For the Lord delivered them into the hands of their enemies. His anger waxed against them. He hid his face from them on the day of their reckoning."[28] Once more the phraseology is highly reminiscent of the prologue to the entire collection.

The lengthiest editorial gloss is reserved—not surprisingly—for the end: "The master of vengeance will avenge in our own days and before our eyes the blood of his servants that has been spilled. May their merit and their piety serve us positively; may they protect us on an evil day."[29] This again sounds very much like what we have encountered already, in this instance in the editor's epilogue to the collection.

Thus, the Trier unit was introduced largely because it was yet one more available description of the events of 1096. Its precise contours did not fit well with the central themes of the collection, as the editor conceived them. Nonetheless, he utilized the Trier narrative, appending once more glosses that stressed his own perceptions of 1096: the tragedy was not rooted in the alleged Jewish sin of deicide or in an alleged divine abandonment of the Jews; it was, rather, grounded in the unique capacity of the Jews of 1096 to withstand persecution and remain true to their faith. Given this understanding of the tragedy, it could have only one reasonable outcome. God would surely enact appropriate vengeance upon the enemy and shower requisite reward upon the heroic Jewish martyrs and their descendants.

COLOGNE

As noted already, the Cologne unit of the *Solomon bar Simson Chronicle* is the only element in the composite account that carries any dating.[30] In a curiously placed statement of authorship, we are told that a Jew named Solomon bar Simson authored the Altenahr segment of the Cologne unit in Mainz in the year 1140. In order to gather this information, he "asked the elders about the entire incident. From their mouths I ordered all the elements properly. They told me this incident of sanctification [of the divine Name]."[31] There is yet a second reference to information supplied by elders. After depicting the remarkable events in Xanten, one of the most moving of the incidents affecting Cologne Jewry, the author of the Cologne unit has the gifted Jewish spokesman ending his hortatory address by returning to the grace after a meal and adding a series of requests for divine assistance. Our narrator concludes: "He further added many benedictions related to the event, because of the decree about to overtake them, as my ancestors and the other elders occupied with the matter—who saw this great event—have told me."[32] These two interpolations concerning oral sources reinforce the explicit statement of authorship in 1140. The Cologne unit was surely written many years after the events themselves and was based on recollections still alive in the older stratum of the Rhineland Jewish population. The later date of the Cologne unit of course had an impact on the range of interests exhibited by its author.

The organization of the Cologne unit is simple and effective. It begins fairly abruptly with reports of the Mainz tragedy reaching Cologne. The response of the Jews of Cologne is somewhat surprising: "The Jews fled

to their Christian acquaintances and remained there through the two
days of Shavuot."[33] Now, flight to Christian acquaintances is hardly
shocking in and of itself; it constitutes a consistent pattern of Jewish
reaction in 1096. What is shocking is that, after the debacles in Worms
and Mainz, Jews should still be choosing a course that seemingly should
have been abandoned. At this late date, it is highly surprising to find
Jews still fleeing to individual Christian neighbors.

On the day after the Jewish holiday, violence broke out in Cologne.
The author of the Cologne unit, writing many decades after the events
of 1096, was not at all interested in specifying the perpetrators of the
attacks. In describing the very first outbreak in Cologne itself, he identifies the attackers as simply "the enemy." Despite this lack of interest
on the author's part, we can comfortably assume that the initial violence
did not involve the crusading band of Count Emicho. Whether this violence involved merely the burghers of Cologne, as suggested by Albert
of Aachen, or involved some random crusaders as well is uncertain.[34] In
any case, the threat was not a potent one and there were few Jewish
casualties. The archbishop of Cologne took precisely the steps instituted
by his counterpart in Speyer. He moved his Jewish subjects out of the
city and into seven fortified towns to assure their safety.

The bulk of the Cologne unit of the *Solomon bar Simson Chronicle*
is then given over to a description of the fate of each of the seven enclaves
of Cologne Jews, a description organized chronologically.[35] These seven
segments of the Cologne unit differ from one another considerably. In
the first place, the seven events are described differentially in terms of
auctorial attention, with some (Wevelinghofen, Altenahr II, Xanten, and
Moers) depicted in great detail, some (Neuss and Kerpen) reported fairly
briefly, and one (Altenahr I) recounted in but one long sentence. The
fate of the seven Jewish enclaves varied as well. In five cases, most of
the Jews met their deaths (Neuss, Wevelinghofen, Altenahr I, Altenahr
II, and Xanten); in one case (Moers), the bulk of the Jewish group was
forcibly converted; in the final case (Kerpen) most of the Jews survived
the ordeal.[36]

We have noted in the *Mainz Anonymous* a striking literary technique,
the interplay of broad description with detailed individualized portraits.
We first encountered this effective technique in the second Worms episode in the *Mainz Anonymous* and found that it enabled the author to
highlight broad developments and reinforce them with specific, emo-
tionally moving episodes. The Cologne report likewise interweaves the

general and the specific, although somewhat less effectively. The generalized portrayal of the seven Jewish enclaves is by and large extremely sparse; only the broad flow of events in Moers is depicted in any detail. Instead of counterpointing the general and the specific, the author of the Cologne report focuses heavily on the individual. The great power of the Cologne report lies in its impressive narration of striking individual episodes.

As noted earlier, our author—again unlike the author of the *Mainz Anonymous*—is not seriously interested in either the identity or the motivation of the attackers.[37] In most instances, our author does make it clear that an invading crusader band was responsible for the assault or near assault on the Jewish enclaves.[38] Given the proximity of these assaults to the Mainz attack and given the parallel commitment on the part of the crusaders in question to total destruction of the Jews, there can be no real doubt as to the identity of these crusaders. They almost certainly were the minions of Count Emicho.

The focus of our author's interest was the Jewish victims of Emicho's murderous assault. As noted, what is particularly striking about the Cologne unit is the profound emotional impact of some of the narrative depictions of the Jewish martyrs, which convey their behaviors and thinking. Most affecting of all is the powerful portrayal of events in Wevelinghofen and Xanten.

The Wevelinghofen description opens with general observations on the fate of the Jews gathered in that fortified town. Alerted to the arrival of the crusading band, many of these Jews took their own lives and the lives of their kinsmen in a variety of ways. Special attention is accorded those Jews who ascended the town's towers and threw themselves into the Rhine River. Most of these Jews perished quickly. Two young men, however, survived the plunge into the waters of the Rhine, and their story is told in considerable detail and with remarkable force.

Featured in this account of Samuel ben Gedaliah *ha-ḥatan* and his friend Yehiel ben Samuel is their resolute intention to martyr themselves and the anguished assistance offered by the father of the latter and the beadle of the Cologne synagogue. The two young men perished at the hands of the father and the beadle, the father then entreated the beadle to dispatch him, and the beadle finally took his own life. This bare outline of the story hardly begins to capture its power, however. That power lies overwhelmingly in the soliloquies placed in the mouths of the four martyrs by the author. They are among the lengthiest and most

moving addresses found in any of the Hebrew narratives. Let us cite
only the opening soliloquy of the two friends, as they prepared to throw
themselves into the waters of the Rhine:

> When it occurred to them to throw themselves into the water, they kissed
> one another and grasped one another and hugged one another by their shoul-
> ders and cried to one another: "Woe for our youth, for we have not been
> worthy of seeing seed proceed from us and we have not reached the years of
> old age. Nonetheless, let us fall into the hands of the Lord, for he is a God
> who is kingly, steadfast, and merciful. It is better for us to die here for his
> great Name, so that we might walk with the righteous in paradise, rather
> than have these unclean and uncircumcised seize us and sully us against our
> will with their wicked waters."[39]

Throughout this episode, the Jewish martyrs address one another and
the reader with their anguish and their convictions. It is one of the most
moving episodes in the composite narrative.

Yet more artistic and skillful is the segment on the Cologne Jews
sequestered in Xanten. Our author portrays the arrival of the crusaders
on the eve of the Sabbath, with the Jews readying themselves for their
festive meal before the prepared Sabbath tables. Interrupted by the
threat of violence, a leader in the group is called upon, and he delivers
a brilliant address (formulated as we have it by the narrator of course)
that weaves together themes of Sabbath, table, Temple ritual, and afterlife. Throughout the *Solomon bar Simson Chronicle*—as well as the
Mainz Anonymous—there is a constant thrust toward linking the mundane and the heroic, toward rooting the extreme behaviors of the martyrs in the everyday obligations of Jewish existence. Grounding the extreme in the mundane is one of the regular techniques employed by the
various narrators in justifying the lengths to which the martyrs of 1096
went. Nowhere is this tendency manifested more compellingly than in
the Xanten episode. Let us focus briefly on the address of Rabbi Moses
ha-cohen.[40] The group of Jews gathered in Xanten had ostensibly begun
their meal with the blessing regularly intoned at this juncture, thanking
God for the food to be consumed. To be sure, these Jews were precluded
from enjoying the actual repast itself. Nonetheless, the ritual obligation
of reciting the closing benedictions to a meal remained, and it was with
this everyday obligation that Rabbi Moses began, invoking the normal
formula for beginning the grace after meal. "Let us intone the grace after
meal in honor of the living God, our father in heaven."

Immediately, Rabbi Moses drew the attention of his followers to the
table spread before them, transforming that table into a surrogate altar.

The relationship of the everyday table to the Temple altar is a constant of traditional Jewish thinking, but it took on special significance at Xanten. "For the table is presently set before us in place of the altar. Now let us rise up and ascend to the house of the Lord and accomplish speedily the will of our Creator." In physical terms, it is the crusaders who are on their way up to Jerusalem; for Rabbi Moses, however, the genuine spiritual ascent is about to be undertaken by the Jewish victims of misguided crusader zeal. With this image of ascent to Jerusalem, Rabbi Moses calls upon his followers to slaughter themselves and their loved ones. Temple imagery abounds. "Let us offer up ourselves as a sacrifice to the Lord, as a whole burnt offering to the Most High, offered up on the altar of the Lord."

At this point, Rabbi Moses turns his attention to the rewards for these acts of self-sacrifice. The sense of reward projected invokes the special temporal circumstances of the Jews in Xanten: the onset of the sacred Sabbath.

> We shall exist in a world that is entirely daylight, in paradise, in the [light of] the shining speculum. We shall see him [God] eye to eye, in his majesty and his greatness. Each one [of us] will be accorded a golden crown upon his head, in which will be set precious stones and pearls. We shall sit there among the pillars of the universe and shall dine in the company of the righteous in paradise. We shall be part of the company of Rabbi Akiba and his associates. We shall sit upon a golden throne, under the tree of life. We shall each point with a finger and say: "Behold this is our God. In him have we trusted. Let us rejoice in his salvation." There we shall [properly] observe the Sabbath, for here—in this world of darkness—we cannot [truly] rest and observe it properly.

Overflowing blessing will be the reward for the acts of self-sacrifice about to be undertaken.

From the grace after a meal, to the table, to the surrogate altar to the afterlife—such is the trajectory of this remarkable soliloquy, which ends by bringing Rabbi Moses's auditors and our narrator's readers back to the earthly starting point, the special grace after a meal. Moving to one of the later segments of the grace after a meal, Rabbi Moses intoned: "May the merciful avenge in the days of those who remain after us and in their sight the blood of your servants that has been spilled and that is yet to be spilled. May the merciful save us from wicked men and from conversion and from idolatry and from the impurity of the gentiles and their abominations." According to our narrator, Rabbi Moses continued to intone such special pleas, appropriate to the occasion.

Our narrator closes his description of this remarkable address by suggesting that it achieved its purpose, moving the Jewish auditors to the anticipated acts of martyrdom. He emphasizes in particular the glee and zest with which these acts of martyrdom were undertaken. Rabbi Moses had created a mood that carried the Cologne Jews gathered at Xanten much beyond themselves, into a frenzy of desire to serve the Lord in what seemed the highest possible manner.

I have focused on two of the most successful passages in our narrator's depiction of the fate of Cologne Jewry. Other instances of heroic behavior and artful rhetoric abound. The author of the Cologne unit was uninterested in a number of facets of the events of 1096; he was, however, highly skilled in his effort to depict Jewish martyrdom in the richest terms.

At this point, we should shift from the ostensibly independent Cologne unit to the editor's use of his source and the ways in which he adapted it to his overall objectives for the collection as a whole. A question, however, intrudes: is this in reality an independent unit, or are the author of the Cologne unit and the editor of the collection in its entirety in fact one and the same? We have earlier noted the curious passage—at the end of the description of the fate of the Cologne Jews gathered in Altenahr—that identifies the author as one Solomon bar Simson. At an earlier point, I indicated that it has not been clear whether this Solomon bar Simson was the author of the Altenahr passage, the author of the Cologne unit in its entirety, or the editor of the entire compilation.[41] At this juncture, I see no foolproof way of solving this riddle, although I am inclined to the view that the author of the Cologne report and the editor of the *Solomon bar Simson Chronicle* are one and the same.

In a general way, there are more editorial glosses in the Cologne unit than elsewhere in the collection, suggesting that perhaps the author and editor are one. The glosses are suffused with the same themes and much the same terminology found in the editor's prologue and epilogue. To be sure, this similarity may merely reflect an editorial penchant for glossing the Cologne unit more richly than the others, perhaps in part because this unit was more appropriate to the editor's overall concerns.

More significant is the fact that the content of the Cologne unit corresponds rather fully to the central themes of the editorial prologue and epilogue. I would draw attention, for example, to the heavy emphasis on revenge in the soliloquy of Rabbi Moses in Xanten, noted just above. Revenge hardly appeared as a significant element in either the *Mainz*

Anonymous or the Trier unit; it is certainly central to the Cologne unit, perhaps indicating again that author and editor are one and the same.

Equally significant is the recurrence of key images from the editorial prologue in the Cologne report. Thus, for example, we recall the prologue imagery of God creating an obstacle to the ascent of the prayers of the Jews of 1096, so that these prayers might not reach him and sway him from his decree. Precisely such imagery is found early in the description of the fate of those Cologne Jews who sought refuge in Xanten, a point in the narrative that is so integral to the tale that it can hardly be viewed as an editorial gloss. The evidence is hardly overwhelming, and the point is not at all central to the theses of this study. I would suggest tentatively, however, that the Cologne report was penned by the editor of the broader chronicle.

In any case, we do have, in the Cologne unit, an account that is clearly distinct from the Speyer-Worms-Mainz narrative and the Trier narrative, embellished with glosses that reinforce the central message of the *Solomon bar Simson Chronicle* in its entirety: The Jewish martyrs were the great heroes of the First Crusade; their merit would surely serve their descendants in future straits; the Christians responsible for the anti-Jewish atrocities deserve the fullest measure of divine punishment, which would not be long in coming. All this is highly appropriate to the atmosphere of the 1140s, when Christendom was poised on the brink of yet another crusade. For both the author of the Cologne unit and the editor of the compilation in its entirety—or for the single individual responsible for both—the new crusade would surely eventuate in the punishment so richly deserved. This individual (or these individuals) at the very least wished to lay before God a case for making the new crusading venture the occasion of divine redress and to advance an impassioned entreaty for so doing.

CHAPTER SIX

The *Eliezer bar Nathan* *Chronicle*

The *Eliezer bar Nathan Chronicle* has been the best known of the three 1096 Hebrew narratives. It has survived in multiple manuscripts, which is not the case for the other two. More important, it was cited first in 'Emek ha-Bakha' of Joseph *ha-cohen* and then in the *Ẓemaḥ David* of David Gans, thereby becoming the source of most early modern knowledge of the events in 1096.[1] The broader impact of the *Eliezer bar Nathan Chronicle* is in all likelihood rooted in the combination of its literary format and qualities and the renown of its purported author.

Like the *Solomon bar Simson Chronicle,* so too the *Eliezer bar Nathan Chronicle* has reached us in its entirety. The latter narrative begins in precisely the same fashion as the former: "It came to pass in the year 4856 since the creation of the world, the year 1028 of our exile, in the eleventh year of the two hundred fifty-sixth cycle, . . .[2] that the arrogant, the barbaric, a fierce and impetuous people—French and German—rose up against us."[3] It ends with a rich portrait of the celestial rewards for the Jewish martyrs of 1096, with the closing hope that "their worthiness might sustain us forever, selah. [May their worthiness] hasten the day of redemption, speedily and in our own time, amen. And so may it be [God's] Will."[4] Unlike the *Solomon bar Simson Chronicle,* however, the narrative of Eliezer bar Nathan does not seem to be a composite work. The structure of the work—four poems, which constitute the original element, plus a surrounding narrative—suggests one author who absorbed a preexistent source, modified it considerably, and extended it through the addition of his own independent dirges.[5]

What is original and unique in the *Eliezer bar Nathan Chronicle* is its combination of prose and poetry. It is the poetry that has furnished the clue to the authorship of the narrative. Each of the four poems is organized in the form of an alphabetical acrostic that spells out Eliezer bar Nathan. Generally, it has been assumed that this Eliezer bar Nathan is the well-known twelfth-century halakhist and poet, who seems to have lived most of his life in the reconstructed Jewish community of Mainz.[6] This identification has not, however, been without its opponents. There are data that support the identification of our author with the famed halakhist and poet, but also grounds for questioning that identification. A brief discussion is in order, although the results will not be decisive.

Curiously, the first major student of the renowned Eliezer bar Nathan denied his authorship of the chronicle. Shalom Albeck, in an exhaustive introduction to his edition of Eliezer bar Nathan's important halakhic work, argued that our 1096 Hebrew narrative was written by someone other than the famed halakhist.[7] Victor Aptowitzer, in his introduction to the halakhic work of Eliezer bar Nathan's grandson, Eliezer bar Joel, reexamined carefully all members of the family, including the grandfather. Aptowitzer came to the conclusion that the 1096 narrative was in fact authored by the well-known Eliezer bar Nathan, a conclusion espoused also in the most recent study, that of Ephraim Urbach.[8]

A number of factors point to the well-known Eliezer bar Nathan as the author of our 1096 narrative. Perhaps most persuasive is the evidence that the halakhic expert had deep interests in liturgical poetry. He was vitally involved in poetic exegesis. Evidence of his creativity in this area is indisputable.[9] Moreover, almost thirty poems by Eliezer bar Nathan have survived, and in each the same acrostic system can be found.[10] To be sure, there is no certainty that all these poems were written by the famous Eliezer bar Nathan. Nonetheless, the combination of poetic exegesis and poetic creativity (although not beyond dispute) certainly suggests that identification of the halakhist with the author of the third of our narratives is highly likely.

The analysis to be undertaken shortly will provide one disconcerting detail. As we shall see, the author of our narrative clearly chose to highlight the fortunes of the Jewish community of Cologne—a distinct shift from the *Mainz Anonymous*'s focus on Mainz and the *Solomon bar Simson Chronicle*'s focus on Speyer-Worms-Mainz.[11] Given the association of the well-known Eliezer bar Nathan with Mainz, it is difficult to reconcile that known datum with the central importance of Cologne in the narrative. Nonetheless, despite this reservation, attribution of the third narrative to the renowned Eliezer bar Nathan seems reasonable. It is, in any case, highly likely that medieval Jews made this identification, thereby providing the third narrative with a basis for admiration and preservation lacking in the other two. For our purposes, identification of the author of our narrative with the halakhic expert contributes little, since the evidence available for reconstructing his life adds nothing of substance to our understanding of the prose-cum-poetry account.

Much attention has focused on the relationship of the *Eliezer bar Nathan Chronicle* to the *Solomon bar Simson Chronicle*. Again, there is a broad divide between those who see the two as independent of each other and those who see them as related. We recall that the case for independence has been made in two ways—either that the two were based on communal letters, which account for their sharings, or that the two were rooted in a common *Urtext,* from which each drew.[12] That the *Solomon bar Simson Chronicle* and the *Eliezer bar Nathan Chronicle* represent parallel drawings from earlier communal letters is implausible, because the characteristics common to the two narratives involve much more than simply identical information. The opening section, which must surely reflect the hand of the composer, is shared almost word for word. Moreover, the sequencing of the two narratives is precisely parallel. They both move from Speyer to Worms to Mainz to Cologne, adding reference to four further communities, again parallel in both accounts. This level of sharing precludes the possibility of common data shaped by two authors into independent compositions. The notion of an *Urtext* is also highly problematic. It simply adds another hypothetical layer to the relationship of the two texts.[13]

The remaining alternative is that one of these two narratives must be the source of the other. Solid evidence suggests that the *Solomon bar Simson Chronicle* served as the source for the narrative of Eliezer bar Nathan. Material in the Cologne unit of the *Solomon bar Simson Chronicle* shows it to be an original composition or at least the copy of an original composition. As we have seen, the author of the Cologne unit (who may or may not have been the editor of the entire narrative) went to some length to identify the oral sources of his account.[14] Were the *Eliezer bar Nathan Chronicle* the original, these references to oral sources should by rights have been in it. These references in the *Solomon bar Simson Chronicle* indicate that it was in fact the original.

At the same time, the *Eliezer bar Nathan Chronicle* shows unmistakable signs of being derivative, especially in some of the clarifying commentary it offers. Thus, it portrays, as did the *Solomon bar Simson Chronicle,* the dispersing of the Jews of Cologne into seven fortified outposts in a failed attempt to provide safety. After describing the fate of these seven sets of Jews, the *Eliezer bar Nathan Chronicle* notes that "they [the Christians] did likewise in the town of Geldern—they [the Jews] were plundered and destroyed, and there was no one to save them."[15] This certainly looks like an addition to the original number of seven enclaves found in the Solomon bar Simson original. Yet clearer is the following observation: "There were two Altenahrs in which the holy ones of Israel were killed. The first is the town of Altenahr near Julich; the other is the town of Altenahr somewhere or other."[16] This obviously represents clarification of a preexistent source, which must have been the *Solomon bar Simson Chronicle.*

Establishment of the *Solomon bar Simson Chronicle* as the source for the *Eliezer bar Nathan Chronicle* opens the way for brief speculation on the dating of the latter. We recall the suggestion that Solomon bar Simson edited his composite account on the eve of the Second Crusade and that his lengthy closing section on the destruction of the crusading bands of Peter the Hermit and Count Emicho projected their downfall as the first signs of anticipated divine revenge. The *Solomon bar Simson Chronicle* ends by indicating that "the enemy has not desisted from its evil designs—every day they set forth for Jerusalem."[17] This leads the editor of the composite narrative to plead with God to visit full punishment on those responsible for the atrocities of 1096. The fact that the *Eliezer bar Nathan Chronicle* is based upon that of Solomon bar Simson and omits entirely the account of early defeats of the crusaders and the attendant prayers for continued punishment combine to suggest a post–Second Crusade time frame. While the Second Crusade was in many ways disastrous to the crusading endeavor,[18] it was certainly not the massive failure for which Solomon bar Simson had fervently hoped and prayed. The slightly later *Eliezer bar Nathan Chronicle* simply omits the Jewish hopes espoused before the Second Crusade.

Having established that the *Solomon bar Simson Chronicle* served as the source for the account of Eliezer bar Nathan, we would do well to recall how medieval Jewish authors treated narrative materials at their disposal. As indicated earlier, a striking instance of such utilization of preexistent narrative material is afforded by the Orléans depiction of the Blois incident of 1171 and the revised version of the same event adapted by Ephraim ben Jacob of Bonn for his catalog of late-twelfth-century anti-Jewish incidents. We have noted in the later retelling the addition of further details, culled from other sources, and—far more striking—the rearrangement of data in a manner that, to many readers, seems to entail loss of some of the artistry in the Orléans account. Clearly, Ephraim ben Jacob felt considerable latitude in his utilization of a preexistent narrative.[19]

Our earlier analysis of the *Mainz Anonymous* and the Speyer-Worms-Mainz unit of the *Solomon bar Simson Chronicle* affords yet another instance of later utilization and manipulation of prior materials. Given the dating of the *Mainz Anonymous* as early and the *Solomon bar Simson Chronicle* as stemming from the 1140s, it seems obvious that the editor of the latter utilized the former. In chapter 4, I analyzed in some detail the latitude with which the *Mainz Anonymous* was absorbed. Changes evident in the *Solomon bar Simson Chronicle* include additions at the end of the source, compression at the beginning, and—most striking—insertions throughout. Again, many of these alterations entail, at least to the modern eye, diminution of the artistic power of the source.

How then did Eliezer bar Nathan treat his source? Overall, the later narrative shortens the first four elements of the *Solomon bar Simson Chronicle:* an explanatory prologue, repeated almost in its entirety;[20] a somewhat shortened depiction of events in Speyer, Worms, and Mainz;[21] a somewhat shortened account of events in Cologne;[22] and cursory mention of four further affected Jewish communities—Trier, Metz, Regensburg, and Prague.[23] At this juncture, the *Solomon bar Simson Chronicle* proceeds to add a statement in praise of those forcibly converted and an editorial epilogue that describes in considerable detail the alleged destruction of the bands led by Peter the Hermit and Count Emicho and beseeches further punishment for those guilty of spilling Jewish blood. The *Eliezer bar Nathan Chronicle* moves from the cursory mention of four further afflicted Jewish communities to a closing and fairly brief paean of praise for the Jewish martyrs of 1096. The closing two elements of the *Solomon bar Simson Chronicle* are deleted entirely. Thus, the most noteworthy overall change in the derivative narrative is the considerable compression of its source.

A closer look at the treatment of the *Solomon bar Simson Chronicle* reveals further facets of the adaptation of the earlier source. The editorial

prologue is reproduced by Eliezer bar Nathan in its entirety. This includes the fairly brief description of the call to the crusade, the arousal
of anti-Jewish sentiment in some of the crusading armies, Jewish prayers
to God beseeching his mercy, the divine refusal to heed those prayers,
and the grounding of that refusal in God's choice of the generation of
1096 to expiate the sin of the golden calf. Once again, the harsh divine
decision is grounded in God's sense that this generation of Jews was
uniquely qualified to serve his will in the most radical manner. Eliezer
bar Nathan seems to focus, at the outset, on the difficult issue of the
basis for the catastrophe and to advance for his readers the audacious
theological views of his predecessor, the unknown Solomon bar Simson.

The second segment of the *Eliezer bar Nathan Chronicle* opens with
the continued close reproduction of its source. The account of events in
Speyer is almost precisely that found in the *Solomon bar Simson Chronicle*. Curiously, the Worms report of Eliezer bar Nathan is lengthier than
its source, with two discernible elements added from the *Mainz Anonymous* account.[24] It is with Mainz Jewry that the internal foreshortening
begins. As noted, the report on Mainz Jewry constituted the heart of the
Mainz Anonymous (which included specific reports on only Speyer,
Worms, and Mainz) and the lengthiest single element in the composite
Solomon bar Simson Chronicle, fuller than the latter's extensive depiction of events in Cologne.

We specified earlier the constituent elements in the lengthy Solomon
bar Simson report on Mainz.[25] Eliezer bar Nathan excised most of that
lengthy account. He incorporates only the slaughter in the courtyard of
the archbishop's palace, omitting entirely the riveting stories of events
in the upper chambers of the palace, the assault on the burgrave's palace,
and the follow-up incidents involving David ben Nathaniel and Samuel
ben Naaman. We recall that the Solomon bar Simson narrative added
a number of elements to its source, the *Mainz Anonymous;* Eliezer bar
Nathan cuts these added elements drastically as well. There is, in effect,
only brief reference to the band saved by the archbishop[26] and the two
Jews—Isaac ben David and Uri ben Joseph—who perished while burning down the synagogue of Mainz. The overall tendency then is toward
shortening. Indeed, the Mainz unit in the *Eliezer bar Nathan Chronicle*
is no longer than the Worms unit, whereas the Mainz unit in the *Solomon bar Simson Chronicle*—the source—is something like thirty times
as long as its Worms unit. More specifically, all the dramatic speeches
that gave the Mainz episode in both the *Mainz Anonymous* and the
Solomon bar Simson Chronicle its enormous power were eliminated by

Eliezer bar Nathan. The end result—as regards the Speyer-Worms-Mainz unit—is a shorter, sparer, almost entirely third-person narration that is less dramatic and moving than the earlier account.

Let us proceed to Eliezer bar Nathan's adaptation of the Cologne unit of the *Solomon bar Simson Chronicle*. Here too there is shortening and—especially noteworthy—excision of the moving soliloquies that gave the Cologne unit so much of its emotional power. To be sure, the shortening is less radical than that in the Mainz unit. Whereas the Mainz unit in the *Solomon bar Simson Chronicle* is approximately double the size of its Cologne counterpart, in the account of Eliezer bar Nathan the balance is reversed, with the Cologne unit approximately four times the length of the Mainz account. The thinking that animated the differential compression of the two units cannot be reconstructed.[27]

The basic structure of Eliezer's Cologne unit follows the *Solomon bar Simson Chronicle*. Both begin with a report on the relative safety provided by Christian neighbors in Cologne itself, followed by the decision of the local archbishop to divide his Jews among seven rural fortifications. The sequence of attacks in the two narratives is precisely parallel, moving through Neuss, Wevelinghofen,[28] Altenahr I, Altenahr II,[29] Xanten, Moers, and Kerpen; Eliezer bar Nathan adds Geldern as well. Once more, the sequencing suggests the dependence of Eliezer bar Nathan on the *Solomon bar Simson Chronicle*. Again, however, Eliezer permits himself considerable latitude in shortening and rearranging his source.

Eliezer's Neuss story follows its source fairly closely, at least in its opening incidents. The *Solomon bar Simson Chronicle* includes the lengthy story of a Jew who converted, returned briefly to his home in Cologne, and then drowned himself in the Rhine River. According to this account, his body eventually washed up in Neuss, alongside that of one of the Neuss martyrs.[30] For reasons that are not clear, Eliezer bar Nathan transfers that story to Altenahr I.

Eliezer bar Nathan clarifies the next assault on the Cologne Jews dispersed by the archbishop: he replaces Solomon bar Simson's "a town" with identification of Wevelinghofen as the locus of the second attack. Although Eliezer adds some specific Jewish names not given in the *Solomon bar Simson Chronicle*, the broad tendency is again toward abridgment. The extraordinary story of the two young friends, Samuel ben Gedaliah and Yehiel ben Samuel, is condensed into a far briefer account of the demise of Yehiel and his father. The tale of the triple death—Yehiel, his father, and the beadle—is certainly powerful enough;

it does not, however, match the pathos of the lengthier and fuller account of four deaths—embellished with moving soliloquies—in the *Solomon bar Simson Chronicle*.

As noted, Eliezer's account of events in the first Altenahr adds the story of Isaac *ha-levi*, which was placed by Solomon bar Simson in his account of Neuss. Eliezer tells us—as did Solomon bar Simson—that in the second Altenahr there was an organized killing. Indeed, he provides the names of the five stalwarts who took this gruesome responsibility upon themselves. While fuller than his source on this matter, he omits a number of specific stories from the *Solomon bar Simson Chronicle*, each of which has considerable dramatic and emotional impact. The Xanten story, certainly one of the jewels of the Cologne unit of the *Solomon bar Simson Chronicle*, is shortened by Eliezer bar Nathan into a brief and fairly pallid account of yet another slaughter.

According to Eliezer bar Nathan, in the remaining two of the seven sites into which Cologne's Jews were dispersed, the fate of the Jews was overwhelmingly forced conversion. This is, in fact, what Solomon bar Simson reported for Moers. Eliezer, however, replaces Solomon's more positive report on Kerpen—that the Jews were saved without baptism—with an emphasis on forced conversion. He says that such forced conversion was the fate of yet another group of Jews sequestered in Geldern. For reasons that are again not clear, Eliezer bar Nathan chooses to tell the story of Moers in great detail, following his source very closely. Indeed, the story of the effort to force conversion upon the Jews in Moers exceeds Eliezer's reports on Worms and Mainz. As has been noted, it is impossible to fathom the grounds for Eliezer's decisions to provide or omit detail.

As already indicated, the concluding segment of the *Eliezer bar Nathan Chronicle* is extremely brief. The author simply asserts parallel persecution in four further locations—Trier, Metz, Regensburg, and Prague—and then closes with lavish praise of the Jewish martyrs of 1096 and the hope that their merit will protect their descendants and hasten the advent of redemption.

This close look at the relationship of the derivative narrative to its source has provided us with a third and final example of the freedom that medieval Jewish authors arrogated to themselves in reproducing narrative materials at their disposal. Ephraim of Bonn, Solomon bar Simson, and Eliezer bar Nathan all reshaped earlier narratives. To an extent we can follow the thinking that led to this reshaping; often, how-

ever, we can simply not comprehend what precisely moved them to
shorten or to lengthen the depictions with which they began.

Having followed Eliezer's utilization of his source, we must now proceed to examine his product. What do the prose sections of the *Eliezer
bar Nathan Chronicle* look like in their aggregate? They in effect provide
a relatively brief sequential narrative of a series of assaults on Rhineland
Jewry during the spring months of 1096, highlighting Speyer, Worms,
Mainz, and Cologne. The narrative lengthens as the sequence progresses: the Speyer story is the shortest and the Cologne account the
longest. The narration is by and large third person—the gripping soliloquies that studded the *Mainz Anonymous* and the *Solomon bar Simson
Chronicle* have been excised. The focus is exclusively on the Jewish victims of crusader atrocities, with no real interest in or attention to the
variety of Christian behaviors manifest in 1096 or—for that matter—
to the variety of Jewish responses to the assaults. Conversion is mentioned only fleetingly, and political negotiations disappear entirely. In
effect, as we move from the *Mainz Anonymous* to the *Solomon bar
Simson Chronicle* to the *Eliezer bar Nathan Chronicle,* we encounter a
growing narrowness of focus, with the last of the three by far the most
constricted in its vision. The reader of the *Eliezer bar Nathan Chronicle*
encounters essentially an account of Jewish suffering and heroism, a far
cry from the complexity of the *Mainz Anonymous.* To be sure, the farther removed Jews became from the tragedy, the less interested they
might have been in those complexities and the more comfortable they
might have been with generic depiction of suffering and heroism.

The poetic insertions in the *Eliezer bar Nathan Chronicle* reinforce
many of the conclusions drawn from an examination of the prose adaptation of the *Solomon bar Simson Chronicle.* There is, first of all,
precisely the same developmental sequence. Just as the prose material
lengthens considerably as we proceed from Speyer to Worms to Mainz
to Cologne, so too do the dirges become longer. The briefest by far is
that devoted to Speyer Jewry. Again, the Worms and Mainz poems—
like the Worms and Mainz prose sections—are about equal in length.
Finally, the Cologne dirge is by far the fullest of the four.[31] Again, we
have no way of understanding precisely why Eliezer bar Nathan chose
to allocate writing space in this manner.

More interesting is the style of the poetic insertions. Lamentation
poetry can be written in a number of ways, ranging from the somewhat
specific to the most generic. We have noted, in the prologue, the dirge
written by Ephraim ben Jacob of Bonn in honor of the Jewish martyrs

of Blois. In this poem, we encounter fairly specific reference to Count Theobald, to some salient aspects of the persecution, and to identifiable features of the heroic Jewish response.[32] There are similarly specific dirges written in memory of the martyrs of 1096 as well.[33] While such poems do not show the precision and specificity achievable in prose narrative, they do conjure up broad outlines of the events and figures memorialized. At the other end of the poetic spectrum are dirges that simply bewail in the most general terms the martyred, drawing imagery from traditional Jewish lamentation literature, but making no effort to depict the events in question.

The prose-poetry structure of the *Eliezer bar Nathan Chronicle* might well lead us to anticipate the more detailed kind of lamentational poetry. Such, however, is not at all the case. The four dirges inserted into the narrative fall very much toward the generic end of the spectrum. They tell us nothing of the perpetrators of the massacres, the identity of the Jewish martyrs, or the specifics of their heroic acts. The imagery is highly allusive, drawn from the rich treasury of traditional Jewish lamentations. The best way to provide a sense of Eliezer's poetic style is to offer in translation the shortest of the four dirges, which honors the Jews of Speyer.

> Lament, O great community,
> > That proclaimed the unity of its Rock,
> > Like the ten martyrs to Roman oppression!
> You appointed her guardian [of the commandments].
> > Wholeheartedly and in unison,
> > She stretched forth her neck.
> You have excelled in beauty among the heavenly and the earthly,
> > O community of Speyer,
> > A comely portion.
> A fortunate congregation, always in divine favor,
> > You have been set apart as atonement,
> > As a guardian of the divine vineyard.
> A sacred pair, in the month of Ziv,
> > Was united in its glory
> > And proclaimed in the book of eternal life.
> It was enrolled and sealed [in the book of eternal life],
> > Bound up as a diadem
> > With the divine king, [who decreed] the persecution.[34]

Striking in this poem—and its three companion pieces as well—is the utter lack of any specific reference to the actual events of 1096.

Crusaders, Jerusalem, purported Jewish guilt for the crucifixion, Jewish reviling of Christianity, martyrdom by suicide, killing of friends and relatives—all these special features of 1096 that, in different measure, fill the prose accounts of the *Mainz Anonymous,* Solomon bar Simson, and Eliezer bar Nathan have been effaced in favor of generic wailing that memorializes by adapting imagery from a rich prior literature.

On the one hand, this generic lamentation is surprising, given the prose setting into which it is inserted. At the same time, it is precisely this prose setting that permits the generic lamentation since the facts—in brief format at least—have been provided in the framing narrative. Perhaps we are best off treating the *Eliezer bar Nathan Chronicle* as an esthetic whole, as a combination of prose and poetry, as an effort to provide minimal detailed description enhanced by utterly timeless poetry. It is perhaps this combination, the fusing of the minimally time-bound with the thoroughly timeless, that accounts for the relatively greater long-term impact of the *Eliezer bar Nathan Chronicle.* Obliteration of the specific qualities of the 1096 catastrophe—for example, the evidence of conversion on the one hand, and the radical and somewhat questionable Jewish martyrdom on the other—made the *Eliezer bar Nathan Chronicle* the vehicle of choice for long-term memorialization.[35]

As we come to the end of the first half of this study, we might well take a fleeting look backward. Within the three Hebrew 1096 narratives we have found four or five discernible post-1096 voices, whose interests range from the rigorously time-bound to the utterly timeless. The most time-bound of these voices is the anonymous author of the Trier unit of the *Solomon bar Simson Chronicle,* who is concerned overwhelmingly with explaining to his readers the conversion of the vast majority of Trier Jews. The *Mainz Anonymous* represents the most successful fusion of the time-bound and the timeless. Deeply committed to providing an accurate portrayal of the events of 1096, on both Christian and Jewish sides, the *Mainz Anonymous* saw this information as crucial for the community of survivors. At the same time, the author told his story in a manner that addressed timeless issues as well, with a sense that the same story would have meaning for the generations to come and, indeed, for a divine audience. The author of the Cologne segment of the *Solomon bar Simson Chronicle,* writing more than four decades after 1096, was far less interested in the details of what transpired and far more concerned with highlighting Jewish heroism and addressing the timeless implications of this heroism. The editor of the *Solomon bar Simson*

Chronicle, who may or may not have been identical to the author of the Cologne unit, absorbed and adapted earlier narratives into a wide-ranging account of the events of 1096, with heavy focus on the timeless meaning of those events. Finally, Eliezer bar Nathan, basing his text on the earlier work of Solomon bar Simson, abridged that earlier narrative and expanded it through poetic interpolation and, in the process, further diminished the time-bound and enhanced the timeless. Armed with this understanding of the four or five voices available to us, we must now proceed to investigate a number of facets of the time-bound and timeless messages that are provided in the narratives.

CHAPTER SEVEN

The Hebrew
First Crusade Narratives

Time-Bound Objectives

The focus of this study is the Hebrew prose narratives written subsequent to the calamity of 1096. Although we know that utterly time-bound communications were written during the period of upheaval itself (and in all likelihood afterward also) and although we have at our disposal a number of poetic dirges over the fallen Jews,[1] the prose narratives, like the 1171 Orléans epistle discussed in the prologue, were intended to address both time-bound and timeless concerns simultaneously. More precisely, the authors of these narratives felt that the prose medium—crucial for transmitting detailed information—could be utilized effectively for constructing an explanatory rationale for the events as well.

Our close analysis of the Hebrew prose narratives has suggested that the traditional emphasis on these narratives as three related compositions is of limited utility. More useful by far is recognition that we are in fact provided with five major Jewish accounts of the events of 1096.[2] Two of these narratives—the Trier report and the *Mainz Anonymous*—were in all likelihood written fairly close to the events themselves; the Cologne report was written in 1140; the balance of the so-called *Solomon bar Simson Chronicle* was compiled by its editor in the early or mid 1140s, on the eve of the Second Crusade; the *Eliezer bar Nathan Chronicle*—the last of the sequence—was written after the Second Crusade.

Each of the five Jewish observers who authored or compiled these works brought his own special perspective and his own set of objectives to the events of 1096. The author of the Trier report was most closely fixed on the time-bound realities of these events, as he sought to rationalize the conversion of Trier Jewry by emphasizing the hopelessness of its circumstances and its steadfastness in the face of the daunting dilemma, and by highlighting the martyrdom of those few Trier Jews who opted for death.

The author of the *Mainz Anonymous,* to my mind the most gifted of our five observers, nicely balanced the time-bound and the timeless. On the one hand, he etched sharply the spiraling animosity and violence of the Christian majority and the increasingly radical stances of the beleaguered Jewish minority. After reading the *Mainz Anonymous,* one comes away with a sense of diverse Christian and Jewish behaviors and perceptions and—yet more striking—a feel for the intensifying patterns of action and thinking during the brief but turbulent period of persecution and martyrdom. This careful plotting of the time-bound has obvious propaedeutic and apologetic value. On the one hand, full knowledge of the crusade, its attendant anti-Jewish ramifications, and the range of Jewish responses was intended to provide guidance for that time when the next threat of anti-Jewish hostility would develop. At the same time, this detailed information served to explain a number of problematic aspects of Jewish behavior in 1096. Simultaneously, the author of the *Mainz Anonymous* successfully moves far beyond the carefully delineated temporal and spatial confines of his story to place the assaults and the radical Jewish responses within a timeless framework of the Jewish and human past. By so doing, our author provides an answer to the burning question of the meaning of the persecution and suffering.

With the Cologne segment of the *Solomon bar Simson Chronicle,* the events of 1096 have receded in time and we encounter diminished concern with the time-bound and fuller concentration on the significance of the sanguinary events. Writing in 1140 and relatively unconcerned with temporal realities, the author of the Cologne report focused lavishly on the martyrs, their radical behaviors, and the rich symbolism that undergirded these behaviors.

The editor of the *Solomon bar Simson Chronicle* is deficient in historical sensitivity when contrasted with the author of the *Mainz Anonymous,* but he nonetheless performed an important service by attempting an overall narrative of the events of 1096. He created the fullest picture we have of the persecutions and the Jewish reactions by stitching together preexistent units. For this editor, the varied accounts he incorporated all pointed toward the central meanings of the events portrayed, meanings that he reinforced regularly through his editorial glosses. God had chosen the generation of 1096 to accept punishment for the historic sin of the golden calf. This divine choice was surely not to be attributed to the shortcomings of late-eleventh-century Rhineland Jewry; to the contrary, it was based on the unique fitness of these remarkable Jews to fulfill the divine mandate with unparalleled vigor and commitment. The reward for this valor would be bounteous. The Christian perpetrators of the violence, however unprecedented their actions might seem, were ultimately yet another link in the historic chain of Israel's oppressors and would eventually suffer the same punishment as their predecessors.

The *Eliezer bar Nathan Chronicle* is built upon the collection of Solomon bar Simson; it is expanded occasionally, compressed more often, and supplemented with a series of four highly traditional dirges—poems that totally efface the particularity of 1096 in favor of timeless lament. With the *Eliezer bar Nathan Chronicle* the balance of the time-bound and the timeless is most thoroughly skewed in the latter direction.

The varied perspectives of these five late-eleventh- and twelfth-century Jews provide much data for reflection on a number of issues. Using the spectrum of the time-bound and timeless (both richly reflected in the five compositions), we shall commence with temporally delimited concerns and then proceed to the broader and more wide-ranging issues of theodicy and historiographic assumptions concerning God, humanity, and history. The discussion of temporally delimited issues, to be undertaken in this chapter, will of necessity focus heavily on the two more time-bound narratives, the Trier report and the *Mainz Anonymous*.

GUIDANCE FOR THE FUTURE

The focus on the time-bound in our five distinct Hebrew sources, particularly in the Trier unit and the *Mainz Anonymous*, was intended to serve a number of purposes. Guidance for the future was surely one such objective, although the lessons to be gleaned were hardly clear-cut. Let us begin with the portrait that emerges of the Christian majority, a portrait intended to alert Jewish readers to the dynamics of persecution and thus to provide requisite insight. We will then attend to the depiction of Jewish responses. It is the *Mainz Anonymous*, written shortly after the events themselves, that has, far and away, the sharpest focus on the

Christians' behaviors; all five narratives of course relate to the Jews' responses.

Perhaps the most important lesson to be drawn from the events of 1096 was that crusading could arouse anti-Jewish hostility. To be sure, no one could have known with certainty that the crusade launched in 1095 was to be the first of many such expeditions. Thus, our Jewish authors, especially the author of the *Mainz Anonymous,* could hardly have been certain that Jews would face a second and third repetition of the same explosion. Nonetheless, to describe what happened surely served a purpose. An unprecedented eruption of animus had caught Rhineland Jewry unawares. Telling the tale fully would insure that Jewish readers would know that such an eruption had taken place and could conceivably recur.

A central time-bound message was that the call for an armed expedition to Jerusalem bore the potential for immediately arousing anti-Jewish hostility. To be sure, we know that almost all the crusading armies passed through western Christendom without evoking anti-Jewish sentiment or inflicting damage on the Jews. The Trier report indicates clearly that Peter the Hermit's followers did no damage whatsoever to the Jews of Trier or, in all likelihood, to the other Jewish communities they encountered. The heavy emphasis in the *Mainz Anonymous* on the special wickedness of Count Emicho may well have been intended to highlight his personal idiosyncrasies and the distorted thinking that characterized his following. In a general way, our five narratives probably suggest that crusading agitation had the potential for creating severe problems, although such problems were hardly inevitable.

The major protectors of the Jews were the political authorities of Germany, preeminently the emperor and secondarily the bishops. Unfortunately for the Jews of 1096, the emperor could only thunder at a distance. Real responsibility for Jewish safety devolved upon the bishops of the Rhineland towns.[3] With respect to these bishops, one message is uncontested: they were unanimously committed to providing proper protection. Their capacity to do so, however, varied. In all likelihood this variability had more to do with the size and strength of the anti-Jewish forces than with either the will or capability of the individual bishops. Particularly striking is the depiction of Bishop Engilbert provided in the Trier unit and of Archbishop Ruthard set forth in the additional Mainz material included in the *Solomon bar Simson Chronicle.* In both cases, the prelates in question went to great lengths to protect their Jewish protégés, and in both cases erstwhile protectors had to urge or even force baptism upon their Jews. The picture of Bishop Engilbert is especially poignant. According to the Trier unit, Engilbert's own life was threatened because of his overtly pro-Jewish stance. Even in the painful final moments of the conflict, however, he refused to surrender the Jews to the raging mob in front of his palace, and he forced baptism upon them instead as a means of preserving Jewish life.[4] Clearly, there was not a lot to learn from all this for the future. Christian authority figures might begin as great friends; where they would end in the face of irresistible pressures was utterly unpredictable.

Much the same portrait emerges with respect to Christian townsmen, although here the situation is yet more complex. While the Rhineland bishops were at least united in their determination to save the Jews, the burghers exhibited contradictory inclinations from the outset. Some were staunchly loyal to their Jewish neighbors; others quickly joined the camp of the persecutors. Recurrently, anti-Jewish violence is specifically attributed to a coalition of crusaders and burghers. Townsmen loyal to their Jewish friends could be overwhelmed by the anti-Jewish pressures just as the bishops were, eventually linking themselves with the oppressors. Once again, the clearest message was probably that once violence spun out of control no one could be truly trusted. This is hardly a message that permits much in the way of foresight and planning; it is much closer to a philosophic sigh.

There can be little doubt that the portrayal of the Christian majority in the *Mainz Anonymous* and—to a more limited extent—the other Jewish narratives was intended to be used as a guide to future incidents and as a directive to subsequent patterns of Jewish reaction. To be sure, not all that much could be conveyed. In most instances, Jews and their protectors were overwhelmed by insuperable forces. Nevertheless, knowledge of the variety of Christian behaviors in 1096 might conceivably ameliorate somewhat the fate of Jews caught subsequently in the vortex of crusading passions.

With respect to Jewish reactions to the unanticipated events of 1096, all five narratives tell much the same story of uncertainty, negotiation with the terrestrial authorities, petition to the divine authority, occasional conversion, and heroic martyrdom. Preservation of Jewish life emerges as the objective to be pursued at all costs: when preservation of Jewish life is clearly no longer possible, and the only alternatives are conversion or death, then martyrdom is obviously the preferred response.[5] Here again, however, the guidance offered by the narratives is hardly decisive. The extremely understanding stance taken toward the converts mitigates somewhat the portrait of martyrdom as the reaction of choice.

In a real sense, the authors of our narratives might well have objected to this effort at analyzing the lessons that their stories projected for the future, and perhaps such objections are in fact well grounded. The entire episode was unprecedented and unanticipated. No clear-cut messages can readily be distilled. The best that might be done is to recount the events as effectively as possible, thus providing at least some narrative data that might be useful under future circumstances. A modest goal, but a reasonable one.

APOLOGY AND MEMORIALIZATION

Guidance for the future involved necessarily a focus on majority society—on the perpetrators of the violence, on those normally charged with maintaining order in society, and on the burgher neighbors of the Jews. Jewish responses could add to understanding, but such responses were essentially reactive and highly limited. There were, at the same time, a number of time-bound objectives that related more fully to the Jews themselves. To an extent, some Jewish behaviors had to be depicted and explained, whereas some Jewish behaviors were so impressive that they almost cried out for appropriate memorialization. All the authors of our five Hebrew accounts responded in some measure to these issues, although once more the Trier unit and the *Mainz Anonymous* will figure most prominently in our discussion.

Despite the overwhelmingly positive tone of the depiction of the Jews of 1096, questions could readily be raised about some aspects of their reaction to the unanticipated violence. The most obvious question concerned the forcible conversion of some Rhineland Jews to Christianity.[6] All five Hebrew narratives note unabashedly the reality of conversion. Now, these acts of conversion raised at least two problems. The first was a purely halakhic problem. To be sure, the halakhic dimension of conversion makes no appearance whatsoever in the narratives, an interesting enough phenomenon in its own right. Nonetheless, there was in fact a halakhic issue. By all rights, the Jews of 1096 should have, according to Jewish law, accepted death at the hands of their persecutors rather than convert to Christianity. How could the behavior of the converts possibly be justified?[7] Moreover, the centrality of martyrdom in all five of the narratives posed a subtler problem. If self-sacrifice was in fact the remarkable response of the 1096 Jews and if martyrdom provided the key to understanding the meaning of the catastrophe, then surely conversion undid—at least to some extent—the heroism of the 1096 martyrs and undermined the carefully constructed explanatory structure.

All five narratives address the issue of the converts in more or less direct fashion. The most committed to dealing with this issue was, as we have seen, the author of the Trier report, who made the explanation of the mass conversion of Trier Jewry the central theme of his narrative. As noted, whereas the Jews of Trier might have been castigated by some as renegades, our author argues that they were all heroes. Ultimately, for our author, there was no objectionable Jewish behavior in Trier; what the Jews of that town did could be arranged in hierarchical fashion from forced conversion—lamentable but excusable; to return to the Jewish faith—difficult and revealing; to martyrdom—the most laudable Jewish action imaginable. The story of Trier Jewry was, from this perspective, complex and tragic. Although it was perhaps somewhat less exalted than the record of Worms, Mainz, and Cologne Jewry, the story of the Jews of Trier had to be presented and understood properly. Anyone who truly comprehended the complexities of the situation in Trier would readily grasp what had happened and acknowledge the profound heroism of that harried community. It might well be objected that this constitutes mere assertion of the rectitude of conversion and nothing more, and there is truth to the objection. The author of the Trier unit obviously felt, however, that the best way to make his case was by reconstructing the realities as he perceived them.

A more direct case is made by the editor of the *Solomon bar Simson Chronicle* toward the end of his composite narrative. This later editor eschewed historical reconstruction in favor of direct declaration. Let us note the core of his argument:

> Now it is fitting to speak in praise of those forcibly converted. For all that they ate and drank they mortally endangered themselves. They slaughtered meat and removed from it the fat. They examined the meat according to the regulations of the sages. They did not drink wine of libation. They did not go to church except occasionally. Every time they went, they went out of great duress and fear. They went reluctantly. The gentiles themselves knew that they had not converted wholeheartedly, but only out of fear of the crusaders, and that they did not believe in their [the Christians'] deity, but rather that they clung to the fear of the Lord and held fast to the sublime God, creator of heaven and earth. In the sight of the gentiles they observed the Sabbath properly and observed the Torah of the Lord secretly. Anyone who speaks ill of them insults the Divine Countenance.[8]

Now, this is in many ways a curious case. There is no focus whatsoever on the act of conversion itself. Rather, the author advances the argument that the subsequent behavior of the converts offers testimony to their lack of sincerity in converting, to their uninterrupted commitment to the God of Israel, and to the heroism required to maintain that commitment. To be sure, even this argument is compromised somewhat. These faithful Jews did occasionally have to make an appearance in the local church, and they complied. Again, however, our author chooses to see the matter differently, emphasizing the limited number of such appearances made by the converts. The issue was complex and painful. The author's position, however, is unequivocal: "Anyone who speaks ill of them insults the Divine Countenance."

The *Mainz Anonymous* deals less fully with this problem than does the Trier report and less directly than does the *Solomon bar Simson Chronicle*. In its account of the first assault on Worms Jewry, aimed specifically at those Jews who had remained in their homes, the *Mainz Anonymous* notes that some of these Jews converted in order to bury the dead and to protect those youngsters who had been seized by the Christians. The author of the *Mainz Anonymous* refrains from advancing his own assessment of the rectitude of their actions, preferring to leave such evaluation to the Jews sequestered in the bishop's castle. According to our narrative, the sequestered Jews sent clothing with which to cover the dead and a note of comfort to their converted brethren: "Fear not and do not take to heart what you have done. If the Holy One, blessed be he, saves us from the hands of our enemies, then we shall be with you for death and for life. But do not turn away from the Lord."[9] Since we as readers know that the senders of this message of consolation and acceptance themselves became heroic martyrs, their warm and positive response to the converts takes on yet more force than does the historical reconstruction of the Trier report or the insistent assertion of the *Solomon bar Simson Chronicle*. Once again, the artfulness of the *Mainz Anonymous* makes a compelling case, this time for the rectitude of those forcibly converted.

In the wake of tragedy, it is always easy enough to second-guess the victims. Why weren't they prepared for the crisis? Why didn't they take this or that obvious step in order to protect themselves? Surely part of the apologetic task of the narratives was to exonerate the victims of the 1096 violence from allegations of unpreparedness and ineptitude. The narrative that takes the greatest pains to make this apology is the *Mainz Anonymous*. Central to its case is insistence on understanding the development of the crusade, its unexpectedness, and especially the stunning rapidity with which it overtook an insouciant Rhineland Jewry. We have already noted the *Mainz Anonymous* portrayal of Rhineland Jewry as insulated from the formal crusade propaganda that developed farther westward in France. When addressed by alarmed French Jews, the Rhineland leadership prayed on behalf of their seemingly endangered co-religionists, but overtly expressed their lack of concern for themselves.

Everything in the nuanced *Mainz Anonymous* account maintains the sense that the development of anti-Jewish hostility was rapid and unexpected. Even Mainz Jewry, whose story lies at the end of the chain of events that constitutes the narrative and who enjoyed the advantage of external and internal warnings, was ultimately unprepared for the devastating military assault that represented a new and deadlier twist in the escalation of violence during the spring of 1096. In the face of these unanticipated events and the rapidity with which they unfolded, it was hardly possible to hold the Jewish victims accountable for a lack of foresight and intelligent management. According to the *Mainz Anonymous,* God himself had occasioned the lack of foreknowledge as yet another element in his divine decree. The humans involved were totally exonerated.

Indeed, the *Mainz Anonymous* forcefully drives home this point in its own after-the-fact assessment of the behavior of Archbishop Ruthard of Mainz. In an important closing note on the archbishop's advice to bring the Jews of Mainz and their possessions into his own castle and under his direct protection, the *Mainz Anonymous* concludes:

> They [the archbishop and his functionaries] extended this advice in order to gather us up and to surrender us and to hold us like fish trapped in a net of wickedness. Indeed, the archbishop assembled his barons and servants—great barons, nobles, and grandees—in order to assist us and to save us from the crusaders. For at the outset it was his wish to save us, but in the end he failed.[10]

This is a remarkably convoluted statement for a generally clear writer. I would argue that, by projecting his own uncertainty in this conclusion, our author is subtly reinforcing his message of the difficulty suffered by those caught up in the whirlwind.

There is yet one more apology involved in the five Hebrew narratives, and that concerns the behaviors of the martyrs themselves. As noted, the converts could reasonably be criticized for failing to live up to the demand of Jewish law to choose death over conversion. At the same time, this death, according to Jewish law, was to be inflicted by the persecutors and suffered by the Jews. Such is the precise formulation of the rabbinic injunction, and such is the example afforded by the (relatively few) classic martyr figures that are regularly cited in the Hebrew narratives.[11] One well-known talmudic tale portrays and justifies suicide by drowning under dire circumstances, and there are clear echoes of this story in a number of the martyrdom accounts.[12] Thus, martyrdom by suicide was also within the parameters of the acceptable. However, there was a yet more extreme form of martyrdom prominent in 1096, and that involved martyrdom via murder, especially the murder of youngsters by parents and relatives. Such extreme forms of martyrdom lay outside the norms of Jewish law and were unprecedented in the rich aggadic literature of the Jews. The narrators of the events of 1096 surely had to make some kind of case for the propriety of these extreme manifestations of martyrological zeal.[13]

The complications of this issue are well captured in the *Mainz Anonymous*'s first report on such radical martyrdom. The story, noted already, involved a Worms Jew named Meshullam ben Isaac, his son Isaac, and his wife Zipporah, who had given birth to the lad late in life. The father, Meshullam, put himself in an Abraham-like posture and prepared to sacrifice his son in order to fulfill what he perceived to be divine mandate. His wife implored him to take her life first, a request he denied. He took up his knife and slew his son. The overtones of the biblical story pervade every phrase of this account. Yet any Jewish reader would of course be aware that the biblical Abraham had not taken the life of his son, that he had in fact been ordered by divine mandate not to do so. To be sure, the Hebrew narratives turn this divergence from the biblical record to advantage, suggesting that the martyrs of 1096 exceeded the heroism of their forebears.[14] Nonetheless, the parallels to and divergences from the biblical report become complex and problematic, as does the entire phenomenon of martyrdom through murder.

Nowhere in any of our narratives is there an effort to argue on legalistic or any other grounds the propriety of this extreme form of martyrdom. What the narrators do is simply to portray such behaviors in the most laudatory possible fashion. The most lavishly detailed incidents involve precisely such martyrdom by murder. In the *Mainz Anonymous*, the richest and most moving description of all is that of Rachel of Mainz, who slew all her four children (an act that incidentally evoked the fury of the crusaders who found her). It is precisely the moving quality of the elaborate description that is intended to still doubts. Similarly, the most extensive depiction of martyrdom in the Cologne report involves the two young friends, Samuel ben Gedaliah and Yehiel ben Samuel, the father of the latter, and the beadle of the Cologne synagogue. By the end of the incident, all four of these men were dead, three via murder and one via suicide. The richness of the description constitutes the only real argument for the rectitude of their actions.

As noted, there are a number of reports on events in Mainz that are found in the *Solomon bar Simson Chronicle* but not in its source, the *Mainz Anonymous*. Of these the fullest and most detailed is the description of the death of Isaac ben David of Mainz. Here again, the complexity of the matter can hardly be avoided. On the terrible day of the massacre of most of Mainz Jewry, Isaac chose to convert in order to save his mother and his two young children from the crusaders. Subsequently, he repented of this action and set out on a course of martyrdom for himself and the selfsame mother and children. What precisely made his earlier decision erroneous and his later decision correct? Again, our author does not set forth an argument. Rather, he makes his case through the force of his powerful tale. The suicide of Isaac and his friend Uri ben Joseph (by burning the synagogue) and the murder of Isaac's aged mother and young children are told in a manner that hardly brooks rational objection. In this the author of these additional Mainz episodes—whoever he might have been—followed the lead of his predecessors. The best—indeed the only—justification for the radical forms of Jewish martyrdom in 1096 was the persuasive recounting of the martyrs' stories.

More was involved in the powerful recounting of the martyrs' tales than laying out a case for the propriety of their actions. Part of the motivation for telling these powerful and haunting stories was the author's sense of obligation to those whose heroism demanded memorialization. The drive to memorialize great heroism and devotion on the part of those no longer among the living is a powerful one in most societies. Surely the sense of loss in the wake of 1096 was accompanied by a felt need to tell the stories of great Jewish heroes, a need above and beyond either the need to rationalize some of their extreme actions or the need to comprehend the tragedy.

In reading the extensive and still deeply moving accounts of the martyrs of 1096 in the five Hebrew sources, one cannot escape the palpable sense that these authors felt themselves driven in part by deep feelings of obligation to the men, women, and children whose death they lamented and whose heroism they extolled.[15] Survivors needed to maintain their recollection of the Jews who stretched forth their necks before the swords of the crusaders and burghers, the Jews who threw themselves off the ramparts overlooking the Rhine River or who plunged daggers into their stomachs, and the Jews who took up swords against their own flesh and blood. The glory of these behaviors could not be allowed to dissipate, and re-creating these acts of heroism became a moral and religious obligation.

Again, for these authors the most meaningful outlet for this obligation was the medium of prose, so that they might tell the martyrs' stories as fully and as "accurately" as possible. Poetic hyperbole had its place, to be sure—we have noted the existence of poetic laments over the fallen of 1096. With poetry, however, the possibility exists that readers will make allowance for poetic exaggeration. Given the remarkable devotion and heroism exhibited in 1096, a prosaic rendition of the "actual" events and the "real" behavior of the martyrs represented the most effective mode of enshrining their memory. Readers were to understand that the dirges of 1096 did not represent poetic exaggeration. The actual behaviors of the Jews of 1096 were remarkably inspired and inspiring, to an extent that could only be captured in a "realistic" prose account. Just as the specificity attainable in prose enabled our Jewish narrators to provide requisite—albeit limited—guidance for the future and to present a series of apologies for problematic aspects of Jewish behavior in 1096, so too did it enable these writers to enshrine fittingly the memory of great Jewish heroes.

The key to achieving all these time-bound objectives was adroit utilization of the medium of narrative prose. Data had to be purveyed, imagery had to be created, cases had to be constructed—all by telling the tales "accurately" and movingly. The specificity of the prose narratives and the potential they bore for creating full, "realistic," and intensely moving portraits enabled our authors to provide guidance, to make requisite apologies, and to memorialize properly. As we shall see shortly, our authors also sensed the somewhat surprising potential that the narrative format offered for addressing timeless issues as well.

CHAPTER EIGHT

The Historicity of the Hebrew Narratives

The time-bound objectives of the Hebrew First Crusade narratives lead us ineluctably to the issue of their historicity. If the authors and editors of the narratives, especially the *Mainz Anonymous,* were determined to provide guidance, make requisite apologies, and memorialize properly by adducing extensive evidence on Christian and Jewish behaviors during the crisis period, then what implications flow with respect to the facticity of the data advanced by our narrators. Are these data to be trusted?

As noted, earlier generations of researchers hardly reflected on the historicity of the 1096 Hebrew narratives, assuming their facticity. More recently, growing sophistication in the use of narrative records has resulted in a variety of perspectives, ranging all the way from a continued sense of more-or-less wholesale facticity to thorough skepticism.[1] Our reconfiguration of the three narratives into five identifiable voices and our focus on the time-bound objectives of at least some of the five narrators enable us to advance the discussion considerably.

The two most general issues with which to begin involve the date of composition of the narratives and the goals of the narrators. From these points of view, the *Mainz Anonymous* and the Trier unit show the highest potential for historical facticity. They were both written close in time to the events of 1096, and in both cases the authors were motivated— at least in large measure—by time-bound concerns that dictated accurate reconstruction of the realities. By contrast, the Cologne unit was written four and a half decades later, is heavily dependent on the memory of elderly survivors, and reflects a rather limited range of historical interests. We might reasonably anticipate a lower level of reliability in the Cologne unit than in the two earlier accounts. We have noted the existence, in the *Solomon bar Simson Chronicle,* of material on Mainz not included in the *Mainz Anonymous* and have indicated that it is impossible to determine whether these data were found in the original *Mainz Anonymous.* If not, then the historicity of this material would have to be somewhat suspect as well. The latest of the narratives, the *Eliezer bar Nathan Chronicle,* must be similarly suspect.

In treating in more detail the historical reliability of the time-bound materials in the Hebrew narratives, we will utilize the venerable technique of adducing multiple testimonies and comparing them carefully. The testimonies to be introduced include, first of all, the copious Christian sources available on the First Crusade.[2] For some aspects of our investigation the Christian sources are rich and decisive; for others they are slim to nonexistent. Our analysis of the three Hebrew narratives as five distinct compositions means that, in some instances, we can provide internally corroborating testimonies from the diverse Jewish sources as well.

In addressing the issue of historicity, we might well use once again the distinction between the portrayal of the Christian majority and the depiction of the Jewish minority.[3] With respect to the former, it is the *Mainz Anonymous* that is most fully focused on the Christian majority and that provides the most detailed information. For its own idiosyncratic purposes, the Trier report had to provide considerable reliable detail on the burghers and bishop of that town. Jewish behaviors lie at the core of all five narratives. However, even when we reach discussion of the reliability of the portraits of the Rhineland Jews, there will still be a tendency to utilize more heavily the earlier two narratives, the *Mainz Anonymous* and the Trier report.

THE CRUSADE AND THE CRUSADERS

As we have seen, the *Mainz Anonymous* is most fully focused on the evolution of the crusade and the behavior and thinking of the crusaders. In a number of ways, the *Mainz Anonymous*'s portrait of the crusade in general dovetails strikingly with what we know from reliable Christian sources, both narrative and documentary, of the lay armies that set off to conquer Jerusalem. Happily, there has been a recent spate of study of the behavior and thinking of the lay crusaders who responded to the papal call to arms. This work, particularly that of Marcus Bull and Jonathan Riley-Smith, provides a solid base from which to assess the historicity of the *Mainz Anonymous*'s portrayal of the crusaders who burst so unexpectedly across the Rhineland.[4]

What then are the key facets of crusading that are accurately reflected in the *Mainz Anonymous?* The first is simply our author's sense of the Rhineland Jews being overtaken by a movement that was unprecedented and unanticipated. Historical scholarship is, by its very nature, committed to uncovering continuities and influences, and some of the most valuable crusade research has located the roots of the First Crusade in the heady developments of the vigorous eleventh century.[5] Nonetheless, there is considerable evidence that late-eleventh-century Christians saw the call of Pope Urban II as something radically and excitingly innovative.[6] Indeed, one of the most striking aspects of the early Muslim response to the crusaders' intrusion into the Levant was their failure to appreciate that the crusaders represented a new and different challenge.[7] The Jews of the Rhineland were in a far better position to appreciate the innovativeness of the First Crusade. For the author of the *Mainz Anonymous,* it was a new and shocking phenomenon for which he could discern neither precedent nor evolution.

To be sure, the mind of our author was highly attuned to precedent. Throughout his narrative, he attempted to assimilate the crusader enemy to the past foes of Israel and the Jewish heroes to the great figures in the history of his people. The very language that he used, a biblically grounded Hebrew, moved him in such precedent-seeking directions. Nonetheless, the sense of something new, different, and shocking outweighs the perception of continuity with respect to the Christian enemy and the Jewish victims and heroes. The Jewish people had never been confronted with such an enemy, and Jews had never reacted with such heroic resistance.

Not only was the crusade strikingly innovative, it was breathtaking in its pace of development. Christian sources recurrently portray the unexpectedness of the papal call to the crusade, the exhilaration this call generated, and the excited reaction of the numerous Christians caught up by the magnetism of this new venture. Two well-known incidents evidence the sudden crystallization of the crusade, the lack of preparedness for the new venture, and the exhilarated response. The first involves the call to the crusade at Clermont itself. To be sure, the call was announced at the close of a convocation that had lasted a number of days. Surely something must have been in the air. Nonetheless, all the sources—as problematic as they might be—agree on the wild enthusiasm that greeted the papal call.[8] Similarly, the *Gesta Francorum*, an eyewitness account written by a follower of Bohemond of Taranto, describes the eruption of French crusaders into southern Italy, Bohemond's utter lack of familiarity with the movement, and his instantaneous decision to join it.[9]

The *Mainz Anonymous*, from the Jewish side, portrays precisely the same rapidly unfolding drama. It begins starkly with the sudden eruption of the crusade in France. "It came to pass in the year 1028 after the destruction of the [Second] Temple that this calamity struck Israel. Barons, nobles, and common-folk in France arose, took counsel, and decided to ascend, to rise up like eagles, to do battle, and to clear the way to Jerusalem."[10] This stark opening portrays a movement exploding out of nowhere. We recall that the letter sent off by the leaders of French Jewry to Rhineland Jewry encountered a total lack of awareness and concern in that distinguished community. The author of the *Mainz Anonymous* by no means castigates the Rhineland Jews for human failure. He simply notes the rapid development of the First Crusade and the way in which it caught the Rhineland Jews unaware. For Christian observers, the rapid development of the movement was a sign of divine blessing; for the author of the *Mainz Anonymous*, this rapid development was but another element in the harsh divine decree. Both sets of sources concur in their depiction of the stunning pace of events.

The innovative and seemingly spontaneous First Crusade emerged, according to the *Mainz Anonymous*, in France, an evaluation with which all the Christian sources agree. There is, however, a striking lacuna in the Jewish portrayal of the early development of the crusade. For our Jewish observer, the crusade was a baronial-popular undertaking; the papal initiator of the campaign is nowhere in evidence.[11] This lacuna should not be simply shrugged off as Jewish insensitivity or obtuseness. Recall, rather, that the papal journey of preaching did not include German territory, so the Rhineland Jews would not have had any direct experience with the papal role. Exhortation to the crusade by either papal representatives or self-appointed popularizers of the campaign does not seem to have taken place to any significant extent in German territory. For Rhineland Jews, and probably Rhineland Christians as well, the crusade burst upon the scene, seemingly out of nowhere, with the intrusion of the French crusading bands. Since the crusade first manifested itself in this way, it is little wonder that a Jewish observer would see the enterprise in baronial and popular terms or, more specifically, in terms of a movement of French barons and common-folk.

The social composition of the crusading armies has been an issue of considerable interest to historians of the crusades.[12] While Christian narrative sources indicate regularly that the pope's call attracted men and women of all stations, there has been an inevitable tendency to focus on the highborn, because they seem more important and are better documented.[13] Our Jewish narrator emphasizes regularly and correctly, however, the wide range of Christians who responded to the allure of the enterprise. When describing the emergence of the crusade in France, he speaks of the response of "barons, nobles, and common-folk," and, when depicting the arousal of crusading passions in Germany, he again specifies both "barons and common-folk." In a fascinating incident that captures the evolution of danger in Mainz, the narrative describes the early passage of a crusading group that included a woman and her remarkable goose. Convinced by her pet goose of the divine leadership of the campaign, the woman taunted the Jews and contrasted God's favor for the Christian forces with his abandonment of the Jewish people.[14] The highlighting of a role of leadership for a woman among the crusaders is striking, reinforcing the sense of a movement with wide appeal, a movement that recruited from all strata of Christian society.[15]

A number of well-known physical accouterments of crusading make their appropriate appearance in the Hebrew narrative. Most noteworthy are the cross, which was the personal insignia of the crusaders, and the banner (specific decoration not indicated), which served as the rallying point of the organized group. In the introductory section of the *Mainz Anonymous,* the cross appears prominently in the description of the French crusaders and their German counterparts. In the closing passage of this opening material, which shows random violence breaking out against Rhineland Jews, the crusading banner is highlighted.[16] Subsequently, in describing the one assault carried out by an organized crusading force, the attack on the Jewish community of Mainz, the *Mainz Anonymous* features prominently the movement of the crusaders' banners as they lay siege to the archbishop's palace and the burgrave's palace.[17]

The facet of the First Crusade that has attracted far and away the most attention among recent historians has been crusader thinking—the range of personal and group commitments that gave impetus to the movement. Much initial research focused on the almost inevitable combination of high ideals and base cupidity notable in every large social movement. Clearly, many of the baronial leaders of the First Crusade abandoned the trek to Jerusalem in favor of the establishment of personal rule in the Levant. Some of the twelfth-century Christian chroniclers castigated the purportedly popular German crusading bands for the prevalence of base motivations in their commitment to the undertaking.[18] The rapidly developing First Crusade surely attracted a share of adventurers among its adherents, on all social levels. In its totality, however, the crusade meant for Christian observers a remarkable spiritual arousal in Christian society, an assessment with which the *Mainz Anonymous* grudgingly agrees.

Striking is our author's acknowledgment of lofty ideals among the persecutors of Rhineland Jewry. Earlier Jewish history writing included no such acknowledgment. The biblical Egyptians, Assyrians, and Babylonians were shadowy oppressors operating as God's agents of punishment; Pharaoh, Haman, and the Persian courtiers of the Daniel stories were portrayed as human beings moved by the pettiest of concerns and the basest of desires; the Seleucids and Romans of late antiquity were regularly depicted as tyrannical rulers motivated by the lust for power. Nowhere in these classical depictions of an enemy do we encounter a foe moved by zeal—even misplaced zeal—for high ideals. Yet such is precisely what we encounter in the *Mainz Anonymous*. Our Jewish author may denigrate Christianity by speaking of the goal of the crusade as "the sepulcher of the crucified, a trampled corpse that can neither profit nor save because it is vanity," or as the "unholy sepulcher of the crucified" and by depicting the end result of crusader devotion as the achievement of hell.[19] Although these pejoratives are rich in biblical allusions,[20] once again the linkage to the past is more than outweighed by the accurate portrayal of a persecutor moved by high ideals and objectives.[21]

What then were these Christian objectives? Holy war and armed pilgrimage to Jerusalem are identified in the Hebrew narratives as the two central crusading ideals, and here as well the perspectives of the *Mainz Anonymous* are substantiated by the extant Christian sources. The concept of holy war appears regularly. In the depiction of the initial deflection of crusading zeal onto the Jews of northern France, the French crusaders advance the following rationale for anti-Jewish violence:

Behold we travel to a distant land to war with the kings of the land. [We take] our lives in our hands to kill and to subjugate all the kingdoms that do not believe in the crucified. How much more [should we kill and subjugate] the Jews, whose ancestors killed and crucified him.[22]

This portrayal of the goal of the crusade as the destruction and subjugation of non-believing principalities seems to reflect the popularized holy war thinking of Christians. The alternatives offered to the Jews are specified as conversion or death, a choice that recurs in all the *Mainz Anonymous*'s depictions of anti-Jewish violence. The end result is, of course, the elimination of non-Christian thinkers and thinking.

We might further note, even in the passage just quoted, the introduction of the revenge motif into the broader concept of holy war. In many of the calls to holy war against Islam, the atrocities allegedly perpetrated by the Muslim foe were emphasized. In the same way, throughout the *Mainz Anonymous* the crusaders refer repeatedly to the historic Jewish sin of deicide, a crime advanced by the attackers as providing ample justification for assault.[23]

Much more central than holy war to the Jewish chronicler's perception of crusader thinking is the sense of the First Crusade as an armed pilgrimage to Jerusalem. The crusade is depicted from the outset as an effort "to ascend, to rise up like eagles, to do battle, to clear the way to Jerusalem, the Holy City, and to reach the sepulcher of the crucified." In lamenting the fact that the French crusaders, passing through the Rhineland, aroused the Christian burghers to violence, the author speaks in hyperbolic fashion of burgher persecution "along the entire way to Jerusalem." Shortly thereafter, our narrator portrays the passage of French crusaders, "battalion after battalion, like the army of Sennacherib," alluding to the eventual failure of the Assyrian efforts to conquer Jerusalem.[24] The most striking reflection of Jewish awareness of the centrality of the pilgrimage in crusader thinking is the regular use of the Hebrew *to'im* as the designation for the crusaders. The Hebrew noun denotes those who move about aimlessly and in error, and it is clearly intended as a pejorative response to the Christian sense of the crusaders as *peregrini*.[25] Once more, this dovetails nicely with the information provided on popular crusading in Christian narrative and documentary sources.

The motivation for crusading, according to the *Mainz Anonymous*, involved in part the potency of such ideals as holy war and armed pilgrimage. At the same time, crusaders embarking on the dangerous journey eastward had to be concerned with the personal rewards that would accrue from participation in the sacred undertaking. The Hebrew narrative contains no sense of essentially venal motives within crusader ranks; the crusaders are not portrayed in the *Mainz Anonymous* as moved by material lusts. Where plunder does take place, it is after the fact. Indeed, the *Mainz Anonymous* shows considerable awareness of the spiritual rewards held out to participants in the crusading enterprise and the appeal of these spiritual rewards.

The *Mainz Anonymous* shows us Jewish familiarity with the centrality of the doctrine of indulgence in the crusading ranks, which is in fact highlighted in Christian sources.[26] The Jewish formulation represents a popular distortion in a number of ways of the papal notion of remission of sin: "Anyone who kills a Jews will have all his sins forgiven."[27] It is certain that there was no ecclesiastical support for the killing of Jews. Whether the popular crusading bands adumbrated a doctrine of indulgence for killing Jews cannot be known. Nonetheless, since the notion of indulgence is in any case foreign to Jewish tradition and thus cannot have been superimposed from a Jewish religious perspective, this Jewish report reflects the extent to which the notion of indulgence was very much in the air, penetrating the crusader psyche as one of the major personal rewards for joining the march to Jerusalem.

The *Mainz Anonymous,* which seemingly reflects fairly early popular crusader thinking, features martyrdom as yet another motivating factor among the German warriors contemplating association with the campaign: "For anyone who sets forth on this journey and clears the way to the unholy sepulcher of the crucified will be assured hell [already noted as a Jewish pejorative, reflecting the Christian sense of assurance of paradise]."[28] As we have seen, Jewish willingness to die rather than convert, so prominent in the *Mainz Anonymous,* was heavily rooted in the profound Jewish conviction that death under the special circumstances of 1096 would confer the crown of martyrdom. The descriptions put in the mouth of the Jewish victims and repeated in the third person by the narrator are extremely graphic, highlighting the immediate transposition of the slain Jews into the highest rungs of otherworldly blessing.[29] It seems likely that Jewish convictions of martyrological reward mirror the sense of such blessing among the crusaders themselves.

Thus, the *Mainz Anonymous,* seemingly committed to an accurate portrayal of the developments of late 1095 and early 1096 that would provide requisite guidance to its Jewish readers, does indeed offer a reliable description of the crusade and the crusaders. All the details it musters dovetail nicely with the information available in the rich

Christian narrative and documentary sources. Our Jewish author did not fabricate in his depiction of the crusade and the crusaders; he in fact shows a discerning eye in depicting central features of the explosive movement that took so many Jewish lives. Our expectation of accurate information is fulfilled.

We should close this discussion of the *Mainz Anonymous*'s depiction of the crusade and the crusaders by noting that the remaining four Hebrew sources, while not focused as seriously on the oppressors, do not in fact diverge from the *Mainz Anonymous* portrayal. The accounts of the crusade in our remaining sources are sketchy in the extreme, but they are not fabrications. The *Mainz Anonymous* is unusual in its level of interest in and attention to the details of crusading; however, the Trier report, the Cologne report, the *Solomon bar Simson Chronicle,* and the *Eliezer bar Nathan Chronicle* do not bend the realities of the crusade to Jewish needs. What they tell is limited, but accurate.

The exception to this generalization is the editorial epilogue to the *Solomon bar Simson Chronicle.* As we have seen, the outlines of the story—the difficulties encountered by both French and German crusaders while traversing the kingdom of Hungary—are basically correct. The details, however, for the French forces are surely wrong, and the tale of the demise of the German bands is highly suspect, vitiated by its essentially folkloristic tone. As noted recurrently, the *Solomon bar Simson Chronicle* simply does not exhibit the driving historical impulses of the *Mainz Anonymous.*

ANTI-JEWISH VIOLENCE

As we proceed from the depiction of crusading in general to the portrayal of the anti-Jewish violence that occasionally broke out in 1096, Christian sources against which to measure our Jewish narratives become extremely sparse. This anti-Jewish violence was limited in its extent and did not draw the attention of many of those who set themselves to the task of recording the crusade. The Christian works that describe the anti-Jewish violence in the most detail are the *Liber Christianae expeditionis,* by the early-twelfth-century Albert of Aachen, who focuses on the assaults in Mainz and Cologne, and the much later *Gesta Treverorum,* which portrays events in Trier. Neither of these sources are as detailed as the *Mainz Anonymous* and the Hebrew Trier report, and neither seems, *prima facie,* as reliable.[30] The remaining Christian accounts are fragmentary in the extreme, although not devoid of interest.

Again, our identification of five distinct Jewish narrators means that we can seek corroborative data among them as well.

Following is a list of the locales for which we have evidence of one or another kind of anti-Jewish violence, with the sources available for each.

Rouen: Guibert of Nogent.[31]

Speyer: the *Mainz Anonymous,* the *Solomon bar Simson Chronicle,* and Bernold of St. Blaise.[32]

Worms: the *Mainz Anonymous,* the *Solomon bar Simson Chronicle,* and Bernold of St. Blaise.[33]

Mainz: the *Mainz Anonymous,* the *Solomon bar Simson Chronicle,* Albert of Aachen, the *Annalista Saxo,* and the *Annales Wirziburgenses.*[34]

Cologne: the *Solomon bar Simson Chronicle* and Albert of Aachen.[35]

Trier: the *Solomon bar Simson Chronicle* and the *Gesta Treverorum.*[36]

Metz: the *Solomon bar Simson Chronicle.*[37]

Regensburg: the *Solomon bar Simson Chronicle.*[38]

Prague: Cosmos of Prague and the *Annalista Saxo.*[39]

To this list we should add the brief general observations of Ekkehard of Aura in his *Hierosolymita.*[40] It is worth noting that, for most of these locales, we have more than one source, in many cases involving both Jewish and Christian observers.

There is unanimity among all our sources, both Jewish and Christian, that the wellspring of the anti-Jewish assaults lay in the crusade, although not all the violence was perpetrated by crusaders. There is striking agreement among the Jewish and Christian observers as to the thinking that animated the hostile crusaders. Anti-Jewish crusading slogans are reported in the *Mainz Anonymous,* the *Solomon bar Simson Chronicle,* and Guibert of Nogent, and these versions are remarkably close to one another. In all these versions, there is reference to the lengthy journey involved in the crusade against the Muslim foe in the East and the jarring reality of a more heinous enemy at home. The sense of an immediate enemy nearby leads, in all versions of the sloganeering, to the conclusion that the immediate enemy should suffer Christian vengeance first, with the more distant foe targeted for subsequent attack.

Both Jewish and Christian sources likewise agree that only a few crusading bands were moved by such anti-Jewish imagery. Not one of the eyewitness Christian narrators' reports on anti-Jewish assaults perpetrated by the forces that they chronicled.[41] The available Christian sources in fact pinpoint only one crusading group responsible for anti-Jewish violence—the army of Count Emicho. The Jewish sources are very much in agreement.[42] Both the *Mainz Anonymous* and the Hebrew Trier report indicate that the French crusaders, specifically those led by Peter the Hermit, seemed threatening, but in fact did no physical harm. By emphasizing so intensely the actions of Count Emicho, the *Mainz Anonymous* seems to be pointing to the depth and uniqueness of his anti-Jewish animus.

Both the Jewish and Christian sources suggest that Emicho and his followers attacked the Jews of Mainz in organized fashion, operating as a military band. They also agree that, on occasion, crusaders were involved in anti-Jewish violence that was unorganized and spontaneous. This seems to have been the case, for example, with the French assault portrayed by Guibert of Nogent. We recall also the *Mainz Anonymous* depiction of French crusaders crossing over into Germany and chasing down individual Jews in haphazard fashion.

Both Jewish and Christian sources further agree that the animosity that the crusade generated among some crusaders made itself felt among the burgher population as well. The *Mainz Anonymous* and the Trier account reinforce each other strongly in the claim that crusading set off a wave of anti-Jewish thinking among the local burghers who were not directly part of the movement. The *Mainz Anonymous* statement is brief, albeit quite clear. The Trier report is lengthier and fuller, stressing that relations between the Jews and their Christian neighbors had been most peaceful prior to the arrival of Peter the Hermit and his followers. The author of the Trier report seems to suggest a number of possible factors in the newly developed burgher animosity: crusading propaganda itself, awareness of the precariousness of Jewish circumstances and the resultant potential for financial exploitation, and the notion that Jewish suffering served as an indication of divine abandonment of the Jewish people. While the lesser-detailed Christian sources do not focus on arousal of burgher hostility, they do indicate recurrently that burghers were heavily involved in some of the anti-Jewish violence.

There is considerable evidence that burghers joined forces with crusaders in attacking Jews. In some instances, these attacks were premeditated and organized. Such was the case with the assault on the Jews of

Worms who had sequestered themselves in the bishop's palace. In other cases, the crusader-burgher violence was spontaneous. We have seen this, for example, in the *Mainz Anonymous* account of the limited violence in Speyer and the more devastating first assault on those Jews of Worms who had elected to remain in their homes.

On occasion, burghers alone initiated anti-Jewish violence. The Cologne unit stresses that the initial and very limited violence suffered by the Jews of that town did not involve crusaders; the initial violence was perpetrated by hostile burghers, was chaotic and oriented toward plunder, and cost very few Jewish lives. Albert of Aachen's portrait of the assault on Cologne Jews concurs strikingly in this assessment.[43]

The *Mainz Anonymous* notes repeatedly that not all burghers were swayed by the anti-Jewish sentiment of some of the passing crusader bands. The episode of the woman and the wondrous goose noted earlier eventuated in spontaneous crusader violence that was met resolutely by a number of Mainz burghers. This battle between the two sets of Christians eventually cost the life of a crusader, suggesting the intensity of the clash. Throughout the *Mainz Anonymous,* Jews are depicted as turning in their desperate straits to neighboring Christians, obviously anticipating assistance. Here the Cologne report corroborates the *Mainz Anonymous,* showing the Jews of Cologne responding to the first outbreak of hostility in their town by fleeing to neighboring Christians and finding successful refuge with them. Albert of Aachen tells much the same story; his vilification of Christian anti-Jewish violence opens a window on the kind of Christian thinking that opposed the assaults on Jews.

Both early Jewish sources—the *Mainz Anonymous* and the Trier report—and a number of Christian sources agree on the protective stance adopted by the local bishops of the Rhineland towns. Perceptions of the bishops' opposition to crusader and burgher anti-Jewish violence are widespread and can hardly be doubted. Our parallel Jewish and Christian sources on the events in Trier, however, serve to warn us that perceptions of episcopal behavior could inevitably vary to some extent.[44]

All in all, the Jewish and Christian sources reinforce one another at every turn in their description of the anti-Jewish violence of 1096—its origins, the styles of assault, and the various groupings implicated in the anti-Jewish attacks. Once more, the sense with which we emerge is that of a high level of reliability in our two early Hebrew accounts. Again, the time-bound goals of the *Mainz Anonymous* and the Trier report produced a need for more-or-less accurate detail. Comparison of the available Christian and Jewish sources and the inner consistency among the disparate Jewish sources combine to suggest that our Jewish narrators did in fact sketch their portraits in a way that was faithful to the events they depicted.

THE JEWISH RESPONSES

All five Hebrew narratives focus heavily on the Jewish responses to the persecution instigated and perpetrated by some of the crusading bands in western Germany. Again, the Christian narrative sources are by and large oblivious to or uninterested in this fringe violence and even less interested in the Jewish reactions. What then might be said of the reliability of our narrative records in this area, where corroborating Christian evidence is yet more minimal? It is precisely with respect to the Jewish responses to crusader and burgher violence that the Jewish sources are most suspect. Given their desire to memorialize properly the Jewish victims and given the place that martyrdom plays in the theological solace they propose, exaggeration and outright fabrication might be most readily anticipated in the description of Jewish behaviors and thinking in 1096.

In assessing the reliability of the narrative reports of Jewish responses in 1096, we must note the existence of yet one more set of sources, and those are the Hebrew dirges composed both immediately and long after the events themselves. These dirges are of no value in reconstructing crusader and burgher behaviors, since they are focused so single-mindedly on the Jewish responses, and indeed only on the Jewish response of martyrdom. Their facticity is, of course, far more suspect than that of the Hebrew narratives. Thus it might seem that they provide no assistance whatsoever. However, the existence of descriptive evidence of Jewish actions and—even more strikingly—of motivations and symbols observable among the Jewish martyrs can be useful, as we shall shortly see.[45]

Both the more detailed Hebrew narratives and the less detailed Christian sources agree that Jews reacted in a variety of ways to the unanticipated threat that materialized so suddenly. There can be no serious doubt as to the reality of Jewish dependence on the local authorities, extensive Jewish negotiation with these authorities, the place of financial incentives in these negotiations, and the positive response of the authorities to these overtures. Further, there is no question as to the essential elements of the protection offered, involving sequestering endangered Jews in urban fortifications or sending them forth into rural redoubts. A complex record of success and failure is obvious from both the Jewish and Christian records as well. Finally, there can be no real doubt as to the accuracy of the portrayal of eventual episcopal efforts in some places to dissolve the dangers by cajoling or forcing Jews into baptism. Our sources, both Jewish and Christian, fail us in their assessment of the thinking behind these episcopally argued or forced conversions. Did the bishops actually come to the conclusion that theologically there was no other reasonable course and that the conversions were ultimately genuine conversions? Alternatively, did the bishops view these conversions as contrived and insincere from the outset, meant to serve merely as a vehicle for extricating Jews from their perilous circumstances? While we might tend to suspect the latter, particularly in view of the rapid permission granted the converts to return to Judaism, our sources never fully illuminate the episcopal mindset. In any case, depiction of Jews turning to their episcopal overlords seems again highly reliable in our two early sources, and, by extension, in the later accounts as well.

That numbers of Jews converted is, once more, clear from both Jewish and Christian sources. The Jewish sources regularly attribute noble motives to the conversions, most prominently the desire to protect Jewish youngsters. Interestingly, the Jewish source most fully concerned with conversion, the Trier report, tells us next to nothing about the conversions themselves, except that they resulted from the imposition of physical force and were wholly insincere. We recall that the *Gesta Treverorum* argued, by contrast, that the conversions were occasioned by the eloquent preaching of Bishop Engilbert. To be sure, even in the *Gesta Treverorum,* there is clear indication that conversion was less a result of eloquence and more a matter of deep Jewish fear. It is interesting that, in the *Gesta,* the learned Jew Micha, who responds positively to the bishop's address, is not depicted as focusing on the theological or historical truths of Christianity, but rather on the impossible circumstances of Jewish existence. "Indeed, as you have said, it is necessary for us to adhere to the faith of the Christians, rather than to undergo daily danger to our lives and our possessions." Similarly, when Micha supposedly also asked Bishop Engilbert to spell out the demands of the Christian faith, he did so with a focus on "how the Jews might be saved from the hands of those outside, seeking to destroy us."[46] The bishop supposedly responded by providing a brief conspectus of the essentials of Christian belief. The Jewish leader accepted the requirements of that faith, once again emphasizing his desire to avoid destruction at the hands of the enemy. In any case, the Jewish and Christian sources agree that the conversions were insincere and that the converts quickly returned to the Jewish fold.

Again, both Christian and Jewish sources agree on the prominence of martyrdom in 1096. They furthermore agree on a diversity of forms of martyrdom, ranging from passive acceptance at the hands of the crusaders and burghers, to suicide, to the murder of others—especially youngsters—as a way of protecting these others from baptism. All these forms of Jewish behavior make their appearance regularly in Christian and Jewish sources. The most radical of these forms of martyrdom was surely the murder of others, and we have seen that one of the objectives of the Hebrew narratives was to insist upon the propriety of such innovative and radical behavior. Given Christian depiction of this extreme Jewish action, the reliability of the Hebrew narratives on this score cannot be doubted. It does seem reasonable to ask whether this extreme form of martyrdom or in fact martyrdom in general was as widespread as the Hebrew narratives suggest. It may well be that there is some exaggeration on this score, but there is certainly no fabrication of behaviors that were not at all in evidence.

Most difficult of all is assessment of the narrative reports of the radical Jewish thinking and symbols that motivated the martyrdoms of 1096. It has recently been suggested that many of these symbols represent mid-twelfth-century retrojections to 1096.[47] Here of course the Christian sources are of no assistance, since such matters fall beyond their range of interest. What we can indicate, however, is that the *Mainz Anonymous* account is early, that it is regularly corroborated by the later material in the Cologne report and the additions of the *Solomon bar Simson Chronicle*'s editor to the Mainz material, and is further reinforced by the early Hebrew dirges that are themselves suffused with the same symbols, preeminently the *'akedah* and the Temple ritual. Given the early provenance of the *Mainz Anonymous* and the corroborative Jewish poetry, it is difficult to challenge the depiction of these strikingly innovative motivations and symbols.

Having argued all through this chapter that the data provided in the two early Hebrew narratives is highly reliable and that the data provided in the later two Hebrew narratives is not much less reliable, let me conclude by noting that the Hebrew accounts are of course carefully constructed literary works. In arguing for the facticity of the evidence supplied in the Hebrew records, I am suggesting that our Jewish authors did not fabricate patterns of Christian and Jewish behavior or Christian and Jewish thinking in order to serve apologetic, polemical, or theological goals. The patterns they project are corroborated by external sources and by a high level of agreement among independent Jewish sources.

I am not suggesting, however, that each individual depiction be taken as a precise record of what transpired. The stories of Meshullam ben Isaac of Worms, Rachel of Mainz, David *ha-gabbai* of Mainz, Isaac ben David of Mainz, and Samuel ben Gedaliah and Yehiel ben Samuel of Cologne are brilliantly crafted reconstructions, and the role of poetic imagination must be acknowledged. We can never know precisely what transpired in such instances. The patterns depicted are thoroughly accurate; the specifics cannot be fully authenticated.[48]

In this regard, we must remain cognizant of the issue of language. Our 1096 narratives are carefully contrived reports in a biblically grounded Hebrew of events that involved Christian and Jewish speakers of Rhineland vernaculars. Precisely what was lost and what was added with the move from the spoken vernacular cannot now be fully gauged. Once again, we should be leery of excessive literalism in the reading of our Hebrew narratives. Nonetheless, the findings of this chapter suggest that wholesale fabrication was not undertaken by the Jewish narrators, that their time-bound commitments necessitated an account that was, in the main, "accurate." How this accuracy of depiction came to simultaneously serve timeless purposes will be the burden of the next chapter.

CHAPTER NINE

The Hebrew First Crusade Narratives

The Timeless

I have argued that our Jewish authors did not fabricate patterns of Christian and Jewish behavior or Christian and Jewish thinking in order to serve apologetic, polemical, or theological goals. That is not to suggest that the Jewish narrators were not animated by apologetic, polemical, or theological goals—they surely were. Rather, these Jewish observers seem to have concluded that the accurate detail necessary to achieve their time-bound objectives was not at all antithetical to their broader purposes. Indeed, they seem to have concluded that precisely the accurate detail would serve them well in making their more far-reaching case.

Tragedy under all circumstances necessitates some kind of consolation and explanation. Simply to suffer pointlessly is by and large inimical to human thinking. Certainly, throughout the Jewish past those undergoing persecution have regularly sought the solace conferred by one or another pattern of explanation.[1] In the case of the Jews of 1096, the need to comprehend the tragedy was much enhanced by the fact that their Christian neighbors had their own explanation for the tragedy, a ready explanation that these Christians recurrently shared with their Jewish neighbors, and that the explication advanced by these Christians—some quite friendly in fact—undercut the possibility of remaining Jewish. Given the disheartening and destructive nature of this Christian view of the suffering that Jews experienced in 1096, the search for comprehension took on added urgency.[2]

The end result of this search for comprehension was an innovative view of God, humanity, and history—a sense of the divine, the human, and the interaction between the two—that differed considerably from traditional Jewish thinking, that showed remarkable affinities to the audacious thinking within crusader ranks, and that transformed tragedy into triumph and suffering into victory.

We shall begin by gaining a fuller sense of the challenge posed by the Christian explanation for the catastrophe of 1096, indicating how this explanation served to constrict the range of explanatory models that Jewish observers might invoke. We shall then examine the diverse explanatory patterns advanced by our individual Jewish narrators. While there is much that is shared among these Jewish observers, there are nuanced and important differences as well, differences worthy of attention. Armed with this understanding of the answers provided by our diverse observers to the difficult theological-polemical issues posed by the tragedy of 1096, we shall proceed to investigate the audacious conceptions of God, humanity, and history embedded in the 1096 Hebrew narratives.

THE SPIRITUAL AND THEOLOGICAL CHALLENGE

Earliest Christianity developed within a Palestinian-Jewish matrix and thus shared the widespread Jewish sense of a potent sin-punishment paradigm at work in history. This paradigm is central to the Pentateuchal books, the historical narratives of the First Commonwealth, and the prophetic admonitions and consolations. With the passage of time, as fissures developed in Israelite society, the sense that the correct grasp of the covenant between God and Israel promises great reward while distorted comprehension of the covenant entails dire consequences became increasingly obvious. Sinning Israelites were warned of the most gruesome forms of divine punishment. As we proceed toward the dislocations occasioned by the Roman domination of Palestine, this sense of the harrowing fate in store for those in the wrong seems to have intensified. The literature of the Qumran community shows us graphically this intense perception of "us" and "them," of those Jews destined for reward and those slated for punishment.

We of course lack any historical sources that derive directly from the earliest phase in the history of Christianity, when the followers of Jesus saw themselves as part of Palestinian Jewry and felt themselves to be the correct interpreters of the covenant between God and the Jewish people.[3] It seems nonetheless highly likely that Jesus and his early followers would have fit themselves into the traditional Jewish sense that projected reward for proper comprehension and fulfillment of the covenant and punishment for distorted understanding and behavior. Some of the Gospel fulminations against the Pharisees and Sadducees, while stemming from sources that postdate the splitting off of the Christian community from its Jewish matrix, may well reflect earlier internal Jewish realities and sensibilities.

With the emergence of gentile Christianity and the growing gulf that separated the Jewish and Christian communities, however, the conviction that Christians had appropriated the riches of the Jewish past and that Jews had lost that heritage replaced earlier notions of proper Jewish understanding of the covenant.[4] Not surprisingly, the Acts of the Apostles, the New Testament book that focuses on the movement of Christianity beyond the confines of Palestinian Jewry, is most emphatic in its assertion of Christian reward and Jewish punishment. Indeed, this is the note on which the entire book concludes. The closing episode in the Acts of the Apostles portrays Paul in Rome attempting to attract Jews of that city to the Christian vision. According to the author, "some were won over by his arguments; others remained skeptical." Before the group of Jews dispersed, Paul made a final statement to them:

> How well the Holy Spirit spoke to your father through the prophet Isaiah when he said: "Go to this people and say: 'You may hear and hear but you will not understand; you may look and look, but you will never see. For this people's mind has become gross; their ears are dulled, and their eyes are closed. Otherwise, their eyes might see, their ears hear, and their mind understand, and then they might turn again and I would heal them.'"[5]

This is a vigorous condemnation of Paul's Jewish contemporaries, drawn from Isaiah's great vision of the divine throne room, with God seeking an emissary to his erring people. It is worth recalling the continuation of Isaiah's vision. The prophet has agreed to serve as the Lord's messenger and has received the chilling message noted by Paul, a message of divine wrath so intense that God precludes the possibility of an understanding that might lead to repentance. Seemingly stunned by the intensity of this divine anger, the prophet asks: "How long, my Lord?" How long will this dullness of mind and spirit last? The divine answer is once more harsh in the extreme.

> Till towns lie waste without inhabitants
> And houses without people,

And the ground lies waste and desolate—
For the Lord will banish the population—
And deserted places are many
In the midst of the land.[6]

Now, it is widely agreed that the Acts of the Apostles postdates the Roman-Jewish war, the defeat of the Jews, and all the pain and dislocation that defeat entailed. The Isaiah passage just cited seems to describe a situation of desolation that corresponds nicely to the Christian perception of the Jews after 70, a perception of destruction and exile flowing from sinfulness, specifically the sinfulness associated with rejection of the promised Messiah.

Since we have cited the Acts of the Apostles, which can fairly be called the first history of the Church, we might well note also the fuller and more mature multivolume history of the Church, penned in the fourth century by Eusebius of Caesarea. It is a rich and stimulating work, drawing on a wide range of sources and addressing a broad spectrum of issues. The core objective of this multifaceted work was "to record in writing the successions of the sacred apostles, covering the period from our Savior to ourselves." In this work, it is striking to note the extent of interest in "the fate which has beset the whole nation of the Jews from the moment of their plot against our Savior."[7] Descriptions of the calamities that befell the Jews from the time of Jesus down through Eusebius's own day are extensive, and the rationale for inclusion of these lengthy accounts is clear: the harsh fate suffered by the Jews was projected as sure evidence of the workings of providence in history, with the conviction that it was Jewish sinfulness, specifically the sin of rejecting the promised Messiah, that set the cycle of persecution and suffering into motion.

Over the centuries, with Jewish presence in the historic homeland ever weaker and Jews spread ever more widely across the Western world, this conviction intensified. This sense of Jewish sin and divine retribution was by and large intended for internal consumption: it reinforced, for Christian auditors and readers, the rectitude of their faith. Dolorous Jewish fate served as yet another index of Christian truth.

This historic perception of Jewish suffering took on added meaning and intensity during the period of the First Crusade. One of the striking features of the First Crusade mentality was a simplistic and triumphalist sense of God operating in history on behalf of his chosen followers. The *Gesta Francorum* contains a most revealing passage that reflects the

assessment among at least some crusaders of victory as divine reward
and defeat as divine punishment. This passage depicts the report of Ste-
phen of Chartres, who fled from the vicinity of Antioch. He described
to the emperor the magnitude of the Muslim forces besieging the crusader army; this crusader army had conquered most of Antioch but
subsequently found itself on the defensive and threatened with annihilation. In the face of this depressing report, Guy, brother of Bohemond,

> and all the others began to weep and to make loud lamentation. All of them
> said: "O true God, three in one, why have you allowed this to come to pass?
> Why have you permitted the people who followed you to fall into the hands
> of your enemies? Why have you forsaken so soon those who wished to free
> the road to your Holy Sepulcher? By our faith, if the word which we have
> heard from these scoundrels [the frightening report brought by Stephen of
> Chartres] is true, we and the other Christians will forsake you and remember
> you no more, nor will any of us henceforth be so bold as to call upon your
> Name." This rumor seemed so grievous to the whole army that none of them,
> bishop, abbot, clerk, or layman, dared to call on the Name of Christ for
> many days.[8]

This is a shocking linkage of human action and divine reward; it is not
truly characteristic of the broad sweep of the *Gesta*. It serves to illuminate, however, how firm the association of human virtue and divine
recompense could become, at least in some crusading circles.

Given the traditional Christian sense of God's abandonment of the
Jews and the more immediate conviction of direct divine reward and
punishment, it is hardly surprising to find Christians interpreting the
Jewish suffering of 1096 as irrefutable evidence of divine rejection, with
the conclusion that Jews must see this reality and leave the faith community that God himself had spurned. Our independent Jewish sources
regularly show Christians, generally well disposed to their Jewish neighbors, urging such understanding upon the Jews, with the obvious be-
havioral implication that conversion constituted the only reasonable option for these Jews. It surely seems that Christians did in fact urge such
conclusions upon the Jews of 1096.

As we have seen, the Trier report is a heavily time-bound *apologia*
for the conversion of the Jews of that town. Of the good will of Bishop
Engilbert there can be no real doubt, given the Jewish author's full acknowledgment of a series of episcopal actions on behalf of his Jews.
Overcome by the strength of the anti-Jewish forces in Trier, the embattled bishop turned to the Jews sequestered in his palace in an effort to
end the stalemate by bringing these Jews to conversion. His argument,

which is not as clear as it might be, ran as follows, according to the Hebrew report:

> What do you desire to do? You surely see that, on all sides, Jews have already been killed.[9] It was my desire—and properly so—to keep my pledge to you as I promised, up to the point that I indicated, until there remained no Jewish community in all the kingdom of Lotharingia. But see now that the crusaders have risen up against me to kill me. Indeed, I am still fearful of them. I have now fled from them for fifteen days.[10]

What is not altogether clear is the essential thrust of the bishop's argument, whether the reference to the death of so many Jews involves practical advice (there can be no stopping the killing) or a spiritual conclusion (the killing proves that God has indeed abandoned you Jews). The former seems the more likely case. The bishop seems to be saying that the anti-Jewish forces are insuperable: in the face of such implacable enmity and such overwhelming power, there is no alternative but conversion.

As we recall, the *Mainz Anonymous* adopts, in its portrayal of the second attack on Worms Jewry, the assault on those Jews who had sought refuge in the bishop's palace, a literary technique of highlighting a number of specific incidents. In two of these, the issue of Jewish suffering and its meaning is raised. The first such instance involves the Jew Simhah *ha-cohen*. The young man was urged to convert with the following argument: "Behold, all of them [the Jews of Worms] have been killed and lie naked."[11] Again, this may well be nothing more than practical counsel, although the reference to the corpses lying naked suggests that all this is in fact to be taken as an indication of divine disfavor.

The second instance, however, clearly introduces us to disaster as a meaningful spiritual sign. This second case involves a distinguished Jewess who had been hidden outside of town by friendly Christians during both assaults. When the violence had spent itself, these erstwhile friends approached the Jewess and urged: "Indeed, you are a distinguished lady. Know and see that God no longer wishes to save you. For they [the Jews of Worms] lie naked through the streets and there is no one to bury them. Baptize yourself."[12] Here there can be no real question as to the argument. The slaughter of Jews and their unburied state can be taken as nothing less than a sure sign of God's abandonment of the Jewish people. In the face of divine rejection, the only reasonable course for this important lady was certainly conversion, a course that she resolutely and fatally rejected.[13]

In the *Mainz Anonymous*'s depiction of the events in Mainz, we encounter a striking instance of the argument of divine rejection of the Jews. As we recall, the narrator artfully inserts two incidents intended to convey the sense of growing anxiety among the Jews of Mainz. The first of these incidents recounts the passage of a band of popular crusaders that included a woman with her ostensibly inspired goose, a phenomenon noted and excoriated by Albert of Aachen. According to the *Mainz Anonymous*, the sense of divine favor held within this popular band was shared as the group made its way through Mainz. "She [the owner of the goose] would say to all passersby: 'Behold, this goose understands my intention to go on the crusade and wishes to go with me.'" The remarkable sight attracted a crowd, which rather quickly turned on the Jews of the town with the following question and assertion: "Where is your source of trust? How will you be able to be saved? Behold, these signs are accomplished for us by the crucified"[14]—Christians are supported by God; Jews are clearly not. This challenge eventuated in an outbreak of violence between the crusaders, who were ready to attack the Jews, and the friendly burghers, who were opposed. Here the sense of divine rejection is expressed by hostile Christians and leads directly to assault.

The material seemingly appended to the Mainz account by the editor of the *Solomon bar Simson Chronicle* provides yet another clear-cut instance of the argument of divine abandonment. The setting for this claim was poignant. Archbishop Ruthard of Mainz had promised protection to his Jews, but had abandoned them in the face of Count Emicho and his formidable forces. No longer protected by the archbishop, most of the Jews gathered in the episcopal palace were killed or took their own lives. A band of Jewish warriors, unsuccessful in their efforts to hold back the crusaders at the palace gates, had hidden in one of the subterranean rooms of the extensive palace, seemingly destined for death. Although the archbishop had abandoned his Jews and had fled across the Rhine River, he did not in fact forget his protégés, sending an armed escort to accompany this Jewish band and its leader, Kalonymous, to the other side of the Rhine and safety. Unfortunately, the safety was not all that long-lived. Soon the archbishop found himself incapable yet again of protecting his Jewish clients.

At this point, the archbishop addressed his friend Kalonymous, the leader of the endangered band.

> I can no longer save you. Indeed, your God has abandoned you and no longer wishes to allow you a remnant and a residue. I no longer have the strength

to save you henceforth. Now, consider what you must do, you and the band with you. Either believe in our deity or else suffer the sin of your ancestors.[15]

The Jews had sinned; God had rejected them; this rejection manifested itself in the current persecution; either the Jews must come to grips with this reality and its painful implications or they would suffer for the sins of their ancestors.

Thus, the environment that tended to equate success with divine approbation and the traditional Christian doctrine that viewed Jewish suffering as an unmistakable sign of divine rejection combined to confront the Jewish survivors of the 1096 tragedy with the urgent task of explaining the catastrophe in a manner that would provide support and solace. Any explanation that highlighted Jewish shortcomings would immediately strengthen the widely perceived Christian view. Obviously, compelling rationales for the tragedy had to avoid simplistic emphasis on Jewish sinfulness as the basis for the tragedy. Within these constricted parameters, how did our Jewish narrators advance theological rationales for the events that they portrayed?

SPIRITUAL AND THEOLOGICAL RESPONSES

The most widely cited explanation for suffering in traditional Jewish (and Christian) thinking involved the sin-punishment paradigm. Since this option was complicated by the Christian interpretation of the 1096 tragedy, other alternatives had to be pursued. As we have seen, the Trier report is by far the most time-bound of the five Hebrew accounts. Its author was concerned with the specific image of Trier Jewry, not the broad questions that arose from the persecution. Emphasis on the martyrological instincts of the Trier Jews was intended to exonerate these Jews of any misdeed, not provide some kind of framework for explaining the tragedy.

The *Mainz Anonymous* was profoundly concerned with the meaning of the tragedy. In approaching the *Mainz Anonymous* and its explanation of the catastrophe, we must bear firmly in mind two characteristics of the work that have already been identified in our earlier examination of the narrative and its achievement of time-bound objectives. In the first place, as we have noted, the *Mainz Anonymous* by and large refrains from editorializing; it much prefers to let the story convey its messages. We recall, for example, the artful device of having the martyrs of Worms exonerate the converts of that town, rather than introducing an editorial *obiter dictum*. Secondly, we recall the insistence in the *Mainz Anonymous* on rapidly evolving developments on both sides. There is nothing static about the realities of 1096, according to our narrative. Indeed, rapid change was itself part and parcel of the divine decree. Both these characteristics will inform our analysis of the author's effort to explain the tragedy.

This analysis must begin with the notion of divine decree, which plays throughout the narrative, from beginning to end. The imagery of a divine decree is introduced by both the actors in the drama and the auctorial observer. The first use of this terminology comes early on, when the author completes his description of the insouciant Rhenish reply to the anguished letter dispatched by the Jews of France. "Indeed, we were not intended to hear that a decree had been enacted and that a sword was to pierce us mortally."[16] Early in his description of the fate of Speyer Jewry, the author falls back on the notion of a decree, indicating that "the decree began from there, in order to fulfill what has been said: 'Begin with my sanctuary.'"[17]

The same terminology is introduced by the narrator in his depiction of the anguish of Worms Jewry upon hearing the news from Speyer.[18] At the close of his description of the twin assaults on Worms Jewry, our author puts the notion of a divine decree in the mouths of the Jews of that town: "It is the decree of the King. Let us fall into the hands of the Lord, and we shall thus come and see the great light."[19] When portraying the destruction of Mainz Jewry, the author of the *Mainz Anonymous* once again uses the notion of a divine decree in his third-person narration and in remarks attributed to the Jews of 1096. The latter comes in the report of voices heard in the synagogue, taken to be a sign of impending disaster. The reporter, Baruch bar Isaac, conveys the following message: "Know that truly and surely the decree has been enacted against us, and we cannot be saved."[20]

Thus, from beginning to end, the imagery of divine decree is constant. What then does it suggest? I would urge that this imagery is, in and of itself, neutral. It conveys the sense of a divine decision, but leaves the basis for this decision unclear. Often such a divine decision is predicated on sinfulness, but such is not necessarily the case. Indeed, in two of the instances we have encountered the context is quite positive. In the use of the notion of a divine decree with respect to Speyer Jewry, that Jewish community is compared favorably to the Temple in Jerusalem. Such a comparison hardly projects a decree that emanates from Jewish sinfulness. Likewise, when the Jews of Worms themselves talk of a divine decree that will eventuate in their vision of the great supernal light, the implication can hardly be negative. Thus, imagery of a divine decree is ubiquitous, with no directly negative overtones and an occasionally positive implication.

Are there, then, any negative reflections on the Jews of 1096? Indeed there are—two kinds. The first is direct mention of Jewish sinfulness. Very early on, after describing the Jewish provisioning of the French crusaders, which might have led to peaceful passage across the Rhineland, our author notes: "All this was unavailing. Our sins brought it about that the burghers in every town through which the crusaders passed were incited against us."[21] Ostensibly we find here invocation of the time-honored sin-punishment paradigm.

The second style of negative assessment involves the other partner in the divine-human dyad, God. There are two references to intense divine anger. The first comes in the same opening segment in which we encountered the reference to Jewish sinfulness. A bit further in that opening segment, after depicting the threat posed by both German burghers and German crusaders, the narrator portrays Jewish efforts to appease God through fasting, efforts that proved utterly unavailing. "Nonetheless, our God did not relent in his anger toward us."[22] Similarly, after describing in general terms the second assault on Worms Jewry and the ensuing slaughter of those Jews who had sought refuge in the episcopal palace and, more specifically, the Abraham-like sacrifice undertaken by Meshullam ben Isaac, the narrator utters a prayerful outcry, taken from Isaiah 64: "At such things will you restrain yourself, O Lord, [will you stand idly by and let us suffer so heavily?]" This is followed by: "Nonetheless, he did not relent in his great anger against us."[23]

With respect to these few statements that reflect negatively on the Jews of 1096, I would argue that they must be seen in context, with full awareness of the progression of the narrative as revealed in our analysis of the *Mainz Anonymous*. In fact, our author was providing an early explanation for early persecution, an explanation that fit the facts as they were then known but that would no longer fit the facts as the persecution deepened and Jewish responses intensified. Indeed, the notion of Jewish sinning appears only once and the notion of divine anger appears only twice, in all cases toward the beginning of the narrative. I would urge that their early appearance and subsequent disappearance are hardly accidental. Initially, Jews might have seen the minor dangers from the perspective of sin and punishment; as events so rapidly unfolded, that obviously inappropriate paradigm had to be abandoned. Intensifying realities necessitated a fresh understanding of the events of the tragedy and their meaning. Notions of Jewish culpability would fall by the wayside, especially in light of the remarkable Jewish responses elicited by the intensifying persecution.

To be sure, our narrator offers no ringing theoretical alternative to his neutral notion of a divine decree and his early negative references to Jewish sin and divine anger. There is, however, one recurrent phrase and conception that plays throughout the narrative, and that is the notion of *kiddush ha-Shem,* consecration of the divine Name. Reference to the Jews of 1096 as sanctifying the Name of God abound throughout the narrative, from beginning to end. At the simplest level, Jews so intensely committed to *kiddush ha-Shem* can hardly be projected as sinful, suffering the fruits of their iniquity.

Indeed, the exoneration of the extreme forms of Jewish martyrdom in the *Mainz Anonymous* contains much more than simply the broad assertion of *kiddush ha-Shem.* The moving accounts of Jewish martyrdom are so crafted as to brook no suggestion that they were either halakhically incorrect or that they might have been undertaken by Jews who were culpable of significant misdeeds or even of the misdeeds of their ancestors. The targeted reader—Jewish of course—could only come away with a sense of the breathtaking devotion and heroism of these martyrs. Any serious perception of possible Jewish misdeeds or shortcomings would evaporate in the face of the tales themselves.

At this point, we must return to another important facet of our earlier analysis of the *Mainz Anonymous.* In addition to brilliantly plotting the events of 1096 on an immediate spatial and temporal continuum, our author similarly portrayed these events against a larger spatial and temporal backdrop. The spatial backdrop moved from the Rhineland to the Holy Land to the celestial heights; the temporal trajectory moved from 1096 back through high points of the Jewish past, into the early reaches of human history, and back into the precreation void.[24] Projection of the Jews of 1096 into these exalted places and times once again created a portrait of Jews who could hardly be challenged with respect to their saintliness or could hardly be charged with sinfulness and shortcoming. Jews portrayed as re-creating the Temple sacrifices with their own bodies and the bodies of their loved ones; Jews depicted as the successors of Rabbi Akiba, the mother and her seven sons, Daniel and his friends, Abraham and Isaac—such Jews could hardly be guilty of failings that required divine punishment. Jews who could be described as carrying out an unprecedented 'akedah—a sacrifice of loved ones—one greater than that of the patriarch Abraham, had to be seen as virtuous in the extreme. Our relatively restrained narrator eventually bursts out, toward the end of his narrative: "Behold, has anything like this ever happened before? For they jostled one another, saying: 'I will be the first to sanctify the Name of the King of all kings.'"[25] All such portrayal of the Jews of 1096 was intended to make a case for righteousness and sanctity, a case rooted in the depiction of specific behaviors and the projection of those behaviors onto a larger spatial and temporal canvas.

Ultimately then, the *Mainz Anonymous* certainly rebuts any Christian notion of 1096 as a punishment for Jewish sinfulness. The case made is not theoretical; it is the reality of Jewish behaviors and the terms in which the author insists on seeing and projecting these behaviors. Does the Jewish author offer an explicit alternative to the Christian view? He does not provide a fully elaborated alternative, to be sure; he insists on an element of uncertainty. What happened was a divine decree, with the mystery that implies. The Jewish behaviors in 1096 represented acts of incomparable heroism, however, and from the perspective of the divine-human covenant, these behaviors represented the highest possible level of human fulfillment of divine will.

Why did God choose this generation for such suffering? The author offers no answer. The suffering was surely not the result of sinfulness; it involved the greatest religious commitment and valor in the annals of the world. Again, implicit here is a counter-crusade posture: Christians wrongly believe that their soldiers were the most impressive heroes the world has even known. Not so. The most impressive heroes the world has ever known were the Jewish victims of misguided crusading zeal.

With the Cologne report we encounter much the same thinking and much the same explanation via exposition. The notion of a divine decree makes its appearance, although not so consistently as in the *Mainz Anonymous*. The Cologne report uses the same technique we have already identified in the *Mainz Anonymous,* the technique of impassioned description that leaves no place for questioning. Since the spatial and temporal plotting of the Cologne report is not nearly so tight and impressive as that of the *Mainz Anonymous,* the extensions in space and time lose some of their force. Nonetheless, the author of the Cologne report does project his heroes across the known world to the Holy Land and into the celestial realms. Similarly, he moves them backward in time and links them with the great figures of the Jewish past, again preeminently the patriarch Abraham.

Three slight departures from the *Mainz Anonymous* are notable. The first is a far stronger tendency toward citation of biblical verses. While such verses are occasionally quoted in the *Mainz Anonymous,* their number is paltry when compared with the verses in the Cologne report. A second departure involves the overt introduction of the notion of the calamity of 1096 as a divinely imposed test, inflicted on a generation singled out for its strength. This notion, which is surely implicit in the *Mainz Anonymous,* is made quite explicit in the Cologne report. Finally, the theme of vengeance, so strikingly minimal in the *Mainz Anonymous,* occupies center stage in the Cologne report. All in all, these departures are hardly monumental: they represent slight shifts rather than real change.

As noted recurrently, the editor of the *Solomon bar Simson Chronicle,* who may well have been identical with the author of the Cologne report, was not well focused on the historical realities of 1096; he was a collector and interpreter of the reports of others. To be sure, collection and interpretation of materials is to be cherished as well. Our knowledge of the events of 1096 would be much diminished without the collecting zeal of our editor. Similarly, his interpretive skills surely constituted a significant contribution to post-1096 German Jewry, as it grappled with the meaning of the calamity. As already noted, our editor spins out a fairly full scheme of explanation, a scheme intended to counter Christian claims and provide the solace of meaning simultaneously.[26]

Key to our editor's explanatory scheme was projection of the historic sin of the golden calf as the basis for the divine decree of 1096. Focus on this historic sin achieved two purposes: it negated the Christian claim of Jewish culpability and punishment for the Crucifixion, and it signaled the remarkable place that Rhineland Jewry achieved in the trajectory of Jewish history. The suggestion that this particular generation of Jews should have been singled out by God to bear the punishment for the sin committed at the foot of Mount Sinai, despite the horror of what transpired in 1096, conferred unique dignity on the sufferers. Over and above all the great generations of Jews—those of the conquerors of the Holy Land under Joshua, of David and Solomon, of those who perished in the conquest of Jerusalem by the Babylonians, of Nehemiah and Ezra, of the martyrs of the Seleucid period, of the heroes of the Jewish resistance to Rome, of Rabbi Akiba and his associates, of the codification of the Mishnah, of the crystallization of the two Talmuds—God had seen fit to select the Jews of 1096 to bear the burden of expiating the sin of the golden calf. While the experience of expiation involved enormous pain, the glory of being singled out by God in such a way had to be perceived as unique and noble. The Jews so chosen could only—in the eyes of our editor—have been the very worthiest of all time.

As noted, the essential thrust of the thinking of the editor of the *Solomon bar Simson Chronicle* is toward the future: the roots of the present calamity are in the far distant Jewish past; the present shows a picture of bloodshed and pain; the meaning of the events of 1096 will be fully felt in the future. Moreover, that future will involve great reward, on an individual and group basis, for the heroism of the martyrs; it will likewise entail punishment for the perpetrators of the catastrophe, the crusaders and their burgher allies. Like the other voices we have encountered, this one reflects a striking counter-crusade mentality. Christian triumphalism, which by the 1140s meant deep satisfaction over the conquest of Jerusalem in 1099, was ultimately misplaced self-congratulation. Both Jewish defeat and Christian victory would give way to stunning reversal. It may well be that our editor saw in the agitation of the new crusade the beginnings of such a reversal. Looking back, we may well feel that such projections of the future represented nothing more than a weak rationalization of the present and its pain; again, however, our editor did not project this reversal in the abstract. His central message was that this ultimate reversal of the roles of 1096 was rooted in the inevitable divine reaction to the realities as perceived by all our narrators—unprecedented heroism on the part of the Jewish men, women, and children subjected to the cruelty of the crusader-burgher assault in 1096.[27]

CERTITUDE AND PETITION: THE HUMAN AND DIVINE AUDIENCES

To the extent that the Hebrew First Crusade narratives undertake time-bound objectives, they are of course addressed to an immediate human audience; to the extent that they commit themselves to timeless objectives, their audience is somewhat more complex. Even in undertaking timeless objectives, the Hebrew narratives were surely addressed to a set of human audiences—the immediate survivors of 1096 and, beyond them, succeeding generations of Jewish readers. At the same time, they were addressed to God himself. We have analyzed the thrust of the timeless message addressed to a human audience; we must now attend to the message addressed to the divine auditor.

The *Mainz Anonymous* is somewhat less expressive in this direction than is the *Solomon bar Simson Chronicle*. Nonetheless, even in the *Mainz Anonymous* there are occasional instances of direct outcry and petition to the Lord. These petitions, which are in large measure cries of pain and outrage, are artfully dispersed throughout the narrative. In its early segments, as the tension and level of violence build, there are no such outbursts. It is only after the second assault on Worms Jewry, with the resultant destruction of that great community almost in its entirety, that our narrator permits himself his first outcry, echoing the words of Isaiah: "At such things will you restrain yourself, O Lord, [will you stand idly by and let us suffer so heavily?]"[28] Implicit here is the setting within which the prophetic question was originally raised. This question-assertion is found at the end of a lengthy passage bemoaning the ills of Jerusalem after its destruction by the Babylonians. They cap a sequence of the following images:

> Zion has become a desert,
> Jerusalem a desolation.
> Our holy Temple, your pride,
> Where our fathers praised you,
> Has been consumed by fire;
> And all that is dear to us is ruined.[29]

Implicit here is, once more, identification of Worms Jewry with the Jerusalem of yore; both images evoke an outcry of pain, despair, and even anger addressed to the God who had permitted such tragedies to take place.

A second and lengthier outburst and petition is introduced at the end of the victorious and bloody entrance of Emicho's troops into the palace courtyard of the archbishop of Mainz:

> Sun and moon, why did you not hide your light? You stars, to whom Israel has been compared, and you twelve planets, like the number of the tribes of Israel, the sons of Jacob, how is it that your light was not hidden, so that it not shine on the enemy intending to blot out the name of Israel?[30]

Ostensibly addressed to the sun, moon, stars, and planets, these queries were in fact intended for the divine being that lay behind the seemingly indifferent forces of nature.

A third and last instance of appeal to God is found toward the close of the description of the slaughter of those Jews who had shut themselves up in one of the upper chambers of the archbishop's palace. While that particular story is dominated by Rachel, in fact she and her children were not the only victims of the crusaders' fury in that chamber. After depicting generalized killing, the author notes that the victims were then stripped naked. This evokes once more an auctorial cry of pain and outrage, this time taken from the book of Lamentations. "See, O Lord, and behold how abject I have become."[31] Again, the Jewish victims of 1096 are identified with the destroyed sanctuary, with parallel shock evoked by both.

Just as the outbursts of anguish are addressed to a divine audience, so too is the general argument of the *Mainz Anonymous:* the Jews of 1096 exhibited unprecedented loyalty and devotion in their heroic behavior; God who knows all can hardly be oblivious to this loyalty; the end result must surely be divine reversal of affairs, with the Jewish victims vindicated and the Christian oppressors punished. This is, of course, simply another version of the timeless message addressed to the Jewish survivors. For the latter, this thesis is presented as declarative: God must surely behave this way. For the divine audience, it is laid down in the appropriate form of a petition. The certitude expressed to human readers does not detract from the supplicatory nature of the petitions to God, nor do the supplications diminish the certainty of the message to the human eyes and ears that will encounter the narrative. Divine reward must be forthcoming, and the anguished request for such reward by no means compromises the certainty of that assertion.

The Cologne segment and the larger *Solomon bar Simson Chronicle* of which it is a part both address the double audience just noted. More specifically, they address immediate and subsequent Jewish readers and a divine reader-auditor. Indeed, the outcry to God is, if anything, intensified in these two compositions. We have noted earlier the fuller tendency in the Cologne unit and the prologue and epilogue to the *Solomon bar Simson Chronicle* to address God repeatedly and urgently. In particular, the closing segment of the *Solomon bar Simson Chronicle,* which focuses on the destruction of the popular crusading bands that wrought such havoc among the Rhineland Jews, ends with the citation of a series of biblical verses that urge divine vengeance upon those who had committed such atrocities on innocent Jewish victims. Given our dating of the writing of the Cologne segment as well as the editing of the *Solomon bar Simson Chronicle* to the 1140s, the petitions for divine reward and—especially—for divine vengeance take on special urgency.[32]

The timeless message of these two late Jewish observers is addressed to both humanity and the divinity, and the essentials of the message remain the same: God will surely and/or must please reward the Jewish heroism of 1096 and avenge the Christian bestiality. Once again, there is an interesting interplay between the assertive declarations of divine reward and punishment intended for Jewish eyes and the urgent requests for such reward and punishment intended for divine eyes. While seemingly a contradictory combination, our Jewish observers clearly felt that these related messages in fact effectively reinforced each other.[33]

CHAPTER TEN

God, Humanity, and History

The timeless objectives of the Hebrew First Crusade narratives were shaped by both the normal human desire to ameliorate tragedy through understanding and by Christian insistence that the catastrophe of 1096 should serve as a particularly dramatic sign of divine rejection of the Jewish people. A Jewish explanation that would simultaneously provide the solace of meaning and rebut the destructive Christian contentions was essential. It was, I would argue, no accident that the format chosen for clarifying the meaning of the events of 1096 was the narrative. As we have seen, our five Jewish voices make their cases largely through their stories. The unprecedented (from the narrators' perspective) Jewish behaviors of 1096 ultimately provide the solace of understanding and rebut the damaging Christian assertions.

The Jewish narratives present a striking view of the interplay between God and humanity in shaping the course of history. From the Bible onward, Jewish (as well as Christian) tradition had seen history as resulting from the interaction of the divine and the human. The simplest paradigm for that interaction, as already noted, involved human sin and resultant divine retribution. That simplistic paradigm had to give way to considerable refinement. Indeed, Christianity, with its suffering Messiah, had from its earliest days established more complex notions of the ways in which God and mankind interact. Now the Jewish survivors of 1096 had to produce some alternative to the simplistic sin-punishment model, and they did. In so doing, they inevitably adumbrated

far-reaching views of the crucial interplay between the divine and the
human.

We have identified a multiplicity of Jewish voices reflecting on the
events of 1096. While there is much common ground among these five
voices, there is much that is idiosyncratic to each as well. Although it is
necessary to make allowances for these idiosyncrasies, it is possible, in
tracking the innovative views of God, humanity, and history, to com-
press things considerably. Since we have already seen that the Trier unit
is in fact uninterested in the timeless questions associated with 1096, we
can comfortably omit consideration of that voice from this chapter.
Likewise, since there is so much shared between the narrator of the
Cologne unit and the editor of the *Solomon bar Simson Chronicle,* it is
easy enough to treat these two voices in tandem. Indeed, when we compare these two voices with the earlier *Mainz Anonymous* and the later
Eliezer bar Nathan Chronicle, we find little difference with regard to the
issue at hand. As a result, the analysis in this chapter will be simplified
in some measure. With but a few exceptions, we shall not have to attend
to a series of discrete voices. I shall focus this discussion on the *Mainz
Anonymous,* but I will cite particularly striking illustrative material from
the Cologne unit, the editorial views in the *Solomon bar Simson Chronicle,* and the *Eliezer bar Nathan Chronicle,* especially when these narratives offer a slightly different perspective.

GOD AND HIS ROLE IN 1096

God is surely central to the *Mainz Anonymous.* He is the will that enacted the requirements for human behavior that the Jewish martyrs of
1096 were so profound in deciphering and so relentless in realizing, and
he is the force that, in the eyes of the Jewish narrator, will reverse the
seeming catastrophe of 1096, with the Jewish victims rewarded for their
allegiance and the Christian aggressors punished for the pain they inflicted. In both the past and the future, God dominates the historical
scene.

Beginning with the past, we find that God's role in the events of 1096
can be traced as far back in time as it is possible to envision. We recall
the striking passage that connects events in Worms with the precreation
void. There God crafted heaven, earth, and humanity, setting in motion
all the forces that played themselves out in 1096. More important, long
before fashioning heaven, earth, and humanity, God spelled out the requirements that would shape the destiny of his chosen people. In the

Torah, crafted long before the physical universe, the following key obligation was articulated: "You have affirmed this day that the Lord is your God, that you will walk in his ways, that you will observe his laws and commandments and rules, and that you will obey him."[1] The relationship between God and Israel was founded on the readiness of the human associates to the covenant to know and carry out the will of their divine partner.

Throughout the *Mainz Anonymous,* the Jews of 1096 are regularly portrayed as attempting to live up to this set of obligations, even though the precise requirements of the covenant demanded excruciatingly difficult behaviors. Thus, the Jews assembled in the courtyard of the archbishop of Mainz are described as recapitulating the loyalty of their ancestors at Mount Sinai, who responded to the divine demands by saying, "We shall do and we shall hear"—that is, that the commitment to fulfill the demands of the covenant was so profound that it preceded any knowledge of the covenant's details. A bit further on, the Mainz Jews are portrayed as proclaiming the following

> Ultimately, one must not question the ways of the Holy One, blessed be he and blessed be his Name, who gave us his Torah and commanded that we be killed and slaughtered for the unity of his Name.[2]

In the same vein, Rachel of Mainz, the most lavishly depicted of the Jewish martyrs, is described as slaughtering her two daughters in the following terms:

> She [Rachel] took her two daughters, Bella and Madrona, and sacrificed them to the Lord God of hosts, who commanded us that we never abandon fear of his pure and awesome nature and that we remain faithful to him.[3]

God had set out his demands from the beginning of time; these demands were radically fulfilled by the Jewish martyrs of Speyer, Worms, and Mainz in the spring months of 1096.

The aftermath of the calamity of 1096 was filled with pain, and that anguish is regularly expressed in the narratives. Alongside the pain, however, there was also a measure of certitude as to the future. Radical Jewish fulfillment of the demands of the divine-human covenant necessarily implied obligations on God's part as well. We noted just now Deuteronomy 26:17, in which Israel is described as accepting its obligations toward God. It is not accidental that our author chose this particular formulation of human responsibility, for it is immediately followed by its correlative: "And the Lord has affirmed this day that you are, as he promised you, his treasured people who shall observe all his commandments and that he will set you, in fame and renown and glory, high above all the nations that he has made." Given the losses of 1096, it hardly seemed that the Jews had been set high above all the nations. Indeed, their Christian neighbors thought that they had reached the very nadir of their historical experience. Yet our narrator was quite convinced—and sought to convince his readers—that the relationship spelled out in Deuteronomy 26 could mean nothing other than subsequent reward. The Jews had clearly fulfilled their part of the covenant; God could surely do no less. This is the ultimate message of the narrative, one designed to uplift its Jewish readers. God was still, after all, the God of history. Just as he had set the course of events in motion eons ago, so too would he bring the course of events to its requisite conclusion sometime in the future. Precisely when God would reemerge to take control of history remained a mystery. That he would do so was indisputable.

To be sure, the God whose crucial actions stretch back into the pre-creation void and who will reengage himself in the indeterminate future is noticeably absent during the period of the persecution itself. Unlike the earliest of the prior Jewish tales consciously evoked throughout the narrative—the stories of Abraham and his son Isaac and of Daniel and his friends—the account of 1096 shows no God emerging to set things right. The most obvious and striking reflection of this has been noted. Meshullam ben Isaac of Worms invoked the precedent of Abraham in preparing to sacrifice his son Isaac, the lad born in old age to his wife Zipporah. As indicated, the story is a jarring one, since in the biblical account God intervened before Abraham and Sarah's Isaac was slain. In Mainz there is no staying voice; no ram suddenly appears as a substitute. God is silent, and the slaughter of the lad takes place.

In fact, the *Mainz Anonymous* suggests at only two points in its account any form of divine involvement whatsoever. In its account of the fate of Speyer Jewry, the *Mainz Anonymous* first tells of the ill-planned assault on Sabbath morning and the energetic intervention of Bishop John. This positive action, according to our narrator, can ultimately be attributed to divine intervention. "The Almighty caused protection and safety through him [Bishop John of Speyer]." The initial protection proffered by Bishop John in the face of a weak and disorganized threat did not end the story. Properly concerned with more ominous dangers, the bishop sent his Jews out into fortified areas where they might be effectively guarded. The dangers were real, but the episcopal ploy was successful. "For the Lord moved his [the bishop's] heart to maintain them without bribery, for this came about through the Lord, in order to provide us a residue and remnant through him [the bishop]."[4] Thus, the most positive outcome included in the *Mainz Anonymous,* the effective protection of Speyer Jewry, is attributed to divine intervention.

To be sure, since little such effective human protection is recounted in the *Mainz Anonymous,* there are few references to divine intervention. A second instance did not eventuate in the successful protection of Jews. Even before the arrival of Count Emicho and his troops, most of the Jews of Mainz had made their way to the archbishop's palace or to the palace of the local burgrave. A few Jews had sought safety in other venues. Some, like Baruch ben Isaac and his son-in-law Judah, had even opted to remain in their homes. The *Mainz Anonymous* tells the following tale about these two Jews.

> He [Baruch] said to us [the precise referent is not clear]: "Know that truly and surely the decree has been enacted against us, and we cannot be saved. For tonight I and my son-in-law Judah heard the souls praying here in a loud voice that sounded like weeping. When we heard the sound, we thought that perhaps they [the Jews] had come from the court of the archbishop and that some of the community had returned to pray in the synagogue at midnight out of pain and bitterness. We ran to the door of the synagogue and it was closed. We heard the sound but understood nothing. We then returned, shaken, to our house, for it is close to the synagogue."

The Jews to whom this report was communicated understood its meaning immediately: "When we heard these things, we fell on our faces and said: 'Woe, Lord God! Are you going to destroy utterly the remnant of Israel?' They went and recounted these events to their brethren in the court of the burgrave and in the court of the archbishop. They likewise wept greatly."[5] God thus did provide Mainz Jewry with foreknowledge at this critical juncture; the message was one of destruction, and the Jews of Mainz understood the message and lamented its content. Here God functions largely as a revealer of information, rather than an active agent. Even this relatively restricted role, however, is not reprised in the narrative. By and large, God is removed from the scene.

The Cologne segment and the *Solomon bar Simson Chronicle* in its entirety share the same sense of God as the controller of history, who set the events of 1096 in motion long ago by creating the world and its human inhabitants and by advancing a set of regulations for his special people that entailed difficult and dramatic actions on the part of the Jews of 1096. Likewise, the Cologne segment and the *Solomon bar*

Simson Chronicle share the sense that the Jewish behaviors of 1096 imposed, as it were, obligations on God himself. These two voices also assume the inevitability of divine reward for the Jewish martyrs, and they are far stronger than the *Mainz Anonymous* in their emphasis on the complementary component of the divine reaction to the events of 1096, the visitation of vengeance on the Christian perpetrators of the violence.

Like the *Mainz Anonymous,* the author of the Cologne unit and the editor of the *Solomon bar Simson Chronicle* depict God as playing a relatively inconspicuous role in the events of 1096. Strikingly, the few instances in which God intervenes involve revenge upon Christians. The Cologne unit concludes its depiction of the fate of the seven Jewish enclaves with the one set that emerged both alive and Jewish, the small number of Jews sequestered in the fortress of Kerpen. There is, not surprisingly for the Cologne unit, no real focus on the actions that resulted in the protection of these Jews. Rather, the author veers off into an unrelated issue. He tells the story of the local authority's decision to use the gravestones from the Jewish cemetery of Cologne for erecting a building. In the process of carrying out this plan,

> it came about through the Lord who is zealous and vengeful that a stone fell on the head of the enemy, the ruler of the town, smashed his head, and shattered his brain and he died. Subsequently, his wife went mad; his consort lost her mind; she died from her illness. Thus, the zealous and vengeful God provided a hint to us, by taking revenge upon them for what they did. Thus may he avenge speedily in our days the blood of his servants shed daily on his behalf.[6]

Here divine intervention comes in the form of incipient vengeance, understood as merely a foretaste of the requisite recompense that will eventually be exacted.

The entire *Solomon bar Simson Chronicle* ends, we recall, on the note of broader Christian catastrophe, again presented as a foretaste of the divine revenge that will surely eventuate. The tale, told with great relish, involved the alleged destruction in Hungary of two large popular crusading bands, those of Peter the Hermit and Count Emicho. The depiction, which we have had earlier opportunity to note and question, emphasizes heavily the thorough obliteration of these two sets of crusaders. The editor concludes with intense pleas for fuller revenge and for the rich rewards that the Jewish heroes of his story so obviously deserved.[7]

God had set in motion the events of 1096 long ago and would reconfigure the skewed realities of 1096 at some point in the future. During the crisis period itself, however, he was essentially passive and silent. The same is true with respect to any mediating or alternative heavenly figures. At no point, for example, does the devil or any parallel force make an appearance. Satan is in fact mentioned once, in the additional material introduced by the editor of the *Solomon bar Simson Chronicle* into his expanded Mainz account. Our editor immediately identifies Satan as the pope, however, thus again emphasizing the terrestrial dimensions of the 1096 events.[8] The immediate events of 1096 are thoroughly dominated by human figures, whether hostile Christians or heroic Jews.

HUMANITY AND ITS ROLE

The vacuum created by divine withdrawal in 1096 was, as it were, filled by a set of human protagonists. In the absence of an intervening God or even an active Satan, the Christians and Jews of 1096 dominate the *Mainz Anonymous,* the Cologne unit, the composite *Solomon bar Simson Chronicle,* and the *Eliezer bar Nathan Chronicle.*

As noted earlier, the human villains of 1096 are exactly that: they are intensely human and by no means function as unthinking agents of a divine plan. The *Mainz Anonymous* opens with a striking portrait of the inception of the First Crusade. This mammoth and eventually harmful enterprise was set in motion by genuine religious enthusiasm. Let us look once more at the description in the *Mainz Anonymous,* purposely truncated for the moment:

> It came to pass in the year 1028 after the destruction of the [Second] Temple, that this calamity struck Israel. Barons, nobles, and common-folk in France arose, took counsel, and decided to ascend, to rise up like eagles, to do battle, and to clear the way to Jerusalem, the Holy City.[9]

Breaking for a moment at this point, we are surely inclined to see the undertaking in a positive light. This certainly looks like a movement inspired by laudable goals. More important, our author clearly perceives history as set in motion by the arousal of human will and spiritual passion.

Although history was set on its course by the arousal of human will and although the goal of the enterprise seemed noble, there was in fact a profound problem with the precise objective of the campaign, which to the Jewish observer could only have been seen as hopelessly misguided. The specific goal of the crusade was to attain "Jerusalem, the Holy City [for both Christians and Jews] and to reach the sepulcher of

the crucified, a trampled corpse that can neither profit nor aid, because
he is vanity.''[10] Intense spiritual sensitivities set the crusade into motion;
the depth and impact of these feelings were, for the Jewish observer,
beyond question. It was the orientation of these sensitivities or, more
precisely, the erroneous goal of these feelings that transformed piety into
folly, religious enthusiasm into vanity. Humans set in motion the events
of 1096 and controlled the direction of these events. The tragedy of 1096
lay in the fundamental errors of the Christians and their worldview.

As noted, the crusaders responsible for the atrocities of 1096 are not
portrayed as moved by venal motivations. They were cruel in the extreme, but their cruelty was rooted in their intense commitment to a
misguided religious vision. We recall, for example, the story of the lad
Daniel ben Isaac of Worms. This young man, upon refusing baptism,
had a rope slipped around his neck and was dragged throughout the
town, up to the church. All the while, the crusaders and burghers urged
him to relent in his devotion and to convert, which he steadfastly refused
to do.[11] Likewise, in Mainz, after storming the chamber in which a number of Jews had found refuge, the crusaders of Count Emicho killed all
those whom they found, stripped the corpses naked, and threw them to
the ground below. Those victims who had somehow survived the attacks
and were lying in their death throes were yet again urged to convert,
even at this very last moment.[12] The Christians thus exhibit intense and
consistent commitment, a commitment that the Jewish author seems to
admire for its intensity and consistency, while excoriating it for its va-
cuity and error. Most important is the sense that it was this driving
human will on the majority side that set the tragedy into motion. Humans—in this case the crusaders and their allies—supply the energy that
sets history on its—in this instance tragic—course.

What is true for the Christian persecutors and their role in 1096 is
yet more obvious for the Jewish heroes, their actions in 1096, and the
impact these actions will exert upon the further course of history. The
Jewish hero figures are, like their Christian counterparts and persecutors, intensely human, with their will and commitments looming large.
They may not seem to dominate the scene in 1096, at least in military
and political terms, but to our Jewish authors they in fact constitute the
most significant facet of this tumultuous period. They more than match
their Christian counterparts in the intensity of their commitment and
the depth of their devotion. More important by far, they supersede their
Christian counterparts in the propriety of their goals. Christian aspira-
tions are focused on a human deity that is a sham; Jewish eyes are set

upon the one God, creator of heaven and earth, enunciator of the covenant and its demands, and shaper of history in ultimate terms. The behaviors of the Jews of 1096 will, in the long term, turn history in new directions. It is hard to imagine a profounder respect for human potential and a deeper sense of the human role than that expressed by our Jewish narrators.

The Jewish hero figures of 1096 are drawn far more fully and forcefully than their Christian counterparts. They are, first of all, real people, and their behaviors are realistically portrayed. While many of the descriptions are painfully graphic, there is nothing folkloristic or unbelievable about the accounts. This is in striking contrast, for example, to the stories of Daniel and his associates and of the woman and her seven sons, who are cited recurrently in the narratives as precursors to the martyrs of 1096. In both these earlier stories, the depictions of the Jewish hero figures are grossly exaggerated, projecting human behaviors that extend far beyond the reasonable.[13] Not so with the *Mainz Anonymous* and the other Hebrew narratives. The human behaviors re-created are extreme, but still essentially realistic and believable.

These realistically drawn hero figures have identity and individuality. They are located in Speyer or Worms or Mainz; they are old or young, male or female, learned or unlettered, wealthy or poor, honored or despised. The descriptions are not extensive, but they suffice to anchor the particularity of each figure. This individuation reinforces the sense of these figures as real people, performing in the real historical arena. Through their realistic portrayals of the Jewish martyrs, our narrators are able to address a combination of time-bound and timeless objectives.

As committed as these people are to what they perceive to be their duty—the fulfillment of divine will—they have an intense zest for life. They are not stoically resigned to dying: they do everything in their power to maintain their grip on life, although they never compromise their core commitments in order to do so.

The *Mainz Anonymous* regularly emphasizes the will to live. The Jews of France beseech the assistance of their brethren in the Rhineland; the leader of the Jewish community of Speyer exerts all his influence on the local bishop to save his fellow Jews; Worms Jewry tries a number of different ploys to secure its safety; the Jews of Mainz enter into serious negotiations with Archbishop Ruthard in order to win requisite protection. Indeed, Jews negotiate directly and forcefully—although unsuccessfully—with Count Emicho in order to ward off danger, and when

Count Emicho's troops storm the courtyard of the archbishop, Jews flee into the upper chambers of the compound in hopes of yet saving themselves. There is no hint of resignation to death among these Jews, except at the point when all other options were exhausted and the only remaining choice was conversion.

This zest for living expresses itself yet more poignantly through the individual portraits that are so important to the narratives. The *Mainz Anonymous*, for example, attempts to create real human beings, with genuine feelings, passions, and this-worldly rootedness. The martyrdom of these Jews does not flow from a weak hold on life: the greatness of their martyrdom lies in the capacity to overcome the strongest possible yen to remain alive. Thus, the very first individual portrait drawn in the *Mainz Anonymous* involves the Jew Meshullam ben Isaac, his wife Zipporah, and their son Isaac. As we recall, Meshullam ben Isaac adopts an Abraham-like posture, prepared to offer his son to God. At this point, there is an intrusion not found in the biblical narrative. The wife Zipporah challenges her husband in a way that the matriarch Sarah does not. Zipporah does not attempt to dissuade Meshullam ben Isaac from his horrific act; rather, she simply asks that he slaughter her first, so that she cannot witness the death of her son. This haunting request, denied by the husband, serves to bring us back to a set of human realities. The intensity of the moment and the biblical prototype aside, this is an incident in which a young lad is about to be killed by his father. All the horror of this act is suddenly brought home to us as readers. There is no possibility of losing sight of these human realities. The greatness of Meshullam ben Isaac, for the *Mainz Anonymous*, lies not in the absence of human emotions, but in his capacity to repress these human emotions in the name of his ultimate commitment.

A truly striking instance of this same awareness of the human dimension of the act of killing—indeed, one that highlights the human dimension—is found in the most stunning of the incidents in the *Mainz Anonymous*, the story of Rachel of Mainz. Caught in one of the upper chambers of the archbishop's palace, which was clearly failing as a refuge, Rachel was determined to sacrifice her four children. She announced her determination to slaughter these four youngsters "lest these uncircumcised come and seize them and they [the children] remain in their [the Christians'] erroneous faith." The stirring announcement of intention moved one of Rachel's companions to produce a knife for the killing. The sight of the knife reoriented the distraught woman—and it reorients the reader as well—to the gruesome realities. "And it came to pass that, when she saw the knife, she let loose a great and bitter cry. She smote her face and cried out and said: 'Where is your loving kindness, O Lord?' " This is no cardboard figure, unfeelingly ready to give up her children. Indeed, the intensity of the story is augmented by the lad Aaron's efforts to escape his mother. Once again, the author reminds us graphically of the horror of the acts performed. The normal will to live is fully expressed by the youngster attempting unsuccessfully to hide. The final element in this tense and riveting drama is supplied by the crusaders, who—upon discovering that slaughtered children were covered by the billowing sleeves of the distraught Jewess—responded to the sight of the slaughtered children with fury.[14] Our narrator does not for a moment allow us to become oblivious to the horror of the act undertaken. Again, it is the capacity of the Jewish martyrs to overcome their normal emotions that makes them the heroic figures that he claims them to be.[15]

The Jewish behaviors reported in the *Mainz Anonymous* show more than just the capacity to suppress normal human emotions in order to fulfill the demands of divine will. There is a striking aggressiveness in carrying out these actions. The traditional Jewish posture in the face of persecution is decidedly passive. Daniel and his friends, the mother and her seven sons, Rabbi Akiba and his associates—the stereotypic martyrs noted recurrently in the Hebrew narratives as role models—respond to demands for violation of divine mandate by allowing themselves to be killed by their persecutors, rather than transgress Jewish law. Indeed, for all its complications, the famous halakhic ruling on the response to persecution is clear in enjoining that, in the face of demands to transgress essential dictates of Jewish law, Jews must allow themselves to be killed rather than transgress.[16]

Some of the Jewish martyrs of 1096 adopt this essentially passive posture, dying at the hands of the crusaders and their burgher allies. We recall, for example, Isaac ben Daniel and Minna of Worms, two of the specific figures cited by the *Mainz Anonymous* to highlight Jewish behaviors in Worms. In both cases, strenuous efforts to bring these two to baptism are resisted, and the two meet their deaths at the hands of Christian persecutors, exactly as specified in the famous halakhic injunction.[17] Likewise, at the outset of the conquest of the archiepiscopal courtyard in Mainz, the crusaders led by Count Emicho encounter and slaughter immediately a group of Jews who are seated, passively awaiting their demise.[18] Finally, the very last tale told in the *Mainz Anonymous* involves an important Mainz Jew named David ben Nathaniel, who had sought safety for himself and his family with a friendly cleric. After the destruction of the major Jewish enclaves in the archbishop's palace and the burgrave's palace, these Jews too met their deaths at the hands of Count Emicho's followers.[19] All this again corresponds to the dictates of Jewish law and the historic precedents cited regularly in the Hebrew narratives.

The story of David ben Nathaniel, however, alerts us to the fact that even among those Jews who accepted death at the hands of their enemies there was more happening than simply passive acceptance of death at the hands of oppressors. David ben Nathaniel exploited the hopeless circumstances in which he found himself by announcing his readiness for conversion, thus attracting a group of Christian onlookers who were delighted at the prospect of witnessing the baptism of a leading Mainz Jew. He then publicly excoriated Christianity in the final act of his life. While technically he allowed himself to be killed rather than transgress, in fact he engaged the Christian enemy in a highly aggressive manner. David ben Nathaniel emerges as a warrior: he is portrayed by the Jewish author as the victor in an intense verbal engagement. The crusaders may have, for the moment, won the battle of arms, but David was the victor in the arena of ideas. To cite once again the earlier hero figures who appear in the Hebrew narratives, David's behavior was far more aggressive than that of Daniel and his friends, the mother and her seven sons, or Rabbi Akiba and his circle. In none of these prior instances do we encounter the militance of David ben Nathaniel.

There is yet another Jewish martyr who died at the hands of Christians, yet nonetheless deviated considerably from the halakhic mandate and the aggadic precedents, and that is the young man Simhah *ha-cohen*. Simhah *ha-cohen* chose an innovative path. He feigned willingness for conversion in order to bring himself into the bishop's chamber. Once there, he took out his knife and attacked a number of highly placed Christians, killing three before succumbing to assailants. After detailing the death of Simhah, the *Mainz Anonymous* concludes: "There was killed the young man who sanctified the Divine Name. Indeed he did what the rest of the community was not able to do, for he killed three uncircumcised with his knife."[20] The innovative and highly aggressive behavior of the young Simhah is obviously viewed and projected most positively by our narrator. He clearly wishes that more Rhineland Jews had followed the example of Simhah *ha-cohen*.

Most of the Jewish behaviors highlighted in the *Mainz Anonymous* diverge even further from the halakhic norms and the behaviors of traditional Jewish martyr figures. As we have seen recurrently, it is the aggressive and activist Jewish martyrs, the ones who preempt the Christian persecutors in spilling blood, that dominate the *Mainz Anonymous* and the other narrative records. These Jewish hero figures are even more radical than David ben Nathaniel and Simhah *ha-cohen*. In the narratives their actions are bellicose and martial; they are warriors in the service of God, ranged against another set of warriors who deem themselves also servants of God, but who are in fact thoroughly misguided in that regard. Indeed, the bellicosity of the Jewish martyrs is matched by the aggressive air of the depiction of their martyrdom.

Activist and aggressive Jewish martyrdom is highlighted in the depiction of Jewish group behaviors in Worms and Mainz provided in the *Mainz Anonymous*. For Worms, the narrator offers a brief description of pitched battle at the gateway to the episcopal palace, with the Christian forces—composed of crusaders, burghers, and villagers—eventually victorious. At that point, the Jews who were now exposed directly to their enemies "accepted the divine judgment and put their trust in their Creator and offered up true sacrifices. They took their children and slaughtered them willingly for the unity of the Name that is revered and awesome."[21] The same emphasis is to be found in the portrait of group behaviors in Mainz. There the description is somewhat fuller, including extensive reconstruction of the utterances of the martyrs, with an accelerating stress on self-sacrifice rather than submission to the weapons of others. When all the speeches come to a close, the narrator concludes: "They then all stood, men and women, and slaughtered one another."[22]

What is true for the portrayal of the group—highlighting the activist and aggressive style of Jewish martyrdom—is equally true for the individual portraits that dot the *Mainz Anonymous*. Although the author acknowledges a variety of styles of Jewish martyrdom, the activist martyrs dominate. As noted, the most prolonged and moving of all the individual portraits is that of Rachel of Mainz, who represents the epitome of aggressive, self-inflicted martyrdom.

Throughout this study, I have noted recurrently the adroit movement from group depiction to individual portraiture, with the latter deepening and intensifying the impact of the former. At this point, it would do well to signal a further significance to this interplay. Most martyrological literature is profoundly individualistic, with great figures holding center stage. This is the case with the precursor figures so regularly cited in our Hebrew narratives. Daniel and his three friends, the woman and her seven sons, and Rabbi Akiba and his associates are all outstanding figures who embody high virtue in the eyes of those who depicted them. To be sure, there is a certain hollowness to such depiction of individual giants. To what extent do they represent a norm? Put more negatively, to what extent do they merely represent personal idiosyncrasy?[23]

For our Jewish narrators, all such questions are unthinkable, for to them the uniqueness of the events they describe lay in the mass character of the Jewish martyrological behavior. The Jewish heroes of 1096 were individuals in all their specificity; the phenomenon, however, was a group phenomenon. For the *Mainz Anonymous,* this was the overwhelming reality in Worms and Mainz, where massive martyrdom involved every element in a diversified community. Indeed, this is the closing and truncated note on which our present version of the narrative ends:

> All these things have been done by those whom we have specified by name. The rest of the community [of Mainz] and the leaders of the congregation [perhaps a reference to Meshullam ben Kalonymous and his followers]— what they did and how they acted for the unity of the Name of the King of kings, the Holy One, may he be blessed, like Rabbi Akiba and his associates.[24]

There is much more to tell, because every element in the community sanctified the divine Name. The reference to Rabbi Akiba and his associates is striking. The willingness for martyrdom may be parallel, but (without explicitly saying so in this particular case) our author surely felt that the Jewish martyrdoms of 1096 represented far more of a group phenomenon than did those of the Hadrianic persecutions.

Once again, it should be recalled that our authors do not claim that every Rhineland Jew sanctified the divine Name. Much attention is lavished on efforts to survive, and some Rhineland Jews did survive. Likewise, despite the sense of battle that dominates the Hebrew narratives, there is unflinching testimony to spiritual defeat—that is, conversion (to be sure, justified and exonerated). All this complexity notwithstanding, the overwhelming impression fashioned by our narrators is one of mass martyrdom. As noted, the editor of the *Solomon bar Simson Chronicle* thought that an entire generation had been chosen by God as his special portion because of their unparalleled spiritual strength. This generation was not an abstraction; our authors and editors make the members of this special generation real and particular. Conversely, the specificity of the individuals could not be allowed to obscure the group nature of the Jewish martyrdom of 1096.

The Jewish hero figures of 1096—as groups and as individuals—are extremely articulate. Such articulateness is hardly surprising for martyrological literature. Martyrs generally tend to be portrayed with heavy emphasis on their thoughts and motivations. On the spectrum of slightly articulate to highly articulate, the Jewish martyrs of 1096 clearly flow toward the latter end of the range. Their high level of verbal expression is related to a number of the features of the Jewish hero figures identified thus far.

In the first place, the articulateness of the martyrs serves to anchor them as individuals. One of the last of the Mainz martyrs, a certain Jacob bar Sulam, is briefly but strikingly depicted by the author of the *Mainz Anonymous* as "not from a noble family—indeed his mother was not a Jewess." This Jacob is then made to cry out: "All my life, up until now, you have despised me. Now I shall slaughter myself."[25] The two young friends depicted at length in the Cologne segment of the *Solomon bar Simson Chronicle* tell us much about themselves in their speeches. Especially noteworthy is their sense of lost youth: "Woe for our youth, for we have not been worthy of seeing seed proceed from us and we have not reached the years of old age."[26] This is a poignant lament that serves to deepen our sense of the loss of young and unfulfilled lives. We have just now noted the way in which the author of the *Mainz Anonymous* reveals the Jewess Rachel to us as a thoroughly distraught mother, deeply sensitive to her maternal role and feelings. Much of the particularity of the lifelike hero figures is achieved by creating such quotations for them.

The articulateness of the 1096 martyrs is also related to their bellicosity. Since 1096 clearly involved a military defeat for the Jews, the only avenue left for immediate and successful engagement was to attack the enemy verbally. As noted, David ben Nathaniel lost the physical battle, but—according to the *Mainz Anonymous*—won the war of words. His statement, like those of so many of the martyrs, involved both a positive and negative thrust.

> Lo, you are the children of harlotry. You believe in one born of harlotry. But I believe in the God who lives forever, who dwells in the heights of heaven. In him have I trusted to this very day and to the expiration of my soul.

> If you kill me, my soul will repose in paradise, in the light of life. You, however, will descend to the pit of destruction, to eternal disgrace. In hell you will be judged along with your deity, who was a son of lust and was crucified.[27]

This carefully crafted chiastic structure moves us from the shortcomings of Christianity to the truths of Judaism and then from the attendant

rewards to be bestowed upon the Jewish heroes for their grasp of the
truth to the inevitable punishments to be visited upon the errant Christians for their distortion of the truth. All this involves verbal battle, with
the Jew portrayed as victorious. David ben Nathaniel perished in the
face of superior physical force; he was, for the *Mainz Anonymous,* the
spiritual and thus ultimate victor in the engagement.

The articulateness of the Jewish martyrs has yet a third implication.
The martyrs' speeches afforded our authors their most effective vehicle
for making the timeless case they wished to advance. The martyrs
themselves lay out the case, directed—as we have seen—at both
humanity and God: the Jews of 1096 remained faithful to the true dictates of the covenant between God and Israel; in order to achieve this
loyalty to the covenant they paid a fearful price, repressing in the process all normal human inclinations; the divine-human covenant is decidedly reciprocal; thus God must surely reward this remarkable Jewish
faithfulness, individually through immediate afterlife and corporately
through a reversal of the skewed realities of seeming Christian triumph
and ostensible Jewish defeat. This message is reinforced by the third-
person observations of the Jewish narrators; it is advanced most effectively, however, through the speeches constructed for the martyrs themselves.

As a group comprised of distinct, real individuals and as a set of
individuals that constitute an impressive group, indeed a complete generation, the martyrs of 1096 ultimately possess the power to shape history in the most meaningful terms. Christian piety and spirituality, mired
unfortunately (for both Christians and Jews) in profound error, was
nonetheless potent enough to alter the flow of late-eleventh-century history. Although they dispute its ultimate significance, the Jewish narrators reluctantly acknowledge the scope and impact of the crusade, which
flowed from an outburst of religious zeal. The narratives stress that the
Jewish martyrs of 1096 represent parallel zeal, in this case rightly directed, although the immediate trajectory of history does not permit
clear evidence of the power of such giants to shape the course of historic
development. The Christians seem victorious and the Jews defeated, but
the immediate trajectory is terribly misleading. The narratives promise
that the longer trajectory (precisely how much longer is of course not
clear) will be far more revealing. When that longer trajectory is finally
manifest, God's role in history will be reasserted; the hiatus will have
come to a close; Jewish loyalty and heroism will be rewarded; Christian
error will find its recompense. In this sense, the Jews of 1096 are ac-

corded enormous power on the world historical scene. They will emerge as the ultimate shapers of human destiny.

There is of course an element of extreme arrogance in all this. A tiny minority on the European scene presumes to suggest that it represents true understanding and real virtue and that the one and only God will ultimately reenter the stream of historical affairs, hear the pleas of this righteous minority, and reset history on its proper course. This is an audacious claim, but it is profoundly felt by our Jewish authors and editors, and it constitutes the requisite message of comprehension and solace in the wake of a devastating tragedy.

Indeed, there is a further element of audacity in the view of God, humanity, and history that we have analyzed. Not only do the Jewish martyrs of 1096 loom large over the immediate historical scene, they in fact stand among the loftiest figures of the Jewish past. Indeed, in their most radical formulations, our Jewish narrators have the 1096 martyrs dwarfing the very greatest heroes of the Jewish and human past. We have noted the brilliant linkage created in the *Mainz Anonymous* between the Jews of 1096 and the giants of the Jewish past.[28] Now, at the close of this analysis of the sense of God, humanity, and history manifest in our Hebrew narratives, the time has come to indicate how breathtakingly innovative this linkage is.

Generally speaking, medieval Jews shared with their neighbors the sense of a historical process that involved considerable decline in human capabilities and achievements. For the Jews and their neighbors, great human achievement lay in the dim past. This decline was manifest physically in the lengthier years achieved by many of the biblical figures. More important by far was the sense that the early greats had enjoyed a level of communication with the divine that was no longer possible under contemporary circumstances.

For Jews, this broad sense of decline was of course related to the dolorous circumstances noted alike by Christian and Jewish observers— loss of homeland, disintegration of political integrity, exile, and persecution. The same perception of decline was expressed in and reinforced by the system of legal thinking that lay at the heart of organized Jewish religious life. The encompassing outlines of this legal system were laid in the direct divine-human communication between Moses, the first and greatest of the prophets, and his somewhat lesser successors. The system was then cut loose from direct revelation and vested in a set of rabbinic interpreters, the earliest and greatest of whom were responsible for the Mishnah. The rabbis of the Talmud became interpreters of the Mishnah, and their successors became interpreters of the Talmud. All this strongly privileges the early over the later and reinforces a mindset that equates progression in time with deterioration.

In the face of all this, the audacity of the 1096 narratives is simply remarkable. The traditional denigration of present in favor of past is stunningly reversed. Jews living in the Rhineland in 1096 are put onto the same historic plane with the great figures of the Jewish past. Their acts are every bit as heroic; their personal reward will ensconce them in the circle of historic luminaries accorded the choicest places in the afterlife; they will alter the present pattern of Jewish suffering through their heroic devotion. Indeed, in their most extreme moments, the Jewish narrators have their heroes exceeding all prior generations. For the *Mainz Anonymous,* there had never in history been an 'akedah like the one prepared by the Rhineland Jews. Taken quite literally, this can only mean that these Rhineland Jews had in fact exceeded the patriarch Abraham in devotion. For the editor of the *Solomon bar Simson Chronicle,* God had chosen this particular generation over all others to expiate the sin of the golden calf because the Jews of 1096 had a spiritual strength possessed by none of their predecessors. The arrogance of this claim in a sense exceeds that of putting the tiny Rhineland Jewry at the heart of worldwide developments at the end of the eleventh century.

It is easy enough to attribute this 1096 audacity to the hyperbole of lamentation literature. This seems to me, however, to miss the essential point. Our narratives do not constitute a generalized literature of lamentation; they represent, rather, a striking response to a sharp challenge. The Christian interpretation of the debacle of 1096 required a Jewish alternative, which these narratives supplied. In the course of providing this alternative explication of the Rhineland bloodshed, our narrators spun out a radical interpretation of the relation of God, humanity, and history. It should hardly come as a shock that this innovative sense of God, humanity, and history shows striking affinities to the aggressive, militant, and audacious views circulating in majority Christian society at the time.

CHAPTER ELEVEN

Comparative Dimensions

The 1096 Narratives
and Classical Jewish Tradition

We have noted, from early in this study, the effort of our 1096 narrators to link their hero figures with great personages of the Jewish past. These linkages served multiple purposes, some time-bound and some timeless. With respect to the time-bound objectives of the narratives, association of the First Crusade hero figures with their predecessors served to erase any questions that might be raised over their radical martyrological behaviors. If the martyrs of 1096 were recapitulating the actions of prior Jewish stalwarts, then obviously their behaviors—however unprecedented and radical they might seem—were more than justified. With respect to the timeless objectives of the narratives, the linkages with the giants of the past served to highlight the glory of the martyrs of 1096, which in turn proved that Jewish suffering was not rooted in sinfulness, but rather resulted from the unique capacity of this particular generation to endure pain in service of divine will. As we have seen, this thrust of the narratives led ultimately to an innovative sense of the relationship of God, humanity, and history, eventuating in audacious claims as to the preeminence of the heroes of 1096 over their contemporary crusading foes and—more strikingly—their venerated Jewish predecessors.

The difficult issue we must now explore involves the relationship of the narratives of 1096 and their conceptualization of God, humanity, and history to classical Jewish tradition. To what extent are the Hebrew First Crusade narratives well rooted in classical Jewish historical thinking and writing? Alternatively, do they in fact break new ground? In order to undertake such a discussion in a reasonably limited manner, we shall follow the lead of our protagonists and authors themselves and focus on a small number of classical narratives: those that treat the earlier hero figures consistently cited in the First Crusade narratives—the patriarch Abraham, Daniel and his associates, the mother and her seven sons, and Rabbi Akiba and his fellow martyrs. In comparing our narratives to the classical renditions of these hero figures, we shall attempt to highlight similarities and differences in both style and substance. In some instances, it will even be possible to compare and contrast directly the early hero figures with martyrs of 1096 who are closely modeled after them. Such instances permit particularly well-focused analysis.

A word of caution is warranted here. I am not attempting a contrastive evaluation of the two literary corpora, the biblical and rabbinic tales on the one hand and the crusade narratives on the other. Biblical and rabbinic views of God, humanity, and history have long been the subject of extensive analysis. Over the past few decades, there has developed as well considerable investigation first of biblical narrative style and then of rabbinic narrative style. All these analyses have uncovered the compelling vision and esthetic that undergird these literatures.[1] I am not attempting to argue the superiority or inferiority of that vision and esthetic to the substance and style of the narratives of 1096. What I shall try to clarify is whether the conception of God, humanity, and history and the narrative style manifest in these accounts represent a continuation of the classical legacy or an innovation. As I proceed to suggest that certain views and narrative techniques are absent in the earlier materials, I am not arguing for the superiority of the later; I am simply claiming its innovativeness.

PRIOR JEWISH MARTYROLOGICAL LITERATURE

As noted recurrently, Jewish tradition is not especially rich in martyrological literature, with martyrdom understood simply as the readiness to sacrifice life rather than compromise essential religious principles. The slimness of Jewish martyrological literature is made all the more striking by the contrasting centrality of martyrdom in Christian thought and writing.

Martyrdom as we have defined it requires persecution either at the hands of external or internal political-religious authorities. The bulk of the biblical narrative, which runs from patriarchal times down through the destruction of the First Commonwealth and Temple at the hands of the Babylonians, does not really show such persecution, either by external foes or internal authorities. The external enemies seem to be focused exclusively on asserting hegemony.[2] Internally, there might seem to have been a greater potential for persecution involving religious principle, but that potential was not truly realized in the depiction of the vagaries of religious sentiment and behavior through the periods of the Israelite and Judean monarchies.[3] Strikingly, our crusade narratives, so attuned to martyrological precedent, cite none from the period that stretches from the patriarchs down through the destruction of the First Commonwealth and Temple.[4]

The earliest of the Jewish martyr figures cited in our narratives are Daniel and his associates. Stemming from the postdestruction period of exile under Babylonian and Persian rule, the stories in the book of Daniel are cited recurrently in the narratives, suggesting that Daniel and his friends form an initial and important link in the chain of Jewish martyrs of which the 1096 Rhineland Jews are the latest and—our narrators claim—the greatest. For our purposes, what is most striking is the chasm that separates these Daniel stories from the First Crusade narratives.

Recent biblical scholarship has drawn a fairly neat line of demarcation within the biblical book of Daniel, a line between the opening six chapters and the rest of the book.[5] The former are viewed as much earlier, utilized essentially as the narrative matrix into which the closing—and more important—six chapters are embedded. In the first six chapters of the book, the dominant mode is narrative and the heroes of the tales are the young Jewish exiles, Daniel and his three associates. The central motif of these diverse tales is steadfastness in the face of external pressures and the rewards that such steadfastness confers. Daniel, his associates, and their experiences form the focus around which the diverse tales revolve.

One of the elements in the opening stories involves Daniel's capacity for interpreting dreams and signs, a capacity attributed consistently by Daniel to God himself. It is this capacity for dream and sign interpretation that sets the frame for the radically different closing six chapters of the book. In this second set of chapters, the three friends disappear, the narrative framework is lost, and Daniel becomes the dreamer and visionary. No longer the wise interpreter, he requires assistance in understanding the complex and opaque imagery of his own dreams and visions. It is widely agreed that this second half of the book stems from a later period, in all likelihood the period of Seleucid oppression during the second pre-Christian century. The message of the second half of the book thus becomes the extension of eschatological hope to a suffering community. If this dating is correct, then the opening six chapters do a bit more than simply provide the requisite narrative frame to the eschatological dreams and visions: they also reinforce the lesson of steadfastness in the face of externally induced religious oppression.

The stories absorbed by our 1096 narratives come essentially from chapters three and six of the book of Daniel. The two incidents involve persecution of Daniel's three associates, who are thrown into a fiery furnace, and persecution of Daniel himself, who is lowered into the lions' den. Both stories have been widely celebrated in all Western art forms; both stories were clearly in the minds of our narrators as they sought an unassailable precedent for their hero figures. When we place these two tales side by side with the narratives of 1096, the parallels pale, however, and we are most struck by the contrasts in style and conceptualization.

Let us begin with literary style. The two Daniel tales are conveyed in a manner that is folkloristic and highly imaginative. They are overlaid with fanciful data, designed to afford rich background and texture. Thus, the announcement that sets in motion the persecution in Daniel 3 specifies "the sound of the horn, pipe, zither, lyre, psaltery, bagpipe, and all other types of instruments" as the signal for bowing down before the image erected on the plain of Dura. This elaborate set of instruments is repeated two full times during the course of the chapter.[6] More important, the persecution itself is portrayed in highly imaginative and unrealistic terms. The original royal order stipulated that anyone who failed to bow down to the image would be thrown into a fiery furnace. When the interrogation of Shadrach, Meshach, and Abed-nego revealed to the king their unwillingness to make the requisite gestures, "Nebuchadnezzar was so filled with rage . . . that his visage was distorted, and he gave the order to heat up the furnace to seven times its usual heat." The heat was so intense that "a tongue of flame killed the men who carried up Shadrach, Meshach, and Abed-nego."[7]

All the hyperbole in description of the fire is intended to highlight the remarkable divine intervention that saves the heroes. "But those three men, Shadrach, Meshach, and Abed-nego, dropped, bound, into the burning fiery furnace." Immediately, however, the king noted "four men walking about unbound and unharmed in the fire and the fourth looks like a divine being."[8] Hyperbolic description of the fire leads perfectly into the utterly remarkable way in which God rescues his three loyal servants, with a divine figure making an appearance in the furnace itself.

The same stylistic tendencies are manifest in the tale of Daniel in the lion's den. Again, embellishments are the order of the day. The rock used to close the mouth of the lions' den was sealed with the signet of the king and the signet of his nobles, "so that nothing might be altered concerning Daniel."[9] Daniel, like Shadrach, Meshach, and Abed-nego, is saved from death through divine intervention. The basis for this divine intervention is made plain: "Daniel was brought up out of the den, and no injury was found on him, for he had trusted in his God." Delighted with this outcome, the king then gave a further order. "Those men who had slandered Daniel were brought and, together with their children and wives, were thrown into the lions' den. They had hardly reached the bottom of the den when the lions overpowered them and crushed all their bones."[10]

Despite their regular invocation of Daniel and his friends, the Hebrew First Crusade narratives eschew the imaginative, folkloristic style of the Daniel tales. As we have seen, they present their depictions in a manner that is realistic and readily believable. While some of the behaviors described are appalling, none can readily be dismissed as straining credulity.

Likewise, there is a radical divergence in the conceptualization of God, humanity, and history. Clearly, the central figure in the Daniel tales is the God to whom Daniel and his friends remain loyal and who rewards that loyalty directly and immediately, in the eyes of all beholders. God contrives the positive outcomes of both incidents and immediately proves his omnipotence in the eyes of Jews and non-Jews alike. In both cases, the royal figures responsible for the persecution acknowledge publicly and formally the rule of the one and only God in the world. The simplicity of outcome diverges radically from the problematics of 1096 and its aftermath. The God of Daniel who is so immediately present makes no such appearance in the narratives of 1096.

Not surprisingly, the Daniel narratives, in which the central place is accorded to God, have no room for the rich and complex human figures that dominate our narratives. This is true for persecuting non-Jews and persecuted Jews. The persecuting figures of the two Daniel tales have none of the inherent religious zeal that is excoriated, but grudgingly acknowledged in our narratives. The first persecuting figure in the Daniel tales is simply a megalomaniacal King Nebuchadnezzar, concerned with his own glory. In the second case, the persecutor is a hapless King Darius, duped by his courtiers. These latter, ultimately responsible for the danger to Daniel, are portrayed as moved by nothing more than envy of Daniel's successes. These persecuting figures have no depth and no dignity.

The Jewish hero figures are of course laudable, but they hardly dominate the proceedings. The Daniel narratives highlight a small and non-representative slice of Persian Jewry, essentially a few leading figures within a special group of exiles singled out for their nobility and intelligence. This narrowness contrasts markedly with the far broader focus of the 1096 narratives, in which the heroes emerge from all strata of the Rhineland Jewish communities.

Daniel and his three associates are revealed to us partially through third-person description and partially through their own words. They too, like their persecutors, lack reality and depth. They are provided none of the human strokes discerned in the portrayal of the martyrs of 1096. For all their importance, we come away feeling that we know them only superficially, gleaning none of the personalized insight provided for Meshullam ben Isaac, Minna of Worms, Simhah *ha-cohen*, Rachel of Mainz, or David ben Nathaniel.

The lack of reality and depth is particularly notable in the motivation attributed to Daniel and his associates. Their soliloquies contrast sharply with those we have encountered in the 1096 narratives. Let us note the speech attributed to the three friends as they respond to the royal threat of the fiery furnace and to the king's claim that there is no god that can save them from his power:

> O Nebuchadnezzar, we have no need to answer you in this matter. For, if so it must be, our God whom we serve is able to save us from the burning fiery furnace, and he will save us from your power, O king. But even if he does not, be it known to you, O king, that we will not serve your god or worship the statue of gold that you have set up.[11]

This soliloquy differs in a number of striking ways from those encountered in our narratives. The address above lacks the fire of the speeches in the narratives; it breathes quiet certainty of immediate divine intervention, a certainty nowhere to be found in 1096. There is acknowledgment that God may choose not to act, but this elicits only a bland statement rejecting worship of the golden statue. Missing here, first of all, are the lifelike doubt, fear, and uncertainty that characterize the speeches of 1096. The quiet certainty of the three friends contrasts sharply with the intense self-scrutiny and regret we see in Rachel of Mainz or the two Cologne friends, Samuel ben Gedaliah and Yehiel ben Samuel. Equally absent is real engagement with an alternative religious vision. The three friends of the book of Daniel do not feel themselves spiritually threatened by the king and his statue; the threat is physical and political. As a result, there is none of the scathing denunciation of the other side that is the hallmark of the Rhineland martyrs. In so many ways, the thinking reflected in the book of Daniel is worlds away from that of the 1096 narratives.

The second set of historic martyr figures regularly adduced in our narratives is the mother and her seven sons, with a heavy emphasis on the mother. The original version of this story stems from the period of Seleucid persecution during the second pre-Christian century.[12] This version would not have been known directly to the Jews of 1096; it would have been known only through the medieval *Sefer Yosippon*, a work we shall address separately in the next chapter. The early sources from which the Rhineland Jews and their memorializers would have known most fully of the mother and her seven sons were rabbinic.

A number of different narrations of the story of the mother and her seven sons have come down in rabbinic literature.[13] Despite the differences among these alternative accounts, all agree in locating the persecution in Roman times. Since we have no way of knowing precisely which version or versions of the story would have been known to the Rhineland Jews of 1096, I have made the safe assumption that at least the version found in the Babylonian Talmud would have been familiar to them, and I have chosen that account as the basis for yet another comparison and contrast between a classic Jewish tale of persecution and heroic response and the story recounted in the crusade narratives.

In some ways, this comparison and contrast is made more difficult by the fact that the talmudic story is embedded in a distinctly nonnarrative setting.[14] Unlike the Daniel episodes, which were part of a running narrative, the talmudic story of the mother and her seven sons is located in a context that is ultimately legalistic. The issue under discussion involves technical postdestruction issues of land possession. In a manner often encountered in the Talmud, this legal issue gives rise to a series of nonlegal stories, all of them more-or-less unified by the broad theme of the wars with Rome and the suffering occasioned for the Jews. In the midst of this extensive series of tales, we encounter one of the rabbinic accounts of the mother and her seven sons.

The talmudic story of the woman and her seven sons is appended to the tale of four hundred young women and men taken captive and transported to Rome, a story we shall address shortly.[15] This latter tale ends with the martyrdom of the four hundred youngsters, to whom is then applied the verse from Psalms 44: "It is for your sake that we are slain all day long, that we are regarded as sheep to be slaughtered." As we have noted with respect to many such citations, this verse is meant to conjure up the larger context from which it is extracted. The immediately following verses are addressed to God and conclude:

> Rouse yourself; why do you sleep, O Lord?
> Awaken, do not reject us forever!
> Why do you hide your face, ignoring our affliction and distress?
> We lie prostrate in the dust; our body clings to the ground.
> Arise and help us, redeem us, as befits your faithfulness.[16]

Israel suffers; God must redeem. This illuminating verse, it is then suggested by Rav Judah, ought to be applied "to the woman and her seven sons."

The story of the woman and her seven sons is quite simple. Each of the seven sons is brought before the emperor and ordered to bow before an idol. Each son then cites a key biblical verse that outlaws such obeisance and is, as a result, led away and killed. The only slight break in the monotonous routine is afforded by the youngest of the sons. After the youngest son recites his verse, the emperor is moved to suggest a ruse. He proposes throwing down his seal and having the youngster pick it up, thereby creating an impression of obeisance to the idol. The youngest son then excoriates the emperor and refuses. At this point, there is a moment of motherly feeling.

> They were leading him away to kill him when his mother said: "Give him to me, so I might kiss him a little." She said to him: "My son, go and say to your ancestor Abraham: 'You bound one to the altar, but I have bound seven to the altars.' " Then she also went up on a roof and threw herself down and was killed.

At the conclusion of this drama, "a voice came forth from heaven, saying: 'The mother of children is happy.' "[17]

That this talmudic tale played into the consciousness of the Rhineland Jews and their memorializers is clear enough. At the end of the riveting story of Rachel of Mainz, the *Mainz Anonymous* concludes: "She died with them [her children], as that saintly one died with her seven sons. Concerning her [the early heroine and/or Rachel], it is said: 'The mother of children is happy.' "[18]

Now, this talmudic story is surely closer to the 1096 narratives than are the Daniel episodes. In the tale of the mother and her sons, there is no God who appears to save the protagonists; they are—like the Rhineland Jews in general and Rachel in particular—persecuted figures who in fact lose their lives. Nonetheless, there remains a considerable chasm between this tale and the 1096 narrative. This difference becomes quite obvious when we compare the talmudic tale to the story of Rachel of Mainz, which explicitly conjures up recollections of that precedent.

Once more, the narrative style of the earlier account is highly folkloristic. The notion of an emperor bringing seven Jewish youngsters before him strains credulity; the royal ruse is a standard ploy; the stock citations of the seven sons smack of the repetition of a folkish tale. Despite the moment of maternal interaction between the woman and the youngest of the sons, there is none of the personalized detail that humanizes the hero figures of 1096. The speeches attributed to the seven sons are highly stereotypic; once again, there is no genuine engagement with a religiously meaningful enemy.

The tone of the Rachel story is quite different. The setting, a chamber in the episcopal palace in which a number of Jews had sought refuge, is real and concrete, and awareness that the occupants of this chamber are doomed pervades the account. That the enemy is human and moved by human emotions is evidenced by the general savagery of the crusade and the specific rage evoked by the sight of the slaughtered children. The diverse occupants of this chamber are all moved to martyrdom, with Rachel simply the most poignant of a varied group. With a few brief strokes, the author of the *Mainz Anonymous* succeeds in bringing Rachel of Mainz to life in a way that the talmudic source did not attempt. The speeches attributed to her are the antithesis of repetition and stereotype. They are rich, diversified, warm, frightening, and human.

More important than style is substance. Again, there is no reality to the persecuting figures in the talmudic story. The Roman emperor is even less understandable than the Babylonian and Persian kings of the book of Daniel. He is simply a vehicle for persecution and martyrdom. Likewise, the Jewish protagonists—the seven sons and their mother—lack genuine human qualities. There is no hesitation, no regret, no real feeling. Even the mother's brief engagement with the youngest of the sons hardly breaks the mold. She wishes to kiss him, but the words she speaks are not impassioned. They constitute an internal Jewish argument, emphasizing her superiority to Abraham, focusing on the greater sacrifice of seven sons over one son. The worldview of the persecutors is once more worthy of no consideration whatsoever.

All this is radically altered in the Rachel story, as we have had ample opportunity to note. The crusaders who burst into the chamber are real figures. They are moved by the ideals of the crusade and are, in addition, enraged when confronted with the slaughtered youngsters. Rachel of Mainz is a fully realized human figure. She is committed, wavers, is moved to slaughter her children, and eventually does so with firm conviction. Her heroism again lies in the capacity to quash her deepest human feelings out of loyalty to the God of Israel. This heroism, according to the *Mainz Anonymous,* will alter the course of human affairs. Closer to 1096 than the Daniel tale, the rabbinic story of the woman and her seven sons ultimately suggests the innovation of the First Crusade environment, rather than its continuities with the past.

We have noted in passing the story of the four hundred young women and men that immediately precedes the story of the woman and her seven sons in the talmudic series. There are unmistakable echoes of this tale as well in the crusade narratives. A brief look at this account is thus useful. The story is relatively straightforward. In the process of being transported to Rome for immoral purposes, the young women among the captives asked about the fate of those drowned in the sea. In response, a verse from Psalms 68 was cited: "I will retrieve from Bashan, I will retrieve from the depths of the sea." Reassured that drowning would by no means obviate afterlife, the young women threw themselves into the sea. Shamed by the behavior of the young women, who were threatened by sexual defilement viewed as natural, the young men, facing sexual defilement in ways considered unnatural, then followed the girls' example.

In the Rhineland narratives, there are recurrent references to Jews taking their lives by drowning, conjuring up recollections of the story of the four hundred young captives. More specifically, the Cologne unit of the *Solomon bar Simson Chronicle* begins its account of the seven refuges into which Cologne Jewry had been dispersed with a report on the destruction of the group that had gathered in Neuss. Once again, the literary technique of generalization followed by specific incidents is used. One of the individualized figures singled out is Isaac *ha-levi.* Baptized against his will, this Isaac three days later regained his senses, regretted his new status, returned to Cologne, and made his way to the Rhine where he drowned himself. The episode ends: "Concerning him and others like him it is said: 'I shall retrieve from Bashan, I shall retrieve from the depths of the sea.' "[19] Consciousness of the talmudic tale is unmistakable. More striking yet, the Trier unit of the *Solomon bar Simson Chronicle* ends with a (somewhat misleading) focus on martyrdom in Trier, citing specifically four women who took their lives by drowning. The drowning episode ends with a citation of the same verse from Psalms 68, suggesting the impact of the tale of the four hundred.[20]

This tale, like that of the woman and her seven sons that follows it in the talmudic sequence, is closer to the 1096 narratives than the Daniel stories. In addition, this tale introduces conspicuously the theme of afterlife, central to many of the episodes depicted in our narratives. Yet even here difference is more striking than is continuity. With respect to the issue of afterlife, the young women in the talmudic tale pose a question reflecting their concerns. In simplistic fashion, citation and exegesis of a verse reassure them. By contrast, the Jews portrayed in the Rhineland narratives ask no questions. They are infused with a potent conviction of the personal rewards attendant upon their heroism. They know that they will enjoy the richest blessings God has to bestow. In addition, as we have seen, they are equally convinced of the horrible fate awaiting their persecutors. Not surprisingly, this is an issue utterly missing from the milder talmudic tale.

The third set of hero figures regularly cited in the 1096 narratives are the martyrs of the Hadrianic persecution, preeminently Rabbi Akiba. Again, the rabbinic sources are varied. This group of martyrs came to occupy an extremely important niche in the special liturgy for the Day of Atonement.[21] Once more, however, since we cannot be altogether certain of the sources at the disposal of the Rhineland Jews, the safest procedure is to focus on the classical talmudic source for the martyrdom of Rabbi Akiba, with which the Rhineland Jews were surely familiar.[22]

The story told in Tractate Berakhot again has a nonnarrative setting. The Mishnah had stipulated that a Jew is required to bless God for experiences both good and ill and had rooted that injunction in the famous verse that requires love of God with all one's heart, with all one's soul, and with all one's might. A series of explanations of the biblical sequence of heart, soul, and might were offered, including one that uses the Hebrew term for "might" (me'od) as the basis for the notion of the requirement to bless God for both good and ill. In the talmudic discussion, the biblical series is subjected to further scrutiny, with Rabbi Akiba cited as the sage who had suggested that "with all your soul" means even under circumstances in which one's soul (that is, life) is being taken. This bit of exegesis then leads to the narrative.

The talmudic narrative meanders. It begins with a Roman decree outlawing the study of Torah. Discovering Rabbi Akiba teaching Torah in contravention of the decree, a colleague asks why he is not fearful of the Roman edict. Akiba's answer is a parable that portrays a fox attempting to convince fish experiencing difficulty to leave their watery environment. The fish reply in essence that water is where they must live and that to leave it would be far worse than to court the dangers inherent in the setting that is natural to them. For Rabbi Akiba, the life of Torah for Jews paralleled the watery environment of the fish—it is the only setting within which Jews can live.

This dialogue is then succeeded by more ominous developments, the arrest of Rabbi Akiba and his colleague, with the colleague purportedly lamenting the fact that he was arrested for vanities while Akiba had the glory of being arrested for heroic activity. At this point, the mild atmosphere of the meandering tale shifts to the painful death of Rabbi Akiba, with his flesh combed by the Romans. His students were astonished by his equanimity. He explained that all his life he had pondered the commandment to love the Lord even as he took one's soul. At this final point in his life, faced with the opportunity to fulfill that painful injunction, he could only be joyful. He then recited the *shemaʿ*, the statement of Jewish faith in one God only, and, with the pronouncement of the final word, his soul departed.

Whereas the terrestrial story ends at this point, with the death of Rabbi Akiba, the talmudic account continues with a series of developments on the heavenly plane. According to the narrative, a celestial voice celebrated the good fortune of Rabbi Akiba in having his soul depart with the pronouncement of the final word of the *shemaʿ*. The death of Rabbi Akiba, however, caused consternation in the heavenly realm. The angelic host turned reproachfully upon God himself, asking about dissonance between the death of Rabbi Akiba and his lengthy life of Torah. The angels buttressed their question by reference to a verse in Psalms that asks for deliverance from human hands. God is supposed to have replied by citing the very next words of that same verse, words that suggest a portion in life, meaning life eternal.[23] At that juncture, a second celestial voice celebrated the good fortune of Rabbi Akiba in winning eternal life.

Once more, the differences between this narrative and our 1096 accounts are profound. The style here is, if anything, yet more folkloristic than that of the narrative account of the woman and her seven sons. A quaint parable occupies center stage; statements are pithy and aphoristic; a major part of the report is devoted to events in heaven. With respect to substance, the focus here is only minimally upon Roman persecution and Jewish resistance. The story has much more to say about the centrality of Torah study to Jewish life and about the meaning of the biblical verse that require one to love the Lord with all one's soul. The Roman authorities play no role. Rabbi Akiba himself—laudable to be sure—has none of the substance and depth of the martyrs of 1096. The central place of heaven and the heavenly hosts in projecting the meaning of the death of Rabbi Akiba moves us a considerable distance from the human focus in the First Crusade narratives.

Our Rhineland narrators, then, were surely aware of the classical narratives we have analyzed: they make explicit reference to them. They are positively inclined toward the great figures of these narratives and think that identifying the martyrs of 1096 with such predecessors will confer great dignity on their latter-day heroes. At the same time, our narrators regularly express the conviction that their heroes in fact superseded these predecessors. Indeed, they eschew the narrative style used to enshrine the memory of these predecessors in favor of a style that is more realistic, more human, more conflicted, and ultimately more heroic. The conception of God, humanity, and history reflected in these narratives is far removed from that embodied in the classical sources to which the Rhineland Jews were so deeply devoted.

THE ABRAHAM PARADIGM

Of all the giants of Jewish history to whom appeal is made in our narratives, the most important is surely the patriarch Abraham. I have, however, deferred consideration of the Abraham precedent, because he was, after all, not a martyr figure. Invocation of the patriarch Abraham involves an additional mental or spiritual step. Given the notion, so widely expressed in the 1096 narratives, that God requires the sacrifice of life when faced with the alternative of baptism, then Abraham becomes the paradigmatic figure for acceptance of the dictates of divine will under the most trying of conditions. Abraham was not confronted with the exigencies of external persecution; he was faced with God's direct demand for the sacrifice of his beloved son. For our 1096 narrators and their hero figures, Abraham set the precedent of willingness to sacrifice a beloved child out of acquiescence to divine will. The circumstances of 1096 involved, once again, divine will and, once again, the most painful of sacrifices, the killing of children. Hence the centrality of Abraham, the nonmartyr figure.[24]

It should be noted that identification of the martyrs of 1096 with Abraham served both the time-bound and timeless needs of our narrators in precisely the same way as did association with the early martyr figures. Identification with Abraham served to erase any potential questions with regard to the rectitude of extreme Jewish behaviors, while at the same time it reinforced the sense of the 1096 generation as uniquely worthy, rather than especially unworthy.

There is yet another facet to Abraham's importance. Identification of the martyrs of 1096 with the patriarch was intended to wrest yet another major Jewish symbol out of Christian hands and return it to Jewish auspices. The Abraham-Isaac imagery had, from earliest Christianity, formed part of the sense of Christian supersession, of fullest realization in Christianity of the key symbols of biblical Israel.[25] Sensitive to Christian absorption of key Jewish concepts and symbols and determined to contest such absorption, the Jews of 1096 and their memorializers went out of their way to highlight the centrality of these key Jewish concepts and symbols to the Jewish behaviors and thinking of 1096. We have had occasion to note Jewish contestation of the symbol of Jerusalem, so fundamental to the First Crusade. In effect, the Jews of 1096 are portrayed as arguing that the Christians' armed pilgrimage to Jerusalem was meaningless and that the Rhineland Jews were making the true pilgrimage to the sacred precincts through the sacrifices they offered. Similarly, the Jews of 1096 were made to assert their right to the symbols of Abraham, Isaac, and their joint self-sacrifice. Christians may have believed that their history had absorbed these symbols, but such claims were in fact vain.

We have noted, in our analysis of the relationship between classical martyrological tales and the 1096 narratives, a number of instances in which specific episodes from 1096 were modeled after the classical stories, thus allowing especially focused comparison and contrast. Such opportunity is particularly prominent with respect to the Abraham imagery. This imagery plays throughout our narratives, but there is one striking episode that is unmistakably modeled after the Abraham story, and that is the tale of Meshullam ben Isaac of Worms, his son Isaac, and his wife Zipporah. This tale has the protagonist, Meshullam ben Isaac, announcing explicitly his intention to emulate the example of Abraham. "This son God gave me. Zipporah my wife bore him in her old age, and his name is Isaac. Now I shall offer him up, as did Abraham our ancestor with his son Isaac."[26] This explicit indication of parallel circumstances and emulation of the patriarch is solidly reinforced by a series of linguistic usages that inevitably evokes recollection of the famed Genesis narrative.[27] Once more, a close look at the two narratives—the biblical and the 1096—suggest considerable parallel and yet greater divergence.

The brief story recounted in nineteen verses in Genesis 22 is one of the best known tales in the Hebrew Bible and in world literature; it has been subjected to endless scrutiny and analysis.[28] For our purposes, the following salient features of the narrative are significant: the setting involves maximal isolation. Abraham and Isaac set out with two lads on a journey, and, as they approached their destination, the two lads were left behind. Abraham is nearly inarticulate; his response to the painful divine mandate is conveyed by his actions. Uncertainty and ambivalence make no appearance. Divine intervention is central to the story, from the demand for sacrifice of the son through interruption of the killing to the announcement of the rewards that would eventuate from Abraham's loyalty to God and his will.

The Worms story of Meshullam ben Isaac, his son, and his wife, while overtly and linguistically modeled on the Genesis narrative, shows striking differences when compared with the biblical account. The style of the 1096 account is again far more lifelike than that of the biblical narrative. Meshullam ben Isaac is far more verbal, and his wife adds a significant human dimension to the event. The orientation to reality already noted makes its appearance in this story as well.

God, who is so central to the Genesis narrative, works in the Worms story precisely as he works throughout the narratives of 1096. He sets the flow of action through his demanding covenant; he will right the course of history eventually. At the moment, however, he makes no active appearance. In his place, humans occupy center stage. The Worms incident is placed in a setting opposite to that of the biblical tale. The setting is crowded with human figures, friend and foe alike, all of them in a frenzy of activity. Meshullam ben Isaac is deeply conscious of this crowded and bustling setting. He overtly calls for the awareness of the multitudes: "Listen to me, both great and small!"[29] A performative element is very much evident in his behavior. He sets out to recapitulate the actions of the patriarch Abraham. The depiction of his wife, a striking touch, adds the requisite human dimension. She did not actually oppose his plan; she did, however, ask to be slaughtered first, so that she would not witness the death of her son. This request has the same force as the outcry of Rachel of Mainz upon being handed the knife. It brings us as readers back to the painful realities being recorded. A father is about to slaughter a son—there is horror here. Evocation of this horror serves to put the action and the heroism of Meshullam in proper perspective. Like the other heroes of 1096, he is great not because of a lack of feeling, but because of his capacity for overcoming those feelings in service to the divine will. When the drama has been played out with the death of all three members of the family, God does not speak and promise great reward. God remains silent. It is the narrator who cites two important biblical verses (not all that common for the *Mainz Anonymous*) that frame the brief account. Once more, we emerge with a sense of the profound gap between our narratives and the prototypes they highlight.

The Rhineland narratives are deeply rooted in Jewish tradition, its commitments, and its classical sources. The legal requirements, the aggadic personages, and the moving symbols that swirl through the catastrophic months of 1096 are drawn from the classical literature of the Jews. At the same time, our analysis has suggested that something happened to traditional themes, images, and hero figures along the way. A new style of storytelling has made itself manifest. The tales of 1096 differ considerably from the biblical and talmudic precedents we have examined in this chapter. These tales reflect an altered perception of the interaction of God and humanity in setting the course of history. The obvious next step is to pursue this comparative thrust and to seek medieval narratives that might show us closer parallels to the innovative style and conceptualization we have uncovered.

CHAPTER TWELVE

Comparative Dimensions

The 1096 Narratives
and Their Medieval Setting

Comparison of the Hebrew First Crusade narratives with biblical and rabbinic prototypes has shown that the narratives, despite their immersion in the language, images, and symbols of Jewish tradition, made a substantial break with previous patterns of storytelling and conceptualization of the relationship of God and humanity. Now we must examine some medieval narratives for possible parallels in historiographic style and conceptualization.

It has long been maintained that early Ashkenazic Jewry had its roots in Byzantium Jewry and was profoundly shaped by that area's ancient and rich Jewish culture. The Byzantine roots of early Ashkenazic Jewry may well be somewhat exaggerated, since many Jewish immigrants seem to have made their way northward from the more westerly areas of the Mediterranean. In any case, however, we have no cultural artifacts from the Jewish communities of early southern France and Spain; we do have two major historical works from Byzantine Jewry. Careful scrutiny of these two works may reveal parallels that are fuller than those we found in our examination of classical Jewish narratives.

The second major direction to be investigated involves the Latin narratives composed during and after the First Crusade. The historic venture unleashed by Pope Urban II in late 1095 was immediately appreciated as a path-breaking enterprise and attracted observers to try their hand at depicting the campaign or at least what they could perceive and grasp of it. First-hand narratives of the great undertaking have survived.

Perhaps the most interesting of these is the anonymous *Gesta Franco-rum*, written by a follower of Count Bohemond of Taranto. Straight-forward and vigorous, this composition seems in many ways close to the *Mainz Anonymous* and will be regularly cited.[1] Fairly quickly, a set of secondary narratives emerged as well, narratives that remind us of the effort at compilation and explication we have encountered in the *Solomon bar Simson Chronicle*.[2]

It might well be objected that early Ashkenazic Jews, like those of the Rhineland, did not read Latin and were not at all interested in—indeed vigorously rejected—the views of their Christians contemporaries. Both objections have some validity. The Jews who wrote our Hebrew nar-ratives in all likelihood did not read Latin and would not have been interested in the *Gesta Francorum,* if in fact it had been accessible to them. What we are concerned with, however, is not literal borrowing from Christian sources. We have set out to examine an innovative Jewish mindset, and, to that end, some sense of the thinking reflected in the Latin narratives may be useful. It is increasingly clear that the early Ashkenazic Jews did not live hermetically sealed off from their Christian neighbors. They were attracted, repelled, and challenged by the vibrance of the new civilization developing in northern Europe. Jewish behaviors in 1096 show that the radical spirituality manifest in the crusade had considerable influence on the Jews.[3] It is certainly plausible that some of the innovations we have encountered in the Hebrew narratives may similarly show the impact of the patterns of thinking abroad in society at large.

THE BYZANTINE CONNECTION

The two major historical works bequeathed by Byzantine Jewry are the *Sefer Yosippon* and the *Megillat Ahima'az*. The former is a tenth-century survey of Jewish history from earliest times down through the conclu-sion of the war with Rome in the year 73.[4] Ultimately rooted in the writings of Josephus, this work was widely read and cited all through the Middle Ages and on into the modern period. There are clear signs of its widespread use by early Ashkenazic Jewry.[5] The second of these works is a strange family chronicle that traces developments in Byzan-tine Jewry from the middle of the ninth century down into the mid eleventh century. It was little known throughout the Middle Ages.[6]

Let us begin with the latter of the two works, the *Megillat Ahima'az,* simply because there is far less to say with respect to it. The *Megillat*

Ahima'az is focused on the great figures of a distinguished rabbinic family and their extraordinary achievements. While there is an occasional reference to Byzantine oppression, there are no martyrological incidents in the book, incidents that would allow for interesting comparisons and contrasts with the 1096 narratives. In a more general way, however, the difference in style and conceptualization between the *Megillat Ahima'az* and our narratives is enormous. In the *Megillat Ahima'az*, the place of God in the everyday experience of Byzantine Jews and their leaders is central. God regularly intervened to save embattled figures in the Jewish community or to provide the distinguished family members with requisite respect on the part of their Jewish peers.

One specific incident will perhaps illustrate this sense of divine involvement in the affairs of the Jewish community. The rabbis who occupy center stage in *Megillat Ahima'az* were also very well connected to the secular and ecclesiastical leadership of the Byzantine Empire (and other polities as well). One of these rabbis, Hananel, found himself involved in a lengthy conversation with the archbishop of Oria. The vagaries of this conversation took the two men into a discussion of the impending appearance of the new moon, scheduled for the morrow. They eventually disagreed on the precise time of the appearance of the new moon, with the Jew miscalculating. The archbishop flung out a challenge. If he were proved correct, Hananel would accept Christianity; if Hananel were proved correct, the archbishop would give him his horse valued at three hundred pieces of gold.[7] With this agreement in place, Hananel returned home and uncovered his error. Aghast, he directed a moving petition to God, asking divine mercy and assistance. According to the narrative, God answered the prayer of Hananel, intervening so that the moon did not appear until the erroneous time predicted by the rabbi. The archbishop understood precisely what had happened. "You know as well as I that the new moon appeared as I had determined in my calculations; I was not mistaken; I had given much thought to it and knew I had the correct answer. . . . You, however, have gained surcease from your Master, like a son who escapes punishment by caressing and cajoling his father."[8] This kind of divine intervention, so close to that featured in the Daniel stories, is worlds away from the 1096 narratives.

Parallel to the central place of God in *Megillat Ahima'az* is the role played by the rabbis. These rabbis are not heroic figures who fathom divine will and have the strength to meet its extreme demands. They are, rather, much more traditional leadership figures, men who know the secrets of rabbinic and mystical lore and use that knowledge to manipulate the forces at work in the world. Other human figures play minor roles, in striking contrast to the diversified set of heroes who populate the 1096 narratives. Non-Jews are represented, but in relatively quiet ways, often as supporters and allies of the central rabbinic figures. Even when non-Jews turn oppressive, they lack the specificity and power encountered in the hostile crusaders and burghers—or even the friendly bishops and burghers—of 1096. On the human level as well, *Megillat Ahima'az* shows none of the special qualities we have identified in the Rhineland narratives.

The *Sefer Yosippon* offers much more likelihood of significant parallels with the narratives of 1096. To begin, there is sure evidence that the text was known by early Ashkenazic Jews. In fact, the impact of *Yosippon* on the 1096 narratives seems incontrovertible. The Hebrew of the 1096 narratives shows unmistakable signs of the influence of *Yosippon*. The basic Hebrew style of the First Crusade narratives is closer to *Yosippon* than to any of the other texts examined thus far. Both are rooted in biblical Hebrew, although the 1096 narratives show more admixture of rabbinic phraseology.[9]

More important than linguistic style are the concepts that are borrowed from *Yosippon*. For the sake of illustration, let us note two. In both texts, there is much concern with afterlife, expressed in third-person observations by the narrators and introduced by them into the reconstructed speeches of the Jewish hero figures. A recurrent image with respect to the afterlife is the appearance of *ha-'or ha-gadol,* the great or supernal light. This notion appears with frequency in *Yosippon* and likewise in the 1096 narratives.[10] To stay with afterlife imagery, the heroes of *Yosippon* regularly contrast the mean circumstances of this-worldly existence with the glories of other-worldly life. We find remarkably parallel contrasts drawn by the martyrs of 1096 in the soliloquies created for them by our narrators.[11]

Yosippon is much concerned with the oppression of Jews and Jewish responses to such oppression. This central concern affords us an excellent opportunity for comparing and contrasting the tenth-century compilation-translation with the somewhat later First Crusade narratives. Indeed, a number of the figures consistently highlighted in our narratives—specifically Daniel and the mother and her seven sons—are extensively depicted in *Yosippon*.

A preliminary word is in order with respect to our expectations in examining *Yosippon*. The text is, after all, highly eclectic. Efforts to identify a consistent *Weltanschauung* in *Yosippon* are surely misguided.

Such a consistent *Weltanschauung*, however, need not be our goal. For our purposes, it would be sufficient to identify reasonable prototypes for some of the storytelling styles and conceptualizations we have identified in the 1096 narratives.

Let us begin this effort to identify such reasonable prototypes with the story of Daniel recounted in *Yosippon*. The version found there is rather charming. The story of the three friends in the fiery furnace makes no appearance in *Yosippon;* the story of Daniel in the lions' den is considerably lengthened and developed. The end result is a tale that makes the royal figure far more credible and Daniel far more verbal. There is also an effort to connect the Daniel story with the larger developments of the period. *Yosippon* adroitly links the Daniel incident with Darius's support for the effort to rebuild the Jerusalem Temple.[12] Despite these more realistic elements, however, the basic folkloristic style of the tale and its emphasis on immediate divine intervention can of course not be effaced, thus maintaining the chasm between that story and the 1096 narratives.

The mother and her seven sons narrative is considerably expanded in *Yosippon;* it is clearly based ultimately on the Hellenistic original, rather than the brief rabbinic tale. In fact, the story of the mother and her seven sons is embedded in a broader narrative of oppression and heroism, a narrative that includes fleeting mention of two Jewish women who flouted the prohibition against circumcision and were killed along with their infants and a far more detailed story of the aged priest Elazar who was urged to eat of the royal sacrifice in order to influence his Jewish brethren. The fairly lengthy story of Elazar is then followed by the even longer account of the mother and her seven sons.[13] The diversity of this set of characters—a leader of the Jewish community, a family singled out by the king, and two nameless women who flouted the law of the land—moves us at least in the direction of the 1096 narratives, with their sense of an entire community under siege. To be sure, there is still an obvious difference between this limited cast of characters and the remarkable portrait of a total community of martyrs created by the Rhineland authors.

Let us attend briefly to the Elazar incident. The tone is considerably more realistic than that found in either the biblical or rabbinic narratives we have examined. The Seleucid general Philip urges the aged priest to eat of the forbidden food and is rebuffed gently but firmly. Moved by friendship for the elderly Jewish leader, the Seleucid general suggests a ploy that would satisfy him without ostensibly compromising Elazar.

The subterfuge involves announcing that Elazar was eating forbidden food, while in fact allowing him to eat that which was permitted. Elazar refuses this offer, in a lengthy and interesting speech that contrasts markedly with those of the 1096 narratives. The Elazar soliloquy emphasizes the priest's personal integrity and the impact that the subterfuge might have on his younger followers. The speech ends on the following note:

> Indeed, if I were to escape this day from your hands [via the ruse], how would I escape from the hand of my God, from whom neither the living nor the dead can flee? For his rule extends to killing the living and reviving the dead. I shall die valiantly and shall leave a legacy of valor after me to my people and my young followers, as they witness this modest death.[14]

While a strong martyrological statement, this is far removed from the world of 1096. There is no real engagement with an alternative religious vision; there is no sense of religious challenge. There is a modest sense of personal integrity and communal responsibility, rooted in awareness of divine rule and retribution. Most striking of all is the lack of the passion encountered in the speeches in the 1096 narratives and the related sense that Jewish behavior would shape the course of history.

The incident of the mother and her seven sons is told at considerably greater length.[15] It concludes the section on Seleucid oppression and Jewish martyrdom and was clearly meant to serve as the centerpiece of that section. In the effort to embellish this narrative, the folkloristic element is introduced once more. The punishments meted out to the seven youngsters are gruesome in the extreme and are extensively described. In the process, the quiet realism of the Elazar episode is lost. The contrast with the more realistically depicted Jewish suffering of 1096 is sharp. The brief speeches of the first six sons also contrast markedly with the 1096 soliloquies. The central motifs are God's absolute power, Jewish sin, suffering as atonement, and eventual reward for the Jewish martyrs and punishment of the Seleucid malefactor. Although some of these motifs recur in 1096, the speeches are built on a series of abstractions, lacking the rich symbolism that sustained the Rhineland martyrs, the passionate engagement with the faith of the oppressors, and the claims of historic significance for the events depicted.

When the king reaches the seventh and youngest of the sons, the tone of the story shifts a bit. The episode is the fullest by far and involves an effort on the part of the king, parallel to the effort of the general Philip, to forestall Jewish suffering. The king offers the youngster "to make him wealthy with silver, gold, stock, and much wealth and to make him royal vizier and to set him in authority over all his kingdom."[16] Again, this is hardly a realistic portrait. Rejected out of hand by the youngster, the king turns to the mother, who seems willing to attempt to intervene with the lad.

In fact, however, the mother simply uses the opportunity to strengthen the youngster's resolve. She mocks the king and makes a lengthy speech of her own. The themes of this speech are parallel to those of the sons, but are somewhat more developed: God is ruler of the entire universe; he created her son; he fashioned the entire universe; the youngster should emulate his brothers and would surely join them in their great reward. The lad impatiently cuts her off and makes his own address to the king. God, from whom there can be no flight, will surely punish the king for his wickedness. By contrast, the rewards of an other-worldly existence far superior to the vanities of this world await the Jewish martyrs. On that note the youngest son is killed. The mother then stands on the bodies of her offspring and requests to join them, a petition that is granted, seemingly at divine hands. Once again, the ideas expressed are, to an extent, parallel to those expressed in 1096. More impressive, however, is the distance in both style and conceptualization between this story and those that portray the Jewish martyrdom of the First Crusade.

The fullest and most realistic accounts of oppression, Jewish resistance, and Jewish martyrdom come in the final sections of *Yosippon*, the sections devoted to the war with Rome.[17] Here the narrative finds its ultimate roots in Josephus himself. The tone is much more realistic and, in that sense, far closer to the 1096 narratives than anything we have encountered thus far.[18] The suffering cuts across the entire community, although the war setting makes the focus decidedly male-centered. Most important, these stories involve Jews taking their own lives and the lives of their kin, a phenomenon found nowhere else in the martyrological literature we have examined.[19] Three major narrative pieces dominate—the story of the conquest of the fortress of Jotapata, from which Josephus himself emerged to tell his tale; the account of the destruction of Jerusalem in the year 70; and the report on the fall of Masada, the last Jewish center of resistance. In all three, Jews elect to take their own lives, rather than fall into Roman hands, and on occasion they take the lives of family members as well. Thematically, this makes them closer to the 1096 narratives than anything else we have analyzed.

The thematic closeness of these stories raises the difficult question of why these tales should have been omitted from the collective memory of the Jewish martyrs of 1096 and should have been overlooked by the Rhineland narrators in their citation of precedents for their heroes. Again, there seems to be abundant evidence that these Jews were aware of the *Yosippon* and had absorbed some of its language and themes. We earlier concluded that one of the time-bound objectives of the 1096 narratives was to rationalize the Jews' extreme martyrological behaviors. Moreover, we have seen that no real precedents for such behavior as a response to oppression could be produced, and we have noted the somewhat artificial device of holding up the patriarch Abraham as the archetype of such willingness for sacrifice, even though no oppression was involved and even though the biblical narrative indicates clearly that God did not want the sacrifice of the youngster. In view of all this, the failure to cite the heroes of the Roman war seems all the more surprising.

A definitive explanation cannot be provided. In a general way, however, the war against Rome, as portrayed in rabbinic lore and even in the *Yosippon* itself, was hardly projected as a noble effort.[20] Diverse and divergent views circulated within the Jewish community of Palestine, ranging from those of the militants to those of the Jews in favor of accommodation. The militants have come to be lauded in modern Jewish historical thinking, but premodern Jews saw themselves as descendants of the accommodationists. The great rabbinic hero of the war was Rabban Yohanan ben Zakkai, who had purportedly abandoned besieged Jerusalem and established a postwar accommodationist center for reconstructing Jewish life. To make the opponents of Rabban Yohanan ben Zakkai into heroic precursors of the martyrs of 1096 thus involved grave difficulties. In addition, as we shall see, the thinking of the martyrs of the Roman war diverged considerably from that of the victims of the First Crusade. Nonetheless, we are still fully justified in combing the *Yosippon* narrative for signs of parallel and influence.

Let us focus on the incident that has ultimately become the most famous, the Masada incident with which *Yosippon* closes. The dramatic outlines of the story are well known. Aware of a multitude of rebels assembled at Masada, Titus sent his general Silva, with a large army, to eliminate this last Jewish stronghold. The walls were broken down with battering rams. In response, the Jews hastily erected a wooden wall, which the Romans burned. Evening brought about an interruption in hostilities, with the Jews afforded time to assess their plight. It is in this setting that the famous speech of the rebel leader, Elazar, was uttered.

This speech is lengthier and fuller than any we encountered in the 1096 narratives. It begins with the philosophic sense that, in war, there is always a swing of fortunes. "Sometimes one pursues, and sometimes one flees. Sometimes one overcomes, and sometimes one is overcome. He who is overcome should feel no shame, for everything has its appointed time."[21] The truly important goal is to be properly prepared for death. The tone of this opening argument is decidedly Roman, with no Jewish symbolism intruding.

At this point, three historical figures are introduced. The first is the patriarch Abraham, who is mentioned briefly. "Consider what Abraham your ancestor did. He took his only son to offer him up to the Lord. He did not consider in his heart that he was killing the lad; he thought and knew that he was affording him [eternal] life."[22] This brief mention of Abraham is then succeeded by a far lengthier focus on an unlikely predecessor figure, King Josiah, surely an honorable model, but one that hardly has a role in traditional Jewish martyrological thinking. The case made emphasizes the lack of involvement of the Jews in the war that eventually cost King Josiah his life. Josiah, however, was—according to this presentation—determined to win himself the afterlife that comes with noble death. King Josiah leads to a third figure, Abel. Abel, the one who was killed, lost this-worldly existence, but gained afterlife; Cain, the killer, remained alive, suffered in this life, and lost the afterlife to boot. The unusual nature of this argument and these precedent figures hardly needs to be emphasized.

The precedents of Abraham, King Josiah, and Abel introduce a lengthy disquisition on the afterlife. It is convoluted and philosophical, and no Jewish images or symbols intrude. Toward the end, an appeal is made to the wise men of India, who refrain altogether from lamenting death, since they are convinced of the superiority of the afterlife. Again, one could hardly imagine a more striking contrast to the thinking of 1096 and its portrayal in the First Crusade narratives.

The lengthy speech ends with a turn to the immediate circumstances of the Jews who are sequestered in Masada and are about to see their fortress stormed. The rebel leader urges that the life to which they will be exposed in the wake of Roman victory makes death all the more attractive an alternative. He describes vividly the torture and rape to which the subdued Jews will be exposed and argues that honorable death is obviously a more appealing choice. Here it is striking to note the absence of such themes in the 1096 material. For the 1096 narrators, the essential battle is between two religious visions. There is much Christian cruelty, all of it in an effort to bring Jews to conversion. Cruelty for the gratification of human lust makes no appearance.

While it is in a number of ways closer to the 1096 narratives than anything else we have analyzed, the closing *Yosippon* material serves ultimately to indicate one last time how innovative the Rhineland narratives truly are. While this closing *Yosippon* material shares stylistic elements and certain themes, particularly self-inflicted martyrdom, the thinking depicted is utterly removed from the dynamic, aggressive, imagery-laden portraits that fill the narratives of 1096. Failure to locate satisfying parallels and precedents in either classical or medieval Jewish literature makes the examination of the contemporary Latin crusade chronicles all the more pertinent.

THE LATIN FIRST CRUSADE CHRONICLES

As noted recurrently, the First Crusade generated great enthusiasm throughout western Christendom, resulting *inter alia* in the composition of numerous accounts of the remarkable enterprise. These accounts included first-hand narratives, written by participants, and later reconstructions based on a combination of oral and written testimony. The numerous First Crusade histories provide rich data on the events of 1095–1099 and illuminate major aspects of the thinking of late-eleventh- and twelfth-century western Christendom. In this regard, they parallel our Hebrew narratives. Both sets of accounts were intended to relay valuable information on important events, to provide an assessment of these events, and to place these events in a larger historical and metahistorical context.

In the comparative efforts undertaken thus far, in this and the preceding chapter, individual works have been presented for comparison and contrast with the 1096 narratives. Comparison of all the Latin First Crusade chronicles with our four Hebrew narratives is obviously too grandiose an undertaking. I have thus singled out the earliest and, in many ways, most interesting of the Latin chronicles, the *Gesta Francorum,* as a single work that will provide a basis for comparison and contrast.

There is of course an obvious and critical difference between the *Gesta Francorum* and the Hebrew narratives. The *Gesta Francorum* is an exhilarated celebration of Christian victory on both the physical and spiritual plane; the Hebrew narratives, by contrast, tell the tale of a physical defeat that is interpreted and presented as a remarkable spiritual triumph. At a number of points in the ensuing analysis, the impact of these divergent perspectives will be obvious. This important difference notwithstanding, I shall argue that the Hebrew accounts and the *Gesta Francorum* share common assumptions about God, humanity, and the workings of history.

Let us begin with the place of the divine in both the *Gesta Francorum* and the Hebrew narratives. For the *Gesta*, like the Hebrew accounts, there can surely be no doubt as to the centrality of God. Once more, God is the creator of the universe; God controls the workings of history; God will shape the further outcomes of the epic events depicted. Again, as in the Hebrew narratives, God is more than a central subject: he is, in significant measure, also the audience at whom the accounts are aimed. The ten books of the *Gesta* each close with praise of God and petitions to him, in much the same way as do the Hebrew narratives. Let us note, for example, the closing sentences of the first and last books of the *Gesta*:

> This battle was fought on the fourth day of the week, which was Ash Wednesday. Blessed be God in all his works! Amen.

> This battle was fought on August 12th, by the mercy of our Lord Jesus Christ, to whom be honor and glory, now and forever, without end. May every soul say: "Amen!"[23]

To be sure, while Christian victory is the central motif of the *Gesta*, the way to Jerusalem was beset with difficulties and strewn with Christian corpses. On occasion, vengeance was requested for the lives lost, and once again the addressee of such petitions was God himself.[24]

Does God actually manifest himself in the course of the Hebrew narratives and the *Gesta*? Here, of course, we might well anticipate disparity, with God active on the victorious Christian side and eclipsed on the suffering Jewish side. In fact, however, God appears as an active agent only fleetingly in both; when he does intervene, it is in surprisingly parallel fashion. For the Hebrew narratives, we have noted already extremely limited claims of direct divine intervention, with heavier emphasis on God's occasional warnings of impending, usually disastrous, developments.[25]

In the entire *Gesta Francorum*, there is but one major episode in which God is depicted as playing any active role in a Christian victory, and the incident is somewhat ambiguous. In the depiction of one of the key battles at Antioch, the *Gesta* inserts, in the middle of an extensive description of battle formations and tactics, the following:

> Then also appeared from the mountains a countless host of men on white horses, whose banners were all white. When our men saw this, they did not understand what was happening or who these men might be, until they realized that this was the succor sent by Christ, and that the leaders were St. George, St. Mercurius, and St. Demetrius. This is quite true, for many of our men saw it.[26]

These heavenly forces in point of fact play no role in the rest of the author's depiction of the rout of the Muslim forces, which is portrayed once more in distinctly human terms. Ultimately, it seems that the real significance of the apparition lay in its impact upon the Christian troops who claimed to have seen it, strengthening their resolve at a critical point in the engagement.

Interestingly, the *Mainz Anonymous* includes an incident that is similarly interpreted by the crusaders as evidence of divine assistance. For the first two days of the month of Sivan, the troops of Count Emicho camped outside the walls of Mainz, locked out of the town at the order of the archbishop. On the third of Sivan, at noon, as Emicho and his forces prepared to force their way into Mainz, the gates were opened by sympathetic burghers, eliciting—according to the Jewish narrator—the following crusader reaction: "All this the crucified does on our behalf in order to avenge his blood upon the Jews."[27] Once again, the major impact of the purported miracle was to reinforce the conviction of the crusading forces.

Indeed, the most significant modality of God's intervention throughout the *Gesta* involves precisely the alerting of a human audience to divine intentions and reinforcement or weakening of the will of that human audience. Indicative of this kind of divine intervention are three important incidents associated with the struggle for Antioch. The first involves a sign sent primarily to the Muslim foe. After describing the assaults of the Turks upon the beleaguered crusaders, the author of the *Gesta* continues:

> That very night, there appeared a fire in the sky, coming from the west, and it approached and fell upon the Turkish army, to the great astonishment of our men and of the Turks also. In the morning, the Turks, who were all frightened by the fire, took to flight in panic and went to my lord Bohemond's gate, where they encamped. But those who were in the citadel fought with

our men day and night, shooting arrows and wounding or killing them. The rest of the Turks besieged the city on all sides, so that none of our men dared to go out or come in except by night or secretly.[28]

The divine sign was apprehended by both Christians and Muslims, but only a Muslim reaction is indicated. It is interesting that this response was of brief duration and little importance. By and large the Muslims simply kept up their assault.

A striking passage in the *Gesta* depicts a priest vouchsafed a vision of Jesus in conversation with Mary and Peter. The priest begged Jesus for divine assistance for the entrapped Christian forces at Antioch. In the vision, Jesus indicates a record of support for the crusaders, enabling them to win great victories at Nicea and Antioch. However, the crusaders, according to this vision, had abused divine blessing by lustful behaviors with both Christian and Muslim women. In the face of this divine repudiation, the vision has both Mary and Peter interceding on behalf of the crusaders. Jesus relents, sending through the priest a message to his crusading followers: "Go and say to my people that they should return unto me, and I shall return unto them. Within five days, I shall send them a mighty help. Let them sing each day the response 'For lo the kings were assembled,' along with the doxology."[29] This vision seemingly reinforced the commitment of key crusading knights, who took an oath of continued allegiance to the enterprise.

The most famous of the signs vouchsafed to the crusaders at Antioch involved the revelation by St. Andrew of the site of the lance with which Jesus was pierced. This reference would have had a double impact on crusader thinking. Simple reportage of the vision of St. Andrew bolstered crusader morale in and of itself. Subsequently, when the lance was purportedly found in the place indicated by St. Andrew, the relic played a major role in preparing the Christian warriors for their decisive confrontation with the army of Karbuqa.[30] Once again, God's most important role lay in communication with his followers.

If in the *Gesta Francorum* and the Hebrew narratives God rarely appears as an active agent, the central role in both is played by human figures. Humans—both heroic and villainous—lie at the center of the drama portrayed in both the Latin and Hebrew narratives. Like the *Mainz Anonymous*, the *Gesta* begins with no theological preamble; rather, it plunges immediately into the narrative. Let us attend to the opening narrative statements, which are strikingly parallel to those noted earlier in the *Mainz Anonymous*. These opening sentences show

a remarkable blending of underlying divine causation with the immediate efficacy of human will and emotion.

> That time had already come, of which the Lord Jesus warns his faithful every
> day, especially in the Gospel, where he says: "If any man will come after me,
> let him deny himself, and take up his cross, and follow me." There was then
> a great stirring of heart all through the Frankish lands, so that—if any man
> with all his heart and all his mind really wanted to follow God and faithfully
> to bear the cross after him—he could make no delay in taking the road to
> the Holy Sepulcher as quickly as possible.[31]

In the eyes of the author of the *Gesta,* there is an eternal message delivered in the Gospels. Attending to the Matthew passage just cited, we
might usefully note its continuation: "Whoever cares for his own safety
is lost; but if a man will let himself be lost for my sake, he will find his
true self."[32] The crusade is portrayed as a profound response to the
eternal message of the Gospels. Not all generations, however, resonated
to this message. Striking to the author of the *Gesta* is the unusual spirit
that swept Christendom at the close of the eleventh century, the "great
stirring of heart all through the Frankish lands." The message was eternal, but receptivity to this message and willingness to undertake the
sacrifices entailed in its fulfillment were unique features of a particular
time, place, and Christian society. The parallels to the Hebrew narratives
are striking.

The valor of the crusaders is the central theme in the *Gesta Francorum.* It projects an army of well-trained, fierce, and dedicated warriors,
who regularly vanquish forces that are numerically superior. The author
of the *Gesta,* early on, describes the decision of his personal lord, Bohemond, to join the crusading enterprise. Bohemond's purported questions and the answers he receives are revealing:

> He [Bohemond] began to make careful inquiries as to the arms they bore,
> the badge they wore in Christ's pilgrimage, and the war cry they shouted in
> battle. He was told: "They are well armed; they wear the badge of Christ's
> cross on their right arm or between their shoulders; and as a war cry they
> shout all together 'God wills it, God wills it, God wills it!' "

The reply, which artfully combines worldly might with religious enthusiasm, convinced Bohemond, and he immediately "ordered the most
valuable cloak he had to be cut up forthwith and made into crosses."[33]

Descriptions of the crusaders' valiant behaviors dot the *Gesta.* One
passage is particularly noteworthy. It describes an early battle for Antioch, an engagement that pitted a huge Muslim force against the Chris-

tians and that seemed, at the outset, destined to eventuate in Muslim victory. Bohemond, ever the mighty leader,

> gave orders to his constable, Robert Fitzgerald, saying: "Charge at top speed, like a brave man, and fight valiantly for God and the Holy Sepulcher. For you know in truth that this is no war of the flesh, but of the spirit. So be very brave, as becomes a champion of Christ. Go in peace, and may the Lord be your defense!" So Bohemond, protected on all sides by the sign of the Cross, charged the Turkish forces like a lion which has been starving for three or four days, which comes roaring out of its cave thirsting for the blood of cattle and falls upon the flocks careless of its own safety, tearing the sheep as they flee hither and yon. His attack was so fierce that the points of his banner were flying right over the heads of the Turks. The other troops, seeing Bohemond's banner carried ahead so honorably, stopped their retreat at once, and all our men in a body charged the Turks, who were amazed and took to flight. Our men pursued them and massacred them right up to the Orontes bridge.[34]

This important skirmish was, according to the author of the *Gesta*, decided by the sheer militance of his lord Bohemond, out of his profound recognition that "this is no war of the flesh, but of the spirit." A seeming Muslim victory was reversed by the force of a powerful and utterly dedicated Christian warrior. Once more, the view of humanity, its potential for spiritual arousal, and its capacities for momentous achievement are strikingly parallel. As noted, the Christian narrative sees this arousal and achievement as a physical conquest of a more numerous foe, while the Jewish narratives see this arousal and achievement as a spiritual victory in the face of larger numbers and overwhelming strength. What is common to both, however, is the conviction that the potential of human beings for heroic self-sacrifice and achievement is grand.

In the Latin *Gesta* and the Hebrew narratives, portrayal of the enemy is complex and intriguing. Both are keenly aware of the complexities of the enemy camp and distinctions among those in opposition; they avoid lumping the enemy into some conveniently monolithic frame. We have seen already awareness of the specific anti-Jewish forces at work in 1096 in the *Mainz Anonymous* and the Trier unit.[35] The *Gesta* regularly highlights the composite nature of the forces opposed to the crusaders.

> Our men could not understand whence could have come such a great multitude of Turks, Arabs, Saracens, and other peoples whose names I do not know.[36]

> As soon as our knights charged, the Turks, Arabs, Saracens, Agulani, and all the rest of the barbarians took to their heels and fled through the mountain

passes and across the plains. There were three hundred and sixty thousand Turks, Persians, Paulicians, Saracens, and Agulani, along with other pagans, not counting the Arabs, for God alone knows how many there were of them.[37]

In both the Jewish and the Christian accounts, the stances toward this variety of enemies are complex. In large measure, the enemies are looked down upon. They are intellectually lacking, spiritually debased, and morally repugnant. At the same time, there is, in both the Hebrew accounts and the Latin record, evidence of occasional and grudging admiration for the foe. As noted already, the Hebrew narratives, in which the crusaders are ultimately to'im—those consigned to wandering about in error rather than pilgrims making their way to a sacred site—do acknowledge, almost reluctantly, the reality of religious enthusiasm undergirding the crusading venture. Similarly, the Gesta from time to time recognizes the valor of the Muslim foe. Perhaps the most impressive instance of such acknowledgment is the following:

> They [the Turks] have a saying that they are of common stock with the Franks and that no men, except the Franks and themselves, are naturally born to be knights. It is true—and no one can deny it—that, if only they had stood firm in the faith of Christ and holy Christendom and had been willing to accept one God in three persons and had believed rightly and faithfully that the Son of God was born of a virgin mother, that he suffered and rose from the dead and ascended in the sight of his disciples into heaven and sent them in full measure the comfort of the Holy Ghost, and that he reigns in heaven and earth, you could not find braver or more skillful soldiers. Yet, by God's grace, they were beaten by our men.[38]

This is a rather remarkable acknowledgment of the enemy. Put differently, what separates Christian or Jewish heroes from Muslim or Christian enemies is ultimately religious vision and commitment. If only the enemy did not err in their religious vision, then they would in fact be thoroughly laudable.

What follows, of course, in the Christian and the Jewish narratives alike, is linkage of the divine and the human, in the sense that the human heroes are ranged on the side of God and the enemies of these human heroes are the enemies of the deity. Thus, in the Gesta, despite the occasional recognition of Muslim ability and valor, the human foe is essentially God's enemy as well. The perception is precisely parallel in the Hebrew account. Christians of all stripes who assault the Jews are enemies of the Jewish people and are *ipso facto* enemies of the one true God.

The coalescing of human enemies into opponents of the human heroes and the God they serve leads us nicely to the broader issue of the relationship between God and humanity. Both narratives share the conviction that the human commitment and heroism upon which they focus must win divine approbation in one or another way. In the *Gesta* and in the Hebrew narratives, this is an assertion announced often and vigorously; in both, it is also a petition advanced repeatedly. Neither the Christian narrative nor the Jewish accounts see assertion and petition as mutually contradictory.

Given the Jewish circumstances, assertion of and petition for divine reward for the Jewish heroes of 1096 and punishment for the Christian villains were focused entirely on the future. The true outcome of the events of 1096 would only become manifest at that point in time when God sees fit to step more fully into the stream of history and provide appropriate recompense for hero and villain alike.

On the Christian side, the conviction of divine reward is likewise manifest throughout. At the outset of the *Gesta,* we recall the citation of Matthew 16, which calls for human emulation of divine self-sacrifice, with the promise that "if a man will let himself be lost for my sake, he will find his true self." This finding of true self can be and is interpreted in the *Gesta* on many levels.

Surely the simplest of these multiple levels involves immediate military victory. As noted, the *Gesta Francorum* is essentially a celebration of the valor of the crusading warriors and a description of the victories that God bestowed upon them as their just reward. This focus on valor and its immediate recompense leads ultimately to a sometimes mechanical sense of the immediate relationship of human commitment and requisite divine support. We recall the startling incident in the *Gesta Francorum* in which Guy, the brother of Bohemond, and his followers excoriated God for permitting what seemed to be destruction of Bohemond and his army. The conviction of direct relationship between human action and divine recompense is couched in the following stark terms: "If the word which we have heard from these scoundrels [the frightening—but ultimately inaccurate—report of crusader defeat] is true, we and the other Christians will forsake you [God] and remember you no more, nor will any of us henceforth be so bold as to call upon your Name."[39] This assumption of direct linkage between human action and divine response is extreme and does not truly characterize either the *Gesta Francorum* or crusader thinking. It is useful nonetheless in illuminating through its very radicality the more basic conviction that—in one way or another—God must surely reward human devotion.

In fact, the Hebrew narrative provides interesting further evidence of precisely such a linkage, at least in segments of the Christian population. We have recurrently encountered the Christian argument, delivered to Jewish survivors of crusader and burgher violence, that the 1096 disaster itself served as incontrovertible evidence of God's abandonment of the Jews.[40] In the cases of Minna of Worms, Simhah of Worms, David *ha-gabbai* of Mainz, and Kalonymous ben Meshullam, Christians argued that the massacre of their fellow Jews served as indisputable testimony of divine rejection of the Jewish people. Jews should intelligently interpret God's expression of divine will in the realm of historic fact and act accordingly—that is, abandon the rejected faith community. This argument is remarkably parallel to the stance of Bohemond's brother Guy and his associates in the *Gesta*.

To be sure, such is not the only stance toward defeat discernible in the *Gesta*. As noted earlier, the path to Jerusalem was marked by painful setbacks and littered with Christian casualties. Every defeat could not be made the occasion for the abandonment of the enterprise. Sometimes such setbacks were explained as the result of specific crusader shortcomings, which could be identified and rectified. We recall, for example, the vision vouchsafed to the unidentified priest that suggested Christian lust as the basis for a setback at Antioch and proposed specific means for reingratiating the crusading host with its divine protector.[41] This, however, is not at all the dominant approach to the loss of Christian life.

The dominant approach to the loss of Christian life is sounded at the very outset of the *Gesta,* as we have seen. Given Christianity's rich martyrological tradition, which begins with the Crucifixion, it is hardly surprising that the *Gesta* projects the readiness for martyrdom as lying at the very core of the crusade, utilizes the notion of martyrdom as a meaningful explanation for occasional defeat and for extensive loss of life, and asserts a second kind of reward for crusader heroes. Alongside the reward of victory, capped by the conquest of Jerusalem, there existed for the warriors of Christendom an alternative style of divine recompense—other-worldly blessings that were as real as and yet more lasting than tangible conquests on this-worldly terrain.

As we have seen, the *Gesta* opens by rooting the crusade in a new spiritual state in western Christendom, essentially a state of readiness for self-sacrifice and martyrdom. Early on, the *Gesta* makes a fleeting reference to the preaching of Pope Urban II, which it summarizes in the following terms:

> Brothers, you must suffer for the name of Christ many things: wretchedness, poverty, nakedness, persecution, need, sickness, hunger, thirst, and other such troubles. For the Lord says to his disciples, "You must suffer many things for my name," and "Be not ashamed to speak before men, for I will give you what to say." But afterward "great will be your reward."[42]

The crusader insignia—the cross—suggests in and of itself readiness for self-sacrifice—indeed, the ultimate self-sacrifice—out of a sense of ultimate reward.

At the end of the second book of the *Gesta,* where the author notes a lengthy and costly siege, he describes the results in the following terms:

> Many of our men suffered martyrdom there and gave up their blessed souls to God with joy and gladness, and many of the poor starved to death for the name of Christ. All these entered heaven in triumph, wearing the robe of martyrdom which they have received.[43]

Throughout the *Gesta,* there is extensive reference to fallen crusaders as martyrs and to the other-worldly blessings that constitute their just reward. Once more, the parallels to the Hebrew narratives are as obvious as they are striking. Indeed, I would argue that the martyrological language and conceptualization of the *Gesta Francorum* is far closer to that of the Hebrew narratives of 1096 than even the martyrological language and conceptualization we encountered in the *Sefer Yosippon.*

Let us now explore one last index of the parallels between the Christian and Jewish crusade narratives. We noted earlier the end result of the centrality of the Jewish martyrs in the Hebrew narratives. The heroism of these martyrs and their significance in the scheme of history, both universal and Jewish, leads the Jewish narrators to propose that the Jewish martyrs were the towering heroes of the First Crusade, that they loomed far above their crusading contemporaries, that they in fact dwarfed the giants of the Jewish past in the their greatness. This view of the preeminence of present-day figures over their predecessors was noted as highly unusual. Let us conclude with the introduction to yet another eyewitness First Crusade narrative, that of Fulcher of Chartres.

> Although I dare not compare the above-mentioned labor of the Franks with the great achievements of the Israelites or Maccabees or many other privileged people whom God has honored by frequent and wonderful miracles,

still I consider the deeds of the Franks scarcely less inferior, since God's miracles so often occurred among them.

In what ways do the Franks differ from the Israelites or Maccabees? Indeed, we have seen these Franks in the same regions, often right with us, or we have heard about them in places different from us, suffering dismemberment, crucifixion, flaying, death by arrows or by being rent apart, or other kinds of martyrdom, all for the love of Christ. They could not be overcome by threats or temptations. Nay, rather if the butcher's sword had been at hand, many of us would not have refused martyrdom for the love of Christ.[44]

The parallels to the Jewish sense of contemporary heroes who exceed the giants who preceded them constitute a fitting close to this discussion.

The Christians who are the protagonists of the *Gesta* and the Jews who occupy center stage in the Hebrew narratives were profoundly focused on that which distinguished them one from another: the nature of the God they worshipped, the demands their God made upon them, and the identity of the human community that God had singled out for special responsibility and blessing. A close look at these two immediate depictions of the First Crusade experience suggests, however, that beyond these obvious differences there was in fact much that united the two hostile camps. Our analysis of the *Gesta Francorum* and the Hebrew narratives indicates that, differences notwithstanding, they share a common view, first, of God's limited role in what they both perceive as the remarkable developments of the late 1090s and, second, of the centrality of human will, commitment, and action in the drama of the First Crusade. Human will and commitment, as expressed in the crusading venture, could in immediate terms alter the course of history, and this is what the Christian narratives claim the crusaders had done with their conquest of Jerusalem. Beyond the immediately tangible conquest lay the long-term implications of the unique heroism manifest in 1096. For the Jewish narrators, the immediate victory trumpeted by their Christian counterparts was ultimately devoid of meaning. It was Jewish heroism that would—at some point in the future—prove to be the decisive factor in a radical change that would be introduced by God himself.

Epilogue

This study began with a working hypothesis, based on analysis of a valuable Hebrew latter written in the wake of the Blois tragedy of 1171. This hypothesis suggested that early Ashkenazic Jews composed accounts of contemporary events designed to provide important time-bound information while at the same time addressing critical timeless issues. Examining the Hebrew First Crusade narratives from this perspective, we have been able to identify a number of time-bound objectives of the narratives. We have also been successful in understanding the timeless issues faced by the survivors of the catastrophe. In the process, we have learned that the combination of time-bound and timeless concerns reflect an innovative style of historical writing and new views of the relationship of God, humanity, and history.

In fact, the combination of time-bound and timeless concerns involves much more than a technical expedient, a clever means of achieving multiple goals through a single composition. At its core, the combination of time-bound and timeless objectives in and of itself reveals a new sense of the importance of contemporary events and contemporary human heroes. Jewish absorption of some of the values and attitudes of the rapidly developing northern European milieu moved our narrators to see the time-bound and the timeless as inextricably bound up, one with the other.

The Jews who died in the assaults of 1096 and those who survived were part of a vibrant and creative young society that was forging a new understanding of the divine, the world, humanity, and history. The First Crusade was grounded in this new view of human beings, their capacities, and their potential; the crusaders were animated by extreme visions of this human capacity and potential. The Jewish martyrs of 1096, viscerally opposed to the Christian vision, shared nonetheless in this exalted sense of the human potential for heroic commitment and behavior. The Jewish narrators of the events of 1096 shared with contemporary Christian writers assumptions about the limited immediate role played by God during the First Crusade and the correspondingly grand role of human heroes and villains.

Out of the Jewish encounter with this new societal spirit emerged an innovative and intense form of Jewish militance and martyrdom; out of the same encounter emerged also an innovative form of Jewish historical narrative. In the two concluding chapters of this book, we searched in vain for genuine precedents to the Hebrew narratives of 1096 in the previous Jewish historiographic legacy. In the very last chapter, we did locate substantial parallels to the Hebrew First Crusade narratives in the Latin *Gesta Francorum*. The striking convergence of the Hebrew and Latin narratives reveals the extent to which the early Ashkenazic Jews were deeply embedded in their invigorating and challenging environment.

The Jewish encounter with the so-called twelfth-century renaissance produced significant problems for early Ashkenazic Jewry.[1] Some of the new religious themes, like the drive to regain the sacred sites of Christendom or the enhanced focus on the human figure of Jesus, had the potential for exacerbating negative imagery of the Jews, traditionally associated with the persecution and death of Christ.[2] Some of the new patterns of philosophic speculation and investigation, which might conceivably have led in the direction of greater understanding of human difference, in fact reinforced the sense of Christian truth and non-Christian error.[3] Some of the anxieties elicited by rapid change focused attention on the Jews of northern Europe and resulted in the elaboration of damaging new stereotypes of Jewish malevolence.[4]

It would be misleading, however, to see the impact of the "twelfth-century renaissance" in negative terms only. The new patterns of thinking abroad in the Christian majority inevitably stimulated innovative creativity within the Jewish minority. Alongside the new patterns of martyrological behavior and historical writing, both of which have been central to the present study, we might also note innovative developments among the Jews of northern Europe in business, in political organization, and in important sectors of Jewish spiritual and intellectual activity. New forms of biblical commentary, talmudic exegesis, and pietistic spirituality all made their appearance among the Jews of late-eleventh- and twelfth-century northern Europe. While the linkages to majority culture are extremely difficult to track, emergence of all this creativity within a dynamic majority setting can hardly have been accidental. In ways we can no longer document, the Jews participated, absorbed, and created.

The new style biblical commentary, pioneered by the descendants of the great Solomon ben Isaac of Troyes (Rashi), focused on the literal and contextual meaning of the biblical text. It created new insights that seemed to cascade upon one another. It was, in ways not altogether clear, related to parallel thrusts within the Christian majority. There too, a new twelfth-century interest in the literal meaning of the text became manifest, an interest that on occasion sent Christian exegetes in search of the insight that Jewish contemporaries—with their command of Hebrew—might afford.[5]

The innovative talmudic exegesis was yet more far-reaching. The Tosafists, once more led by descendants of Solomon ben Isaac of Troyes, began to treat the sprawling talmudic corpus as a coherent body of law and doctrine. This meant that apparent contradictions were only that— apparent, but not real. The effort to reconcile seemingly discordant texts once more opened up vast new opportunities for human ingenuity. The enterprise, launched again in the twelfth century, proliferated all through the latter decades of that century and on into the thirteenth. A vast corpus of interpretation was created, a literature studied and expanded continuously thereafter all across the Jewish world. Once more, numerous students of this twelfth-century innovation among the Jews of northern Europe have noted striking methodological parallels between the talmudic exegesis undertaken in the Jewish academies and the legalistic and philosophic style of reasoning encountered within majority Christian society. Awareness of the discordant texts, the need to reconcile them, and the capacity of the human mind to solve such problems lay at the heart of the enterprise within both the Jewish minority and the Christian majority.[6]

At about the same time that these new intellectual tendencies were manifesting themselves primarily among the Jews of the western areas of northern Europe, the Jews of the Germanic areas of central Europe were creating a vigorous new pietistic spirituality. This innovative spirituality was, like the martyrological behaviors of 1096, rooted in a sense of human capacity to fathom the dictates of divine will and human strength to fulfill the daunting requirements of that divine will. Like their Christian contemporaries, the Ḥasidei Ashkenaz were convinced of the remarkable potential that committed human beings possessed for insight and heroic behavior.[7]

Again, the striking parallels between these innovative modes of Jewish creativity—martyrological behavior, historical narrative, biblical commentary, talmudic exegesis, and pietistic spirituality—and the contemporary Christian sense of the intellectual, spiritual, and emotional strengths of humanity are not meant to conjure up images of direct interchange, of the kind fully documented for the older and more diversified medieval Muslim world. There were no arenas of open intellectual and spiritual exchange in the rapidly developing areas of northern Europe. The Jews of this area did not command the literary language of their environment and did not have direct access to the literary productivity of majority society. On the other hand, these Jews lived in relatively small enclaves that could not be truly isolated from the surrounding culture. As a result, the Jews of northern Europe came to share many of the fundamental attitudes of the surrounding society, and that sharing is reflected in the new patterns of Jewish behavior, Jewish thinking, and Jewish literary creativity manifest in late-eleventh- and twelfth-century northern Europe.

At the heart of this new creativity lay a high regard for human beings—their capacity to understand the divine will in all its complexity, their capacity to suppress normal human emotion in order to carry out God's dictates, and the capacity of the mind to penetrate the secrets of the Scriptures and of the rabbinic corpus. God surely lay behind all this creativity, but the human partner in the divine-human dyad came to occupy center stage to an unprecedented degree.

Jewish immersion in this vibrant young civilization was not long-lived. The First Crusade, as a manifestation of the new spirit, showed the potential of the innovative mentality for negative implications with respect to the Jews and a number of other minority groups.[8] While the subsequent crusades did not erupt into the same kind of anti-Jewish violence, the anti-Jewish elements in the "twelfth-century renaissance" took quieter, subtler, and ultimately more injurious forms.[9] Jewish presence in northern Europe—or at least the western portions thereof—was increasingly constricted and eventually choked off. In effect, early Ashkenazic Jewry lost its place in the westerly and more advanced sectors of northern Europe, finding new homes in the more backward areas of central and eastern Europe.

In the process of constriction and relocation, much of the vibrancy of the Jewish "twelfth-century renaissance" dissipated. The radical martyrological behaviors of 1096 were rarely recapitulated. Indeed, depictions of oppression and requisite Jewish reactions reverted to earlier and more subdued models. The heroic narrative style upon which this study has been focused was lost with the passage of time. We find occasional late-twelfth-century emulations of the style of the 1096 narratives, but these texts contain no real outburst of the originality that lies at the core of this investigation. The search for the literal and contextual meaning of the biblical text likewise lost its impetus, with the reassertion of older forms of commentary across the Ashkenzic world. The same was roughly true for the new pietistic spirituality, although it did leave an identifiable imprint on subsequent Jewish pietism. The one truly enduring innovation lay in the realm of talmudic exegesis. The Tosafist revolution was complete, and the new style of talmudic study has dominated the Jewish academy from then until now.

Thus, this study has ultimately focused on a failed initiative: the adumbration of a new and exciting narrative style that emerged out of late-eleventh- and twelfth-century Ashkenaz and was shortly thereafter lost to Jewish posterity. Nonetheless, the emergence of this innovative narrative style, like the heroic Jewish thinking and behavior it sought to enshrine, stands as a tribute to the creativity of the small Jewish population of northern Europe and to the impact of the hostile, challenging, and stimulating majority milieu within which it found itself.

Appendix

The Hebrew First Crusade Narratives:
Prior Studies on Relationships and Dating

Since their publication in 1892, there has been considerable investigation of the Hebrew First Crusade narratives, with a focus on their relationships one to another and their dating. A brief review of major studies will serve a number of useful purposes. It will, first of all, permit a close look at prior views, without unduly burdening the body of the text. This chronologically organized survey will also provide a sense of changing stances toward the narratives. Finally, out of this survey will emerge a set of useful guidelines for the present analysis.[1]

1. 1892—Harry Bresslau, "Zur Kritik der Kreuzzugsberichte," in N&S, xiii–xxix. Basing his essay on the German translation, Bresslau examined the relationship of the three narratives and came to the conclusion that they were essentially independent of one another, with the overlaps traceable to common sources. Bresslau saw the *Solomon bar Simson Chronicle* as dating from 1140, the *Eliezer bar Nathan Chronicle* as dating from about the same time, and the *Mainz Anonymous* as a fourteenth-century composition.

2. 1892—Nathan Porges, "Les relations hébraiques des persécutions des Juifs pendant la première croisade," *Revue des études juives* 25 (1892):181–201 and 26 (1893):183–197. Porges was highly critical of the Bresslau effort to analyze the three narratives based on the German translation. Substantively, Porges came to nearly opposite conclusions. For Porges, the *Solomon bar Simson Chronicle,* the beginning of which Porges believed to be lost, forms the basis for the other two.[2] Items in

the *Eliezer bar Nathan Chronicle* or in the *Mainz Anonymous* not now found in the *Solomon bar Simson Chronicle* are assumed by Porges to have been part of the purportedly missing section of the latter.

3. 1916—Ismar Elbogen, "Zu den hebräischen Berichten ueber die Judenverfolgungen im Jahre 1096," in *Festschrift zum siebzigsten Geburtstage Martin Philippsons* (Leipzig, 1916), 6–24. Elbogen provided a most helpful reading for the four Hebrew words in the *Solomon bar Simson Chronicle* that include mention of the year 1140.[3] This reading allowed for the possibility that the date and the authorship of Solomon bar Simson refer only to the relatively brief Altenahr section.[4] As to the relationship of the three narratives, Elbogen remained supportive of the Porges conclusions.[5]

4. 1933—Isaiah Sonne, "Nouvel examen des trois relations hébraïques sur les persécutions de 1096," *Revue des études juives* 96 (1933):113–156. Sonne broke new ground in a number of ways. First of all, he addressed the issue of the precise dimensions of the *Solomon bar Simson Chronicle* and the *Mainz Anonymous*. In both cases, he argued that the text actually begins with the dating provided for the events depicted ("It came to pass in the year 4856" and "It came to pass in the year 1028") and that the prior sentences represent observations of later editors or copyists.[6] Thus, the missing sections in the *Solomon bar Simson Chronicle* claimed by Porges disappear. The evidence for late dating supplied by the supposed opening and closing sentences of the *Mainz Anonymous* likewise dissipates.[7] As a result, Sonne argued for an early dating for the *Mainz Anonymous*. Finally, Sonne reversed the view of Porges, arguing that the *Solomon bar Simson Chronicle* was derived from the earlier *Mainz Anonymous* and *Eliezer bar Nathan Chronicle*.

5. 1945—Abraham Habermann, "Who Wrote Chronicle I Concerning the Persecution of 1096?" (Hebrew), *Sinai* 9, n. 2 (1945):79–84. Habermann recapitulated the views of Bresslau (independent narratives drawing upon common sources), Porges-Elbogen (the *Solomon bar Simson Chronicle* as the source for the other two); and Sonne (the *Mainz Anonymous* and the *Eliezer bar Nathan Chronicle* as the source for the *Solomon bar Simson Chronicle*). Habermann rejected the Sonne view out of hand and argued for the primacy of the *Solomon bar Simson Chronicle*. In the process, he argued that the date 1140 that appears in the text was a copyist error for 1096 and that the *Solomon bar Simson Chronicle* is very early. He also claimed to identify the author of the narrative.

6. 1947—Isaiah Sonne, "Which Is the Oldest Narrative of the Persecution of 1096?" (Hebrew), *Zion* 12 (1947):74–81. Sonne rejected Habermann's dismissal of his views, without adducing truly new evidence. I cite the Sonne study, however, for his insistence that the problems associated with the narratives are extremely complex, that he had amassed a considerable corpus of notes, and that the issues required full-length treatment. In a sense, the present study begins with Sonne's sense of the need for full-length treatment of these important texts.

7. 1953—Yitzhak Baer, "The Persecutions of 1096" (Hebrew), in *Sefer Assaf,* ed. M. D. Cassuto et al. (Jerusalem, 1953), 126–140. Baer in a sense reverted to the original views of Harry Bresslau, but with far fuller justification. According to Baer, there are three identifiable stages in the history of the present texts: communal letters that circulated in the wake of the tragedy; an early composition, now lost; the three later narratives now available, all drawn ultimately from the earlier and better version.[8]

8. 1966—Joseph Hacker, "Concerning the Persecution of 1096" (Hebrew), *Zion* 31 (1966):226–231. In the middle section of his brief essay, Hacker noted the discrepancy between the dates for the two assaults on Worms Jewry provided in the *Solomon bar Simson Chronicle* and the *Eliezer bar Nathan Chronicle* on the one hand and the *Mainz Anonymous* on the other. Since the dating provided in the former is corroborated by a number of mid- and late-twelfth-century sources, Hacker concluded that the *Mainz Anonymous* was late and ill-informed on this matter.[9]

9. 1974—Robert Chazan, "The Hebrew First-Crusade Chronicles," *Revue des études juives* 133 (1974):235–254. I made two methodological observations: (a) All the prior studies had attempted to find one explanatory model—all three narratives independent; one the source of two; two the source of one. Such uniformity is not at all necessary. (b) It is critical to identify the precise boundaries of the narratives, where exactly they begin and end. In the light of these observations, I suggested that the *Solomon bar Simson Chronicle* is the source of the *Eliezer bar Nathan Chronicle,* but that the former and the *Mainz Anonymous* are independent of one another. I suggested that the famous sentence that includes the year 1140 is an interpolation and that the *Solomon bar Simson Chronicle* is quite early. Much of the paper was devoted to a study of the *Mainz Anonymous,* with the argument that it is a superior piece of narrative history.

10. 1978—Robert Chazan, "The Hebrew First-Crusade Chronicles:

Further Reflections," *AJS Review* 3 (1978):79–98. In this study, focused
on the *Solomon bar Simson Chronicle,* I argued for the composite nature
of the narrative. I also reexamined the issue of its dating and came to
the conclusion that this narrative was not in fact early.

11. 1982—Anna Sapir Abulafia, "The Interrelationship between the
Hebrew Chronicles on the First Crusade," *Journal of Semitic Studies* 27
(1982):221–239. Abulafia surveyed the major views of the relationship
between the narratives in a most useful fashion. At the close of the essay,
she indicated her support for a position quite close to that of Sonne.

12. 1984—Robert Chazan, "The Deeds of the Jewish Community of
Cologne," *Journal of Jewish Studies* 35 (1984):185–195. While focusing
on the narrative concerning the Jews of Cologne, I reinforced my earlier
argument that the *Solomon bar Simson Chronicle* is an edited composition and that it is the source of the *Eliezer bar Nathan Chronicle.* I
studied in some detail the ways in which the latter adapted its source.[10]

This review of major studies has, I believe, been useful and instructive.
Let me conclude by identifying a number of methodological conclusions
that flow from this review.

The precise boundaries of each narrative—exactly where each begins
and ends—must be ascertained. Much early argumentation was
based on the contention that the opening section of the *Solomon bar
Simson Chronicle* is lost. Rejection of that contention has had an
impact on the thinking of a number of the researchers reviewed.

Each of the narratives must be examined to discern whether it is the
work of one hand or a composite text. If any of the narratives is a
composite text, then its constituent elements must be carefully identified and analyzed.

Allowance must be made for the uniqueness of each narrative. Many
researchers have assumed that the three texts are interchangeable,
with common objectives and themes. Such an assumption is unwarranted.

The imaginative core of each narrative and primary unit must be
identified. Each of the available sources—whether an entire narrative
or a discernible unit within a composite narrative—must be examined
as a literary and imaginative whole, with major themes and emphases.

Medieval textual borrowing must be properly understood. Much of
the discussion of the relationship of the three texts has been carried

out without sufficient sense of precisely how medieval Jewish authors treated sources at their disposal.

The assumption of a uniform relationship among all three narratives—all independent, or two derived from one, or one derived from two—should be rejected. It is perfectly reasonable to find one relationship between two of the narratives and a completely different relationship between two others.

Abbreviations

The following texts are cited by these abbreviations in the notes and the bibliography.

Chazan   Translations of the *Mainz Anonymous* and the *Solomon bar Simson Chronicle,* in Robert Chazan, *European Jewry and the First Crusade.* Berkeley, 1987.

Eidelberg   Translations of the *Mainz Anonymous,* the *Solomon bar Simson Chronicle,* and the *Eliezer bar Nathan Chronicle,* in Shlomo Eidelberg, trans., *The Jews and the Crusaders.* Madison, 1977.

Habermann *Sefer Gezerot Ashkenaz ve-Zarfat.* Ed. Abraham Habermann. Jerusalem, 1945.

MGH, Ss.   *Monumenta Germaniae Historica, Scriptores.* 32 vols. Hanover, 1826–1934.

N&S   *Hebräische Berichte über die Judenverfolgungen während der Kreüzzuge.* Ed. Adolf Neubauer and Moritz Stern. Berlin, 1892.

RHC, Occ.   *Recueil des historiens des croisades, historiens occidentaux.* 5 vols. Paris, 1844–1895.

Notes

PROLOGUE

1. On this early stage in the history of Ashkenazic Jewry, see Robert Chazan, *Medieval Stereotypes and Modern Antisemitism* (Berkeley, 1997), chap. 1.

2. On this challenge, see Robert Chazan, "Jewish Suffering: The Interplay of Medieval Christian and Jewish Perspectives," in *Lectures on Medieval Judaism at Trinity University,* Occasional Papers 2 (Kalamazoo, 1998); and this volume, chap. 9.

3. This new accusation is illustrated and analyzed in Chazan, *Medieval Stereotypes and Modern Antisemitism,* chaps. 3 and 4.

4. The Blois incident itself has been dissected in Shalom Spiegel, *The Last Trial,* trans. Judah Goldin (Philadelphia, 1967), and in Robert Chazan, "The Blois Incident of 1171: A Study in Jewish Intercommunal Organization," *Proceedings of the American Academy for Jewish Research* 36 (1968):13–31.

5. For a listing of the surviving source material, see Chazan, "The Blois Incident of 1171," 14 n. 3. Susan Einbinder, in an article titled "Pucellina of Blois: Romantic Myths and Narrative Conventions," soon to appear in *Jewish History,* has found a number of additional poetic responses to the Blois episode.

6. For a full discussion of the Orléans letter, see below.

7. I have studied the Blois letters, both the three time-bound missives and the time-bound and timeless communication composed in neighboring Orléans, in "The Timebound and the Timeless: Medieval Jewish Narration of Events," *History and Memory* 6 (1994):5–35. The present chapter draws extensively on that earlier study. The Blois incident is special in providing us examples of rigorously time-bound materials, wholly timeless materials, and the special combination available in the Orléans letter.

8. The four Blois letters were appended by an editor into a series of historical accounts that includes the lengthiest of the Hebrew First Crusade narratives, the

so-called *Solomon bar Simson Chronicle,* and that concludes with some observations on late-twelfth-century Speyer Jewry. They can be found in Adolf Neubauer and Moritz Stern, eds. (hereafter N&S), *Hebräische Berichte über die
Judenverfolgungen während der Kreuzzüge* (Berlin, 1892), 31–35; they were
republished by Abraham Habermann (henceforth Habermann), *Sefer Gezerot
Ashkenaz ve-Zarfat* (Jerusalem, 1945), 142–146. On the sequence of the *Solomon bar Simson Chronicle,* the Blois letters, and the note on Speyer Jewry, see
Robert Chazan, "A Twelfth-Century Communal History of Spires Jewry," *Revue des études juives* 128 (1969):253–257.

9. I have omitted a brief sentence of explication introduced by the narrator,
in order to preserve the continuity of the royal remarks.

10. N&S, 34; Habermann, 145. As will be the case throughout this book,
the translations are my own, unless otherwise noted. A word about translation
policy is in order. The texts of the Blois letters and the three Hebrew First
Crusade narratives that are the focus of this study are all in a dolorous state,
with scribal errors throughout. The N&S text presents a number of emendations
that help make sense of garbled passages, with the manuscript reading foot-
noted. I will regularly make use of the emended readings presented in N&S. On
occasion, Habermann further emends a difficult reading. Where I make use of
such emendations, I shall cite Habermann in the notes. On very rare occasions,
I will offer my own emendations. Biblical texts are almost always cited from the
new Jewish Publication Society translation.

11. The Troyes letter includes a résumé of the information contained in the
Paris epistle, along with mourning regulations to be observed in memory of the
Blois martyrs. The Nathan ben Meshullam letter is a private communication
intended ultimately for Rabbi Jacob Tam and recounts negotiations undertaken
by the author with the archbishop of Sens, a brother of Count Theobald.

12. There is a valuable informational letter sent by the band of Jews who
had elected to remain in Mainz during the difficult days of the organization of
the Third Crusade. On this important letter, see Robert Chazan, "Emperor Frederick I, the Third Crusade, and the Jews," *Viator* 8 (1970):83–93.

13. The Cairo Genizah is of course replete with informational material that
would not normally have survived the ravages of time.

14. There has often been a tendency to depict medieval Jews as bookish and
unworldly.

15. Prose narrative of course lends itself to the transmission of detailed and
accurate information.

16. Again, see Chazan, "Jewish Suffering"; and this volume, chap. 9.

17. I would emphasize the great difficulty in translating these medieval Hebrew poems, so rich in allusion to biblical and rabbinic sources. In making the
following translation, I have been concerned, above all, with conveying a broad
sense of the thrust of the poet's depiction. I would again like to acknowledge
the assistance of my colleague, Baruch Levine, with this difficult translation.

18. This is a difficult line to translate. The author plays on a talmudic argument in T. B. Shabbat 70a, to provide the sense of both distinctiveness and
destruction.

19. Embedded here is a play on the name of Theobald.

20. This is a reference to the prayer that originated in the Yom Kippur liturgy and was eventually transferred to a regular place in the daily service. One of its central themes is the requirement to worship the one true God and the nullity of other faiths. For more on the significance of this prayer, see below, n. 26.

21. This poem by Ephraim ben Jacob of Bonn, chronicler of Jewish fate during the Second Crusade and of a series of late-twelfth-century anti-Jewish incidents that include the Blois episode, can be found in Habermann, 133–137.

22. Recall Chazan, "The Timebound and the Timeless," with its full analysis of the Orléans letter. The Orléans letter can be found in N&S, 31–34, and in Habermann, 142–144.

23. Rabbi Jacob Tam was the great intellectual and political leader of northern French Jewry at this juncture. For a full description of his activities, see Ephraim E. Urbach, Ba'alei ha-Tosafot, 5th ed., 2 vols. (Jerusalem, 1986), 1: 60–113. Rabbi Jacob Tam is reputed to have died during the same Jewish calendar year as the Blois incident, meaning that the letter was ordered and ostensibly written shortly after the incidents depicted.

24. Again, see Einbinder, "Pucellina of Blois."

25. On trial by ordeal, see the recent study of Robert Bartlett, Trial by Fire and Water: The Medieval Judicial Ordeal (Oxford, 1986).

26. The highlighting of the prayer 'Alenu le-shabeaḥ as recited by the martyrs is most innovative and interesting. In the extensive First Crusade narratives, the prayer on the lips of dying martyrs was invariably the shema', the brief formula of Deut. 6:4. Three considerations suggest themselves for the introduction of the 'Alenu le-shabeaḥ:

1. The first is that of altered circumstances. In 1096, the setting was one of popular assault, with little time for Jewish response; in 1171, the setting was one of protracted Jewish preparedness for martyrdom, with the Jews chanting the longer prayer on their way to the pyre.

2. While the monotheistic message of Deut. 6:4 surely implied, from the Jewish perspective, criticism of Christianity, the contrast between Judaism and other faiths is lavishly depicted in the 'Alenu le-shabeaḥ. For a late-twelfth-century version of the prayer with extensive castigation of other faiths (i.e., Christianity), see Yisrael Ta-Shma, "The Source and Place of the Prayer 'Alenu le-shabeaḥ" (Hebrew), in The Frank Talmage Memorial Volume, ed. Barry Walfish, 2 vols. (Haifa, 1993), 1, Heb. sect., 90.

3. Given the original placement of the 'Alenu le-shabeaḥ in the liturgy of the Day of Atonement, the atonement motif, to be discussed shortly, is reinforced through this prayer. In his "Source and Place of the Prayer," 85–98, Ta-Shma discusses the evolution of the 'Alenu le-shabeaḥ and a number of other prayers into the concluding section of the daily services, a development that Ta-Shma traces to the second half of the twelfth century. Ta-Shma argues convincingly for the internal dynamics of liturgical change as the basis for this development, which again goes far beyond the 'Alenu prayer. I would tentatively suggest that the liturgical developments traced by Ta-Shma and the issues treated in my analysis probably reinforce each other. That is to say, the liturgical changes enhanced awareness among the Jews of the late twelfth century of the 'Alenu prayer, while a growing Jewish concern with the contrast between the Jewish and Christian visions and an enhanced awareness of the centrality of sacrifice and atonement influenced the desire to project the 'Alenu prayer into greater prominence in the liturgy.

27. N&S, 32; Habermann, 143.

28. Here I have accepted a Habermann emendation to the problematic manuscript reading.

29. Again I have accepted a Habermann emendation.

30. N&S, 32; Habermann, 143.

31. N&S, 33; Habermann, 144.

32. N&S, 32; Habermann, 142.

33. N&S, 32; Habermann, 142.

34. The story of Gedaliah ben Ahikam can be found in 2 Kings 25:2226. He does not appear in the account of the destruction of the First Temple in 2 Chron.

35. The four minor fasts are specified in Tos. Sotah 6:10 and T. B. Rosh haShanah 18b.

36. Of the four minor fasts, the only one that might have been cited as superseded by the fast for the Blois martyrs had to be the Fast of Gedaliah. None of the other three would have been appropriate. In *Zakhor: Jewish History and Jewish Memory* (Seattle, 1982), 48–52, Yosef Haim Yerushalmi focuses on the fascinating history of the fast of the twentieth of Sivan, a history that continued down into the twentieth century. Yerushalmi rightfully emphasizes the role played in this long history by the halakhic authority of Rabbi Jacob Tam and by the curious and powerful formulation he introduced.

37. N&S, 32; Habermann, 142.

38. For a medieval rendition of the straightforward reading of these verses, see the commentary of Samuel ben Meir, ad loc. For a modern instance of the same sort of straightforward rendition, see Baruch A. Levine, *The JPS Torah Commentary: Leviticus* (Philadelphia, 1989), ad loc.

39. Sifra, ad loc. It is important to note that the commentary of Solomon ben Isaac (Rashi), which would have been highly influential in mid-twelfth-century Ashkenazic Jewry, paraphrases this same midrashic tradition.

40. Recall this item in the letter, as noted above.

41. See, *inter alia,* Sifra, ad loc, and T. B. Sanhedrin 52a.

42. Gen. 8:2021.

43. Recall the poem of Ephraim ben Jacob cited earlier and the centrality of sacrificial imagery.

44. N&S, 32; Habermann, 142.

45. See above, n. 36, for the continuity of the fast, engendered in part by the striking formulations that we have noted.

46. Isa. 6.

47. On the assaults of 1096, see Robert Chazan, *European Jewry and the First Crusade* (Berkeley, 1987).

48. I have once more accepted a Habermann emendation.

49. N&S, 47; Habermann, 93. The three Hebrew First Crusade narratives are available in English translation by Shlomo Eidelberg (henceforth Eidelberg), *The Jews and the Crusaders* (Madison, 1977); two of the three—the *Mainz Anonymous* and the *Solomon bar Simson Chronicle*—are translated as appendices in my *European Jewry and the First Crusade* (henceforth Chazan). Translations of these passages can be found in Eidelberg, 99, and Chazan, 225.

50. N&S, 23–24; Habermann, 51–52; Eidelberg, 59; Chazan, 285.

51. For some of this poetry, see Habermann, 61–71 and 82–92.

CHAPTER 1: THE HEBREW FIRST CRUSADE NARRATIVES

1. The Commission für Geschichte der Juden in Deutschland was organized in 1885 by the Deutsch Israelitische Gemeindebund. This second volume of sources published under its auspices, entitled *Hebräische Berichte über die Judenverfolgungen während der Kreuzzüge,* was edited by Adolf Neubauer and Moritz Stern (cited throughout as N&S). Precisely how these two interacted is not clear. Neubauer was far the more renowned of the pair. The German translation was provided by Seligman Baer, a distinguished philologist.

2. The fourth and fifth pieces are of considerable interest. The fourth is the narrative of Jewish fate during the Second Crusade composed by Ephraim ben Jacob of Bonn, followed by a listing of anti-Jewish incidents from 1171 through 1196. I have studied the Second Crusade narrative in "R. Ephraim of Bonn's *Sefer Zechirah,*" *Revue des études juives* 132 (1973):119–126; I have studied the listing of incidents in "Ephraim ben Jacob's Compilation of Twelfth-Century Persecutions," *Jewish Quarterly Review* 84 (1993–94):397–416. The fifth and closing piece in the volume is a depiction of the fate of Mainz Jewry during the Third Crusade, written by Elazar ben Judah of Worms. I have studied this valuable piece in "Emperor Frederick I, the Third Crusade, and the Jews."

3. It is not clear why the texts were presented in this order. In all likelihood, the choice was dictated by fullness of coverage and length. The order adopted in N&S was repeated in Habermann and Eidelberg. I have long suspected that this ordering may have subtly influenced researchers in their approach to these texts. In the translations I appended to *European Jewry and the First Crusade,* I chose to place the *Mainz Anonymous* first, out of my sense that it is the oldest and most reliable of the accounts.

4. N&S, 1–30; Habermann, 24–59; Eidelberg, 21–71; Chazan, 243–297. The designation *Solomon bar Simson Chronicle* may well be inaccurate. As noted below, the reference to Solomon bar Simson as author may refer to the Altenahr section only, to the entire Cologne section only, or to the entire narrative. I shall, nonetheless, use this widely accepted designation.

5. N&S, 36–46; Habermann, 72–82; Eidelberg, 79–93. In *European Jewry and the First Crusade,* I did not provide a translation of this narrative, because I felt it added little to the investigation of the events of 1096. While the name of the author does not appear in the text, the poems inserted show the acrostic Eliezer bar Nathan. Whether the Eliezer bar Nathan who composed the four dirges and—in all likelihood—the prose framework as well is identical with the famous halakhist of that name will be fully addressed in chap. 6.

6. N&S, 47–57; Habermann, 93–104; Eidelberg, 99–115; Chazan, 225–242. This narrative was given the designation *Mainz Anonymous* because of the length and fullness of the account of events in Mainz.

7. On the manuscripts, see below. Truly popular historical works, like *Sefer Yosippon* (to be discussed in the closing chapter) or Abraham ibn Daud's *Sefer ha-Kabbalah,* are available in a far larger number of manuscript copies.

8. The 'Emek ha-Bakha' was a popular work and was printed numerous times. There is an edition with critical notes by Meir Letteris (Cracow, 1895). It is interesting to note that none of the other well-known Sephardic historians

of the sixteenth century included information on the First Crusade assaults in their compositions. On the relationship of Joseph *ha-cohen*'s account of 1096 to the *Eliezer bar Nathan Chronicle,* see below, chap. 6 nn. 7–8.

9. David Gans's *Zemah David* was also a popular work and was likewise printed numerous times. A critical edition has recently been provided by Mordechai Breuer (Jerusalem, 1983).

10. All the major recent surveys of the First Crusade include mention of the assaults upon the Jews, with regular reference to the Hebrew narratives. See, for example, Steven Runciman, *A History of the Crusades,* 3 vols. (Cambridge, 1951–67); Kenneth M. Setton, ed., *A History of the Crusades,* 6 vols. (Madison, 1969–89); Hans Eberhard Mayer, *The Crusades,* trans. John Gillingham (Oxford, 1972); Jonathan Riley-Smith, *The Crusades: A Short History* (London, 1987). These treatments are all heavily dependent on the influential catalog of events composed by Heinrich Hagenmeyer, "Chronologie de la première croisade," *Revue de l' Orient latin* 6 (1898):214–293 and 490–549, which shows full awareness of the three Hebrew narratives.

11. See, for example, the place accorded the assaults of 1096 in the first volume of the fullest history of antisemitism available to date, Leon Poliakov's *History of Anti-Semitism,* trans. Richard Howard et al., 4 vols. (New York, 1965–85).

12. I have rejected the view of 1096 as a turning point in Jewish history in *European Jewry and the First Crusade,* 197–210. Quite independently, Simon Schwarzfuchs came to the same conclusions—see his "The Place of the Crusades in Jewish History" (Hebrew), in *Tarbut ve-Hevrah be-Toldot Yisrael bi-Me ha-Benayim,* ed. Menaham Ben-Sasson et al. (Jerusalem, 1989), 251–267.

13. I have argued for the influence of the late-eleventh-century environment in *European Jewry and the First Crusade,* 132–136 and 192–197.

14. Without the three Hebrew narratives, reconstruction of the events of 1096 would have to be based on the brief comments of Christian chroniclers and the evidence available from the Hebrew poetry. The results would be most unsatisfying.

15. For the manuscript of the *Eliezer bar Nathan Chronicle,* see N&S, vii–ix.

16. For the manuscript of the *Solomon bar Simson Chronicle,* see ibid., vii; for the *Mainz Anonymous,* see ibid., ix–xi.

17. The edition of Neubauer and Stern has often been severely criticized and amended. Much of the criticism and many of the emendations, however, flow from the parlous state of the manuscripts. For the impact of the defective state of the manuscripts on my translation policy, see above, prol. n. 10.

18. Much—although certainly not all—of the Mainz information is shared by all three narratives. For discussion of the borrowings from the *Mainz Anonymous* by the *Solomon bar Simson Chronicle,* see chap. 4.

19. For the relationship between these two narratives, see chap. 6.

20. For a review of prior analyses of the relationships among the three narratives and their dating, see the appendix.

21. For full discussion of this passage, see chap. 3.

22. Again, for a discussion of the identity of the author of this narrative, see

chap. 6. In the same chapter, the issue of the dating of the narrative will be fully addressed.

23. See appendix.

24. I have examined the variety of Marcus's views in my "The Facticity of Medieval Narrative: A Case Study of the Hebrew First-Crusade Narratives," *AJS Review*, 17 (1991):31–56.

25. Ivan G. Marcus, "From Politics to Martyrdom: Shifting Paradigms in the Hebrew Narratives of the 1096 Crusader Riots," *Prooftexts* 2 (1982):42.

26. This revolution in stance towards talmudic data was initiated by Jacob Neusner and is widely associated with his work.

27. Marcus, in "From Politics to Martyrdom," seems to suggest a rigid set of objectives expressed through a "pre-conceived religious-literary scheme." For a critique of this supposed scheme, see Chazan, "The Facticity of Medieval Narrative," 39–41.

28. Jeremy Cohen, "The 'Persecutions of 1096'—From Martyrdom to Martyrology: The Sociocultural Context of the Hebrew Crusade Chronicles" (Hebrew), *Zion* 59 (1994):169–208.

29. For the literature on this debate, see Jonathan Riley-Smith, *The First Crusaders, 1095–1131* (Cambridge, 1997), 72 n. 116.

30. This is the general thesis of Yerushalmi's important *Zakhor*.

31. Ibid., 37–38.

32. Alan Mintz, Ḥurban: *Responses to Catastrophe in Hebrew Literature* (New York, 1984).

33. Ibid., 89–90.

CHAPTER 2: THE *MAINZ ANONYMOUS*

1. See chap. 1 and appendix.

2. I first argued the superiority of the *Mainz Anonymous* in "The Hebrew First-Crusade Chronicles," *Revue des études juives* 133 (1974):235–254. I utilized the *Mainz Anonymous* quite heavily in *European Jewry and the First Crusade*, out of my sense of its superiority. I analyzed it far more fully in "The Mainz Anonymous: Historiographic Perspectives," in *Jewish History and Jewish Memory: Essays in Honor of Yosef Haim Yerushalmi*, ed. Elisheva Carlebach et al. (Hanover, 1998), 54–69. Portions of the present chapter are taken from this last study.

3. See chap. 6.

4. See chap. 3.

5. N&S, 47 and 57; Habermann, 93 and 104; Eidelberg, 99 and 115; Chazan, 225 and 242.

6. N&S, 47 and 57; Habermann, 93 and 104; Eidelberg, 99 and 115; Chazan, 225 and 242.

7. I would suggest that the *Mainz Anonymous* in fact ended with Mainz. As I will argue fully in chap. 4, I am now inclined to see the Speyer-Worms-Mainz segment of the *Solomon bar Simson Chronicle* as a reworking of the *Mainz Anonymous*. Certainly, the Cologne segment of the former reflects completely

different authorship and historical perspective, indicating that the editor, who made use of the *Mainz Anonymous,* had no continuation beyond Mainz available to him. More closely yet, I would argue (somewhat more tentatively) that the observation about the rest of the community may well have been very close to the end of the entire narrative. The truncated sentence certainly sounds very much like a concluding observation. We have a version of this same sentence in the *Solomon bar Simson Chronicle* (N&S, 14; Habermann, 39; Eidelberg, 43; Chazan, 267). There it serves as something of a conclusion, although the editor then adds a major additional unit to his account.

8. Examples of first-person interjection abound all through the *Solomon bar Simson Chronicle.* See chap. 3.

9. Again, see the suggestion advanced above, n. 7.

10. Because of the clear sequential progression in the *Mainz Anonymous,* I shall make no reference in the following discussion to specific pages in the available editions, except when quoting directly.

11. Note the absence of any awareness of papal initiative in the crusading endeavor.

12. Note in particular the author's awareness of both baronial and popular response to the crusading message. I have studied in some detail the accuracy of the *Mainz Anonymous* depiction of the First Crusade in "The First Crusade as Reflected in the Earliest Hebrew Narrative," *Viator* 29 (1998):25–38. Guibert of Nogent's well-known story of an assault on the Jews of Rouen serves as indication of the deflection of some French crusading zeal in an anti-Jewish direction, although clearly there was little overt expression to such sentiments in France.

13. For the citation in the Trier unit, see N&S, 25; Habermann, 52–53; Eidelberg, 62; Chazan, 287–288. For full discussion of the Trier unit, see chap. 5.

14. Recall the recent controversy over the point at which martyrdom emerged as a central ideal of the crusade. See above, chap. 1 n. 29.

15. The two Christian chroniclers that focus most heavily on popular crusading in Germany are Albert of Aachen and Ekkehard of Aura.

16. Highlighted in the depictions of both Albert and Ekkehard.

17. N&S, 48; Habermann, 94; Eidelberg, 100; Chazan, 226–227.

18. The extensive portrayal of the failed efforts of the bishop of Trier in the Trier unit of the *Solomon bar Simson Chronicle* leaves not a shadow of doubt as to his sincere desire to protect his Jews. See chap. 5.

19. Note the specification of punishment of burghers, not crusaders.

20. For the importance of this reference to the return of converts to Judaism for the dating of the *Mainz Anonymous,* see below.

21. N&S, 48; Habermann, 94; Eidelberg, 101; Chazan, 227.

22. Note the Jewess Minna, cited a bit farther on, who neither remained in her home nor sought refuge in the episcopal palace.

23. The *Mainz Anonymous* and the *Solomon bar Simson Chronicle,* while agreeing on their dating of the assaults in Speyer and Mainz, diverge in their dating of the two Worms episodes. The former dates the first attack on 5 May and the second on 18 May; the latter gives dates of 18 May and 25 May. On

this divergence, see the eighth study listed in the appendix, and app. n. 9. It should be further noted that the latter dating poses internal problems for the narrative. The *Solomon bar Simson Chronicle*, like the *Mainz Anonymous*, dates Emicho's arrival in Mainz on 25 May. He also has Mainz Jewry disquieted over the reports of both assaults in Worms and involved in efforts at self-protection prior to Emicho's arrival. Dating the second assault in Worms on the day of Emicho's arrival thus presents serious internal difficulties. By contrast, the *Mainz Anonymous* sequence is smooth.

24. This item was one of the considerations that led some early analysts of the *Mainz Anonymous* to suggest a late, fourteenth-century dating. However, mention of a well-poisoning accusation by no means necessitates a fourteenth-century provenance. Again, I shall argue below for early composition of the narrative.

25. N&S, 49; Habermann, 96; Eidelberg, 103; Chazan, 230.

26. Recall that these Worms martyrs had more time to ponder an impending assault than did the Jews of Speyer or the victims of the first assault in Worms.

27. Among the intertextual clues are: "Do not raise your hand against the boy"—Gen. 22:12; "Let me not look on as the child dies"—Gen. 21:16; "He bound his son Isaac"—Gen. 22:9; use of the designation *ma'akhelet* for the knife used in the slaughter—Gen. 22:10, while the term *sakin* is regularly utilized throughout all the rest of the *Mainz Anonymous* for a knife.

28. Most of the ten books into which the *Gesta Francorum* is divided end with either God's praise or a prayer directed to the divine.

29. Recall the issue of dating noted above, n. 23.

30. For fuller discussion of this ambivalent portrait of the archbishop of Mainz, see chap. 7.

31. Note Albert of Aachen's excoriation of the popular German crusading bands for their belief in a wondrous goose that would lead them to the Holy Sepulcher. See Albert of Aachen, *Liber Christianae expeditionis*, in *RHC, Occ.*, 5 vols. (Paris, 1844–95), 4:292.

32. For another Jew who chose to remain at home, see below.

33. The identity of this Count Emicho has been reconsidered of late. Long identified as Count Emicho of Leiningen, recent scholars have shifted the identification to Count Emicho of Flonheim. See Ingo Toussaint, *Die Grafen von Leinigen: Studien zur leiningischen Genealogie und Territorialgeschichte bis zur Teilung von 1317/18* (Sigmaringen, 1982), 25–28; and H. Möhring, "Graf Emicho und die Judenvergolgungen von 1096," *Rheinische Vierteljahresblätter* 56 (1992):97–111.

34. Again, these Jews had considerable time to ponder their fate and prepare for death.

35. N&S, 54; Habermann, 101; Eidelberg, 110; Chazan, 238. Jews killing children by strangulation is not mentioned elsewhere in the Hebrew narratives.

36. Recall the prior mention of Jews staying at home, even in Mainz. See above, n. 32.

37. Recall the suggestion that Mainz was the endpoint of the *Mainz Anonymous* in its original form. See above, n. 7.

38. Haim Hillel Ben Sasson, "The Objectives of Medieval Jewish

Chronography and Its Problematics" (Hebrew), in *Historionim ve-Askolot His-toriot* (Jerusalem, 1953), 42–48, emphasizes the political lessons that the 1096 Jewish chroniclers sought to convey.

39. While the focus of the *Mainz Anonymous* and the *Solomon bar Simson Chronicle* is on those communities where the efforts at securing safety were unsuccessful, they do note examples of effective protection. It must be borne in mind that most of early Ashkenazic Jewry in fact emerged unscathed from the turbulence depicted in our narratives.

40. This objective is emphasized by a number of students of the narratives. See most recently Avraham Grossman, "The Roots of *Kiddush ha-Shem* in Early Ashkenaz" (Hebrew), in *Kedushat ha-Ḥayim ve-Ḥeruf ha-Nefesh*, ed. Isaiah M. Gafni and Aviezer Ravitzky (Jerusalem, 1992), 99–130, esp. 119–127.

41. For a discussion of the relevant legal rulings and literary precedents, see chap. 11.

42. For the talmudic story of the four hundred young captives—female and male—who took their own lives rather than submit to Roman defilement, again see chap. 11.

43. The famous story of Masada and its martyrs was known to the early Ashkenazic Jews through the medieval Hebrew *Yosippon*. As to why this precedent was not cited in our narratives, see chap. 12. For a discussion of the legal rectitude and innovative nature of these acts of murder, see Haym Soloveitchik, "Religious Law and Change: The Medieval Ashkenazic Example," *AJS Review* 12 (1987):205–221. While Grossman, "The Roots of *Kiddush ha-Shem* in Early Ashkenaz," challenges Soloveitchik's views on the innovativeness of martyrdom by suicide, he agrees fully as to the unprecedented nature of the martyrological murders.

44. I made a sustained argument for early dating in "The Mainz Anonymous: Historiographic Perspectives."

45. N&S, 48; Habermann, 94; Eidelberg, 101; Chazan, 227.

46. The return of the converts to Judaism in June 1097 is reported by Ekkehard of Aura in his *Chronicon universale*, in *MGH, Ss.*, 6:208.

47. Surely by the middle decades of the twelfth century a more general designation for the empire would have been appropriate.

48. N&S, 48; Habermann, 94; Eidelberg, 100; Chazan, 226.

49. For the failure of the army of Sennacherib, see 2 Kings 18:13–19:37 and 2 Chron. 32:1–22, with the former more fully developed than the latter. Striking in the biblical Sennacherib story are the arrogance of the ultimately unsuccessful Assyrians and their taunting emphasis on the hopelessness of Jewish circumstances; both themes recur in the *Mainz Anonymous* depiction of the popular German crusading bands.

50. See chap. 5.

51. See again, Chazan, "The First Crusade as Reflected in the Earliest Hebrew Narrative."

52. Recall the smooth flow of the dates indicated above, n. 23.

53. N&S, 47; Habermann, 93; Eidelberg, 99; Chazan, 225.

54. On the place of Jerusalem in the Hebrew narratives, see Robert Chazan, "Jerusalem as Christian Symbol during the First Crusade: Jewish Awareness and

Response," in *Jerusalem: Its Sanctity and Centrality to Judaism, Christianity, and Islam,* ed. Lee I. Levine (New York, 1999), 382–392.

55. N&S, 47; Habermann, 93; Eidelberg, 99; Chazan, 225.

56. N&S, 52; Habermann, 99; Eidelberg, 108; Chazan, 235.

57. N&S, 54 (Isaiah) and 55 (Lamentations); Habermann, 101 and 102; Eidelberg, 110 and 112; Chazan, 237 and 239.

58. N&S, 49–50; Habermann, 96; Eidelberg, 103; Chazan, 230.

59. N&S, 55; Habermann, 102; Eidelberg, 111; Chazan, 239.

60. N&S, 50; Habermann, 96; Eidelberg, 103; Chazan, 230.

61. N&S, 53; Habermann, 100; Eidelberg, 109; Chazan, 236.

62. N&S, 53; Habermann, 100; Eidelberg, 109; Chazan, 236.

63. N&S, 55; Habermann, 102; Eidelberg, 112; Chazan, 240.

64. I have here accepted a Habermann emendation. Recall the translation policy indicated earlier, prol. n. 10.

65. N&S, 56; Habermann, 104; Eidelberg, 114; Chazan, 241–242.

66. 2 Maccabees, Josephus, and *Yosippon* all place this martyr in the days of the Antiochene persecutions. The rabbinic sources place her in the days of Roman persecution. See chaps. 11 and 12.

67. N&S, 49; Habermann, 95; Eidelberg, 102; Chazan, 228–229.

68. I have studied this Christian claim from the eleventh through the fourteenth century in "Jewish Suffering." For fuller discussion, see chap. 9. In "The Roots of *Kiddush ha-Shem* in Early Ashkenaz," Grossman—approaching these issues from a somewhat different point of view—notes the serious problem of potential abandonment of Judaism in early Ashkenazic Jewry.

69. N&S, 50 (Worms), 50–51 (Worms), 51 (Mainz), and 56 (Mainz); Habermann, 97 (two Worms incidents), 98 (Mainz), and 103–104 (Mainz); Eidelberg, 104 (Worms), 105 (Worms), 106 (Mainz), and 113–114 (Mainz); Chazan, 231 (Worms), 231–232 (Worms), 233 (Mainz), and 241–242 (Mainz).

70. N&S, 47–48; Habermann, 94; Eidelberg, 100; Chazan, 226.

71. See above, n. 67.

72. Gen. 22:2 and 22:16–18.

CHAPTER 3: THE EDITORIAL PROLOGUE AND EPILOGUE

1. Note the importance of this issue in the prior analyses of the relationship of the three Hebrew First Crusade narratives. See appendix.

2. N&S, 1 and 30; Habermann, 24 and 59; Eidelberg, 21 and 71; Chazan, 243 and 297.

3. See Chazan, "A Twelfth-Century Communal History of Spires Jewry."

4. The later Speyer editor introduces the *Solomon bar Simson Chronicle* as follows: "Now I shall recount the development of the persecution in the rest of the communities that were killed for his [God's] unique Name." The Speyer editor added interpolations twice early on, once at the close of the brief Speyer unit and then at the end of the brief Worms unit.

5. Recall extensive discussion of this material in the prologue.

6. These closing items are extremely valuable also. On medieval Jewish

historical anthologies, see Eli Yassif, "The Hebrew Narrative Anthology in the Middle Ages," *Prooftexts* 17 (1997):153–175. Yassif focuses on the fourteenth-century anthology compiled by Eliezer ben Asher *ha-Levi* and argues that it was much influenced by contemporary German world histories. The briefer and more focused anthology discussed here adds a further dimension to Yassif's important analysis.

7. N&S, 9; Habermann, 33; Eidelberg, 34; Chazan, 257.

8. N&S, 11; Habermann, 36; Eidelberg, 39; Chazan, 262.

9. N&S, 14; Habermann, 40; Eidelberg, 44; Chazan, 268.

10. N&S, 15; Habermann, 40; Eidelberg, 45; Chazan, 268.

11. N&S, 17; Habermann, 43; Eidelberg, 49; Chazan, 273.

12. N&S, 25; Habermann, 52; Eidelberg, 62; Chazan, 287.

13. N&S, 28; Habermann, 56; Eidelberg, 67; Chazan, 293.

14. N&S, 29; Habermann, 57; Eidelberg, 68; Chazan, 294.

15. N&S, 1–2; Habermann, 24–25; Eidelberg, 21–22; Chazan, 243–244.

16. N&S, 3–17; Habermann, 25–43; Eidelberg, 22–49; Chazan, 244–273. For my claim, see chap. 4.

17. N&S, 17–25; Habermann, 43–52; Eidelberg, 49–61; Chazan, 273–287.

18. N&S, 25–29; Habermann, 52–59; Eidelberg, 61–68; Chazan, 287–294.

19. N&S, 29; Habermann, 57; Eidelberg, 68; Chazan, 294.

20. N&S, 29–30; Habermann, 57–59; Eidelberg, 68–91; Chazan, 294–297.

21. Recall the study by Eli Yassif, cited above, n. 6.

22. For extended discussion, see chap. 5.

23. For evidence of the arrival of crusading bands, see N&S, 18 (Wevelinghofen), 21 (Xanten), and 23 (Moers); Habermann, 45, 48, and 50; Eidelberg, 51, 55, and 58; Chazan, 275–276, 280, and 284.

24. N&S, 21; Habermann, 48; Eidelberg, 55; Chazan, 280.

25. Note the important study of the disillusionment occasioned by the Second Crusade by Giles Constable, "The Second Crusade as Seen by Contemporaries," *Traditio* 9 (1953):213–281.

26. It seems that Ephraim of Bonn, in parallel fashion, was moved by an impending crusade—the third—to write up the previous crusade, with high hopes of divine vengeance upon the crusaders. See Robert Chazan, "R. Ephraim of Bonn's *Sefer Zechirah*," *Revue des études juives* 132 (1973):119–126.

27. N&S, 30; Habermann, 59; Eidelberg, 71; Chazan, 297.

28. N&S, 21; Habermann, 48; Eidelberg, 55; Chazan, 280.

29. For fuller discussion, see chap. 5.

30. I have treated aspects of the prologue to the *Solomon bar Simson Chronicle* in "The Hebrew First-Crusade Narratives and Their Intertextual Messages," in *Ki Baruch Hu: Ancient Near Eastern, Biblical, and Judaic Studies in Honor of Baruch A. Levine,* ed. Robert Chazan, William W. Hallo, and Lawrence H. Schiffman (Winona Lake, 1998), 465–480. Some of the material in the following discussion is taken from that study. Since the prologue is fairly brief, I shall not identify the sources for citations.

31. Exod. 32:33–34.

32. Again see Chazan, "The Hebrew First-Crusade Narratives and Their Intertextual Messages."

33. Ezra 8:21.

34. Lev. 16:31, 23:27, and 23:32; Num. 29:7.

35. Deut. 28:49–50.

36. Once more, given the brevity of the closing segment of the *Solomon bar Simson Chronicle*, I shall refrain from identifying specific sources for citations.

37. Albert of Aachen's *Liber Christianae expeditionis* provides the main source for information on Peter the Hermit and his followers. For a fairly full description of Peter's army, including its downfall, see Runciman, *A History of the Crusades,* 1:121–133.

38. Emicho is treated in more cursory fashion than Peter the Hermit in Albert of Aachen and—again briefly—in Ekkehard of Aura. Once more, for a good overview, see Runciman, *A History of the Crusades,* 1:137–141.

39. This mention of an eclipse reinforces the already strong evidence of late editing for the *Solomon bar Simson Chronicle.* The only eclipse at this time was in 1093, suggesting that this observation was written some time after the fact. On the eclipses of this period, see Theodor Ritter von Oppolzer, *Canon of Eclipses,* trans. Owen Gingerich (New York, 1962).

40. Lam. 3:64–66.

41. Ps. 79:12.

CHAPTER 4: THE SPEYER-WORMS-MAINZ UNIT

1. See the appendix.

2. See, for example, the position of Harry Bresslau, as depicted in the appendix.

3. See the position of Yitzhak Baer, as depicted in the appendix.

4. Again see the survey provided in the appendix.

5. On the early dating of the *Mainz Anonymous,* see chap. 2; on the late dating and composite nature of the *Solomon bar Simson Chronicle,* see chap. 3.

6. See the prologue.

7. For the original Orleans letter, see N&S, 31–34; Habermann, 142–144. For Ephraim's reworking of the original, see N&S, 66–69; Habermann, 124–126. For a discussion of the changes introduced by Ephraim, see Chazan, "Ephraim ben Jacob's Compilation of Twelfth-Century Persecutions." For broad reflections on early Ashkenazic copying techniques, with emphasis on the latitude copyists allowed themselves, see Yisrael Ta-Shma, "The Library of the Ashkenazic Sages in the 11th–12th Centuries," *Kiryat Sefer* 60 (1985):298–309, with addenda in *Kiryat Sefer* 61 (1986):581–582. Ta-Shma provided a brief overview of the same matters in "The Library of the French Sages," in *Rashi 1040–1090: Hommage à Ephraim E. Urbach,* ed. Gabrielle Sed-Rajna (Paris, 1993), 535–540. In the latter essay, Ta-Shma identifies the central aspects of the eleventh- and twelfth-century Ashkenazic library as threefold—totality, eclectic use, and active-aggressive adaptation. He defines the third of these tendencies as "the conscious rewriting of words, sentences and whole paragraphs—not to

mention omissions and additions—in whatever book they might be reading."
This description accords well with Ephraim's use of the Orléans letter and with
the *Solomon bar Simson Chronicle's* adaptation of the *Mainz Anonymous.*

8. For the setting in which the *Solomon bar Simson Chronicle* is now found
and for the lost units that preceded it, see again Chazan, "A Twelfth-Century
Communal History of Spires Jewry."

9. On the *Eliezer bar Nathan Chronicle* as an epitome of the *Solomon bar
Simson Chronicle,* see chap. 6. For Eliezer's treatment of Speyer and Worms,
see N&S, 37–38; Habermann, 73; Eidelberg, 80.

10. There is the theoretical possibility that Eliezer was working from the
Speyer collection, but that possibility seems too remote for serious consideration.

11. N&S, 2; Habermann, 25; Eidelberg, 22; Chazan, 244.

12. N&S, 2; Habermann, 25; Eidelberg, 23; Chazan, 245.

13. N&S, 2; Habermann, 25; Eidelberg, 23; Chazan, 245.

14. Recall my earlier suggestion that our present version of the *Mainz Anonymous* may not in fact be seriously lacking. See above, chap. 2 n. 7.

15. N&S, 11–13; Habermann, 36–38; Eidelberg, 39–41; Chazan, 262–265.

16. N&S, 13–14; Habermann, 38–40; Eidelberg, 41–44; Chazan, 265–268.

17. N&S, 14–16; Habermann, 40–42; Eidelberg, 44–47; Chazan, 268–271.

18. N&S, 16–17; Habermann, 42–43; Eidelberg, 47–49; Chazan, 271–273.

19. N&S, 13; Habermann, 38; Eidelberg, 41; Chazan, 265.

20. N&S, 15–16; Habermann, 41; Eidelberg, 46; Chazan, 270.

21. On Godfrey of Bouillon, see John C. Andressohn, *The Ancestry and Life
of Godfrey of Bouillon* (Bloomington, 1947). Andressohn treats the material in
the *Solomon bar Simson Chronicle* in a paragraph on p. 52.

22. N&S, 3; Habermann, 27; Eidelberg, 25; Chazan, 247.

23. N&S, 48; Habermann, 94; Eidelberg, 100; Chazan, 226.

24. On German perceptions of the First Crusade as a French initiative, see
Chazan, "The First Crusade as Reflected in the Earliest Hebrew Narrative,"
32–33.

25. N&S, 3–4; Habermann, 27; Eidelberg, 25; Chazan, 248. The Hebrew
of the first sentence is somewhat problematic. Recall this theme in the *Mainz
Anonymous;* see chap. 2. For further discussion of this important theme, see
chap. 9.

26. N&S, 2; Habermann, 25–26; Eidelberg, 23; Chazan, 245.

27. N&S, 3; Habermann, 27; Eidelberg, 25; Chazan, 247. I have introduced
my own emendation here, reading *mayim* [water] instead of *damim* [blood],
which makes no sense to me. Again, recall the translation policy indicated above,
prol. n. 10.

28. These verses include: Lam. 2:20; Isa. 42:22; Lam. 1:21; 2 Kings 21:12;
Jer. 48:17; Lam. 4:2.

29. N&S, 4; Habermann, 28; Eidelberg, 26; Chazan, 249. The Hebrew for
"divine intention" is taken from 1 Kings 12:15.

30. N&S, 11; Habermann, 36; Eidelberg, 39; Chazan, 262.

31. N&S, 13; Habermann, 38; Eidelberg, 42; Chazan, 265.

32. Isa. 57:1–2.

33. I have accepted a Habermann emendation.

34. I have again accepted a Habermann emendation.

35. N&S, 16–17; Habermann, 42–43; Eidelberg, 47–48; Chazan, 271–272.

CHAPTER 5: THE TRIER AND COLOGNE UNITS

1. The five additional units are: (1) Cologne—N&S, 17–25; Habermann, 43–52; Eidelberg, 49–61; Chazan, 273–287; (2) Trier—N&S, 25–28; Habermann, 52–56; Eidelberg, 62–67; Chazan, 287–293; (3) Metz—N&S, 28; Habermann, 56; Eidelberg, 67; Chazan, 293; (4) Ratisbon—N&S, 28; Habermann, 56; Eidelberg, 67; Chazan, 293; (5) Sh-l-'—N&S, 28–29; Habermann, 57; Eidelberg, 67–68; Chazan, 293–294. The identity of the fifth of these locales has given rise to much conjecture. In general, copyists were highly likely to err in reproducing place-names that reflected a different linguistic milieu and had no real meaning to them—see below, n. 35.

2. On this narrative, see Robert Chazan, "The Trier Unit of the Lengthy Hebrew First-Crusade Narrative," in *Between History and Literature: Studies in Honor of Isaac Barzilay*, ed. Stanley Nash (n.p., 1997), 37–49; some of the following discussion will be taken from that study. I have, however, changed my views on a number of issues, as I shall indicate. I undertook a comparative analysis of the Jewish report on events in Trier and the Christian report included in the *Gesta Treverorum* in a paper titled "Christian and Jewish Perceptions of 1096: A Case Study of Trier," delivered at a conference on the events of 1096 held at Ben Gurion University in June 1996 and scheduled to be published in *Jewish History*.

3. There are major problems with some of the dates provided in the Trier unit. These problems will be addressed at the end of this discussion.

4. N&S, 25; Habermann, 52–53; Eidelberg, 62; Chazan, 287–288.

5. Again, for problems with this dating, see below. Whatever the difficulties, it seems clear that Peter and his followers reached Trier during Holy Week.

6. See chap. 2.

7. N&S, 25; Habermann, 53; Eidelberg, 62; Chazan, 288.

8. For an analysis of some of the crusading ideals and their anti-Jewish implications, see Jonathan Riley-Smith, "The First Crusade and the Persecution of the Jews," in *Persecution and Toleration*, ed. W. J. Sheils (Oxford, 1984), 51–72; and Chazan, 75–80.

9. "They [the Jews] took their money and bribed the burghers individually"—N&S, 25; Habermann, 53; Eidelberg, 62; Chazan, 288.

10. See chap. 2 and chap. 9.

11. As noted (chap. 3), the *Mainz Anonymous* specifies 5 and 18 May as the dates of the two assaults on Worms Jewry, whereas the *Solomon bar Simson Chronicle* indicates 18 and 25 May . Both agree on 27 May as the date of the devastating attack in Mainz.

12. N&S, 25–26; Habermann, 53; Eidelberg, 62–63; Chazan, 288–289.

13. N&S, 26–28; Habermann, 53–56; Eidelberg, 63–67; Chazan, 289–293.

14. N&S, 26; Habermann, 53; Eidelberg, 63; Chazan, 289.

15. In his discussion with the Jews, Bishop Engilbert twice makes reference to crusaders as those threatening the Jews—N&S, 26; Habermann, 54; Eidelberg, 64; Chazan, 290.

16. Note the important study of Sara Schiffman, *Heinrich IV und die Bischöfe in ihrem Verhalten zu den deutschen Juden zur Zeit des ersten Kreuzzuges* (Berlin, 1931).

17. The *Gesta Treverorum*, a composite narrative account of the bishops of Trier, presents quite a different picture of the bishop and his relationship to the Jews. As noted, I have studied this divergence in "Christian and Jewish Perceptions of 1096." For further discussion of this divergence, see chap. 8.

18. Again, the portrait in the *Gesta Treverorum* is strikingly different.

19. N&S, 26; Habermann, 54; Eidelberg, 64; Chazan, 290.

20. Once more, the glaring difficulties with this dating will be addressed below.

21. According to the *Gesta Treverorum,* the insincerity of the converts was patent.

22. Again, I have accepted a Habermann emendation, in line with the translation policy indicated above, prol. n. 10.

23. N&S, 27; Habermann, 55; Eidelberg, 66; Chazan, 292.

24. This point is corroborated by the *Gesta Treverorum.*

25. Such rumination as there is stems, I propose, from the pen of the editor. In "The Trier Unit of the Lengthy Hebrew First-Crusade Chronicle," I suggested that the editor of the *Solomon bar Simson Chronicle* was in fact the author of the Trier unit. I have rejected that view, as will be clear from the ensuing discussion.

26. N&S, 25; Habermann, 52; Eidelberg, 62; Chazan, 287.

27. N&S, 25; Habermann, 53; Eidelberg, 62; Chazan, 288. Note the recurrence of this notion of a divine intention, taken from 2 Kings 12:15, found in the editorial gloss to the Mainz story. See above, chap. 4 n. 23.

28. N&S, 26; Habermann, 53; Eidelberg, 63; Chazan, 289.

29. N&S, 28; Habermann, 56; Eidelberg, 66–67; Chazan, 293.

30. I studied the Cologne unit briefly in "The Deeds of the Jewish Community of Cologne," *Journal of Jewish Studies* 35 (1984):185–195. This brief study included discussion of the Cologne tragedy itself, the Cologne unit of the *Solomon bar Simson Chronicle,* and the relationship of that Cologne account to the parallel account in the *Eliezer bar Nathan Chronicle.* My discussion of the Cologne unit in the *Solomon bar Simson Chronicle* was limited to arguing for it as quite different in focus from the Speyer-Worms-Mainz unit of the *Solomon bar Simson Chronicle.*

31. N&S, 21; Habermann, 48; Eidelberg, 55; Chazan, 280.

32. N&S, 22; Habermann, 49; Eidelberg, 57; Chazan, 282.

33. N&S, 17; Habermann, 43–44; Eidelberg, 49; Chazan, 274.

34. For Albert's description of the assault on Cologne Jewry, see *Liber Christianae expeditionis,* 4:292.

35. As indicated above, n. 1, later copyists would encounter serious difficulties in reproducing place-names utterly unfamiliar to them. The seven locales as specified in our manuscript are: (1) Neuss; (2) "a certain town;" (3) '-y-l-n-'

(depicted very briefly); (4) again '-y-l-n-'; (5) Xanten; (6) Moers; (7) Kerpen. Eliezer bar Nathan, in his narrative, identifies the second site as Wevelinghofen. He further indicates that one '-y-l-n-', which he has as '-y-l-n-r-', was near Julich and the other "somewhere else." Finally, he adds yet one more locale, Geldern. Modern scholarship has been divided on the identification of the sites of numbers 3 and 4. Baer, in his German translation (N&S, 121), opted for Altenahr; Eidelberg, in his English translation (Eidelberg, 53), opted for Eller; Anna Sapir Abulafia, "The Interrelationship between the Hebrew Chronicles on the First Crusade," *Journal of Semitic Studies* 27 (1982):227 n. 25, suggested Ellen. Because of Eliezer bar Nathan's identification of one '-y-l-n-' as located near Julich, I opted for Altenahr in my "The Deeds of the Jewish Community of Cologne," where I drew out a map of the locales, and have maintained that identification throughout this study.

36. For reasons that are not clear, Eliezer bar Nathan depicts the Jewish group gathered at Kerpen as yet another set of casualties.

37. I have noted the lack of concern in the Cologne unit with the precise identity of the attackers above; for the careful identification of the attackers in the *Mainz Anonymous,* see chap. 2.

38. See chap. 3 n. 23.

39. N&S, 19; Habermann, 45; Eidelberg, 51; Chazan, 276.

40. N&S, 21–22; Habermann, 48–49; Eidelberg, 56–57; Chazan, 281–282.

41. See chap. 1.

CHAPTER 6: THE *ELIEZER BAR NATHAN CHRONICLE*

1. See chap. 1. For fuller discussion of the relationship between the *Eliezer bar Nathan Chronicle* and the account in the *'Emek ha-Bakha',* see below, nn. 7–8.

2. I have omitted here a lengthy digression that speaks of Jewish hopes for redemption at this point in time and bemoans the fact that what materialized instead was unprecedented suffering. The digression in the *Eliezer bar Nathan Chronicle* is even lengthier than its counterpart in the *Solomon bar Simson Chronicle.*

3. N&S, 36; Habermann, 72; Eidelberg, 79. Again, I did not translate the *Eliezer bar Nathan Chronicle* in *European Jewry and the First Crusade.*

4. N&S, 46; Habermann, 82; Eidelberg, 93.

5. The four poems can be found in N&S, 37 (Speyer), 38–39 (Worms), 40 (Mainz), 45–46 (Cologne); Habermann, 73 (Speyer), 74 (Worms), 76 (Mainz), 80–81(Cologne); Eidelberg, 80–81 (Speyer), 82 (Worms), 84–85 (Mainz), 91–92 (Cologne).

6. On Eliezer bar Nathan, see Shalom Albeck's introduction to Eliezer bar Nathan, *Sefer Ravan* (Warsaw, 1905), 3a–13a; Victor Aptowitzer's introduction to *Sefer Raviah* (Jerusalem, 1938), 49–57; Urbach, *Ba'alei ha-Tosafot,* 1:173–184.

7. Albeck suggested that the sixteenth-century *'Emek ha-Bakha'* identifies its source as Elazar *ha-levi.* Since the author whose work he edited was Eliezer

(not Elazar) and was not a *levi,* Albeck concluded that the 1096 narrative was written by someone other than his Eliezer bar Nathan.

8. Aptowitzer solved the problem raised by Albeck by asserting that the account drawn upon in the '*Emek ha-Bakha*' was a different and later narrative, with the *Eliezer bar Nathan Chronicle* as we have it the work of the well-known twelfth-century halakhist. Aptowitzer's suggestion that the accounts in the '*Emek ha-Bakha*' and the *Eliezer bar Nathan Chronicle* are two different works is untenable—there is too much in common to allow such a thesis. Urbach simply postulates the authorship of the famed twelfth-century Eliezer bar Nathan.

9. See Ephraim E. Urbach's introduction to Abraham ben Uziel, '*Arugat ha-Bosem,* 4 vols. (Jerusalem, 1939–63), 4:24–39. This Urbach introduction surveys the tradition of poetry exegesis in early Ashkenazic Jewry, assigning a place of honor to Eliezer bar Nathan.

10. For the poetry of Eliezer bar Nathan, see Israel Davidson, *Thesaurus of Mediaeval Hebrew Poetry,* 4 vols. (New York, 1924–33), 4:364–365.

11. See below.

12. See the appendix.

13. Recall my parallel criticism of the *Urtext* hypothesis in the discussion of the relationship of the Speyer-Worms-Mains segment of the *Solomon bar Simson Chronicle* and the *Mainz Anonymous.* See chap. 4.

14. See chap. 5.

15. N&S, 44; Habermann, 80; Eidelberg, 90.

16. N&S, 45; Habermann, 80; Eidelberg, 91.

17. N&S, 30; Habermann, 59; Eidelberg, 71; Chazan, 297.

18. Recall the important study by Constable, "The Second Crusade as Seen by Contemporaries."

19. See chap. 4.

20. N&S, 36–37; Habermann, 72–73; Eidelberg, 79–80.

21. N&S, 37–40; Habermann, 73–76; Eidelberg, 80–85.

22. N&S, 40–46; Habermann, 76–81; Eidelberg, 85–92.

23. N&S, 46; Habermann, 82; Eidelberg, 92–93.

24. N&S, 37–39; Habermann, 73–74; Eidelberg, 81–82.

25. See chap. 4.

26. For reasons that are not clear, Eliezer bar Nathan omits all reference to the leader of the group, Kalonymous the *parnas,* and changes the number indicated in both the *Mainz Anonymous* and the *Solomon bar Simson Chronicle* from fifty-three to sixty.

27. Note that the relative space allotted to Mainz and Cologne in the prose narrative is paralleled by the relative length of the two poems, to be discussed shortly.

28. Eliezer replaces the indeterminate "a certain town" in the *Solomon bar Simson Chronicle* with the precise identification of Wevelinghofen.

29. Recall Eliezer's effort at differentiation, noted earlier. One Altenahr is identified as close to Julich, but Eliezer is uncertain as to the location of the other.

30. N&S, 18; Habermann, 44–45; Eidelberg, 50–51; Chazan, 275.

31. See the specific references for the four poems above, n. 5.

32. Recall the segment of the poem translated in the prologue.

33. Note, for example, the relatively specific poems of an unknown Abraham and the well-known Kalonymous ben Judah—see Habermann, 61–62 and 64–66.

34. N&S, 37; Habermann, 73; Eidelberg, 80–81.

35. Recall the evidence of widespread knowledge of the *Eliezer bar Nathan Chronicle* cited above, n. 1. In Chazan, 143–147, I discuss the broad tendency of post-1096 Ashkenazic Jewry to efface the unique and radical aspects of the tragedy and of the Jewish responses to it.

CHAPTER 7: TIME-BOUND OBJECTIVES

1. For the time-bound communications and poetic dirges, see prol.

2. Recall the three brief reports in the *Solomon bar Simson Chronicle,* cited above, chap. 5 n. 1. These brief reports are too cursory to be of any value in this analysis. Recall also the possibility that the author of the Cologne report may be identical with the editor of the entire *Solomon bar Simson Chronicle.* For the purposes of the ensuing discussion, I shall treat the two as distinct.

3. Recall the classic study of Schiffman, *Heinrich IV und die Bischöfe.* Recall also the emphasis on political advice in the 1096 narratives in Ben Sasson, "The Objectives of Medieval Jewish Chronography and Its Problematics."

4. See chap. 5. Recall the alternative portrait drawn in the *Gesta Treverorum.*

5. Recall Grossman, "The Roots of *Kiddush ha-Shem* in Early Ashkenaz," esp. 119–127.

6. Conversion has begun to emerge as a major and relatively unexplored issue in medieval Jewish history. Note the important essays by Robert C. Stacey, "The Conversion of Jews to Christianity in Thirteenth-Century England," *Speculum* 67 (1992):263–283; and Edward Fram, "Perception and Reception of Repentant Apostates in Medieval Ashkenaz and Pre-Modern Poland," *AJS Review* 21 (1996):299–339.

7. The central halakhic ruling with regard to forced obeisance to another faith can be found in T. B., Sanhedrin, 74a, where acknowledging idolatry even under pain of death is prohibited. Given the widespread medieval Jewish definition of Christianity as idolatrous, the halakhic implications for conversion, even under duress, are clear.

8. N&S, 29; Habermann, 57; Eidelberg, 68; Chazan, 294.

9. N&S, 49; Habermann, 96; Eidelberg, 103; Chazan, 229.

10. N&S, 51; Habermann, 98; Eidelberg, 106; Chazan, 233.

11. According to the central halakhic ruling, cited above in n. 7, the Jew in such dire straits must allow himself to be killed by his persecutors. The classic martyrs regularly cited are: Daniel and his companions; the woman and her seven sons; Rabbi Akiba and his colleagues. For a discussion of the relationship of the 1096 narratives to the tales of these classical heroes, see chap. 11.

12. T.B., Gittin, 57b. The influence of this story is obvious in the Wevel-

inghofen incident—N&S, 18–20; Habermann, 45–46; Eidelberg, 51–53; Chazan, 276–277—and in the Trier unit—N&S, 28; Habermann, 56; Eidelberg, 66; Chazan, 292–293. For fuller discussion, again see chap. 11.

13. Note that the most extreme forms of martyrdom make no appearance in the Trier unit. For problematic aspects of this radical behavior from a halakhic perspective, again see Soloveitchik, "Religious Law and Change: The Medieval Ashkenazic Example," and Grossman, "The Roots of *Kiddush ha-Shem* in Early Ashkenaz." For a sense of the impact that this extreme martyrdom has on twentieth-century readers, see Hillel Halkin's thoughtful review of my *In the Year 1096: The First Crusade and the Jews* (Philadelphia, 1996) in the *Forward,* 26 July 1996, pp. 9–10. Halkin's review includes sensitive reflections on the extreme forms of Jewish martyrdom, which he found appalling.

14. For the importance of this evaluation, see chap. 9.

15. Recall the sense of obligation indicated in the introduction to the Orléans letter, as discussed in the prologue.

CHAPTER 8: THE HISTORICITY
OF THE HEBREW NARRATIVES

1. See chap. 1.

2. The most important Christian narratives are three eyewitness accounts of the First Crusade. They are: (1) the anonymous *Gesta Francorum,* ed. Roger Mynors, trans. Rosalind Hill (Oxford, 1962); (2) Fulcher of Chartres, *Historia Hierosolymitana,* ed. Heinrich Hagenmeyer (Heidelberg, 1913), and the translation by Frances Rita Ryan, *A History of the Expedition to Jerusalem, 1095–1127,* (Knoxville, 1969); and (3) Raymond of Aguilers, *Historia Francorum,* ed. John Hugh and Laurita L. Hill (Paris, 1969), trans. J. H. and L. L. Hill (Philadelphia, 1968). Subsequent twelfth-century accounts are numerous, with many of these providing interesting additional information and perspectives on the undertaking.

3. See the section on guidance for the future, chap. 7.

4. See Marcus Bull, *Knightly Piety and the Lay Response to the First Crusade: The Limousin and Gascony c. 970–c. 1130* (Oxford, 1993); and Riley-Smith, *The First Crusaders.* Recall my essay, "The First Crusade as Reflected in the Earliest Hebrew Narrative." Some of the following discussion is taken from that essay.

5. See the classic study of Carl Erdmann, *The Origin of the Idea of Crusade,* trans. Marshall W. Baldwin and Walter Goffart (Princeton, 1977).

6. This sense of innovation is stressed in the Bull study, *Knightly Piety and the Lay Response to the First Crusade.*

7. See the study of Emanuel Sivan, *L'Islam et la croisade* (Paris, 1968).

8. See Dana C. Munro's classic study of the papal speech, "The Speech of Pope Urban II at Clermont," *American Historical Review* 11 (1906):231–242.

9. *Gesta Francorum,* 7–8.

10. N&S, 47; Habermann, 93; Eidelberg, 99; Chazan, 225.

11. Recall the reference to the pope in the *Solomon bar Simson Chronicle*'s reworking of the *Mainz Anonymous* report on Speyer-Worms-Mainz. As noted in chap. 4, that reference is clearly a later addition, poorly integrated into the flow of the narrative.

12. This issue is highlighted in both the Bull and Riley-Smith books.

13. The tendency to focus on the highborn can be observed in all the Latin First Crusade chronicles. Once again, because of their alternative perspective the Hebrew sources do not share this proclivity.

14. N&S, 51–52; Habermann, 98; Eidelberg, 106; Chazan, 233.

15. It is striking that the diversity in crusader ranks highlighted in both Christian and Jewish accounts is paralleled by the demographic diversity of the Jewish martyr-heroes of 1096, who came from all strata of the Jewish community and prominently included women.

16. N&S, 47–48; Habermann, 93–93; Eidelberg, 99–100; Chazan, 225–226.

17. N&S, 53 and 55; Habermann, 99 and 102; Eidelberg, 108 and 112; Chazan, 235 and 240.

18. Again note Albert of Aachen, *Liber Christianae expeditionis*, 4:292.

19. N&S, 47, 48, and 56; Habermann, 93, 94, and 104; Eidelberg, 99, 100, and 114; Chazan, 225, 226, and 241–242.

20. The "trampled corpse" is an allusion to Isa. 62:14, while the notion that this trampled corpse "can neither profit nor save because it is vanity" is an allusion to 1 Sam. 12.

21. It is precisely the acknowledgment of high ideals that makes the denigration of these ideals so important. On Jewish denigration of crusading and Christianity in the Hebrew narratives, see Anna Sapir Abulafia, "Invectives against Christianity in the Hebrew Chronicles of the First Crusade," in *Crusade and Settlement*, ed. P. W. Edbury (Cardiff, 1985), 66–72.

22. N&S, 47; Habermann, 93; Eidelberg, 99; Chazan, 225.

23. See, for example, N&S, 47, 49, and 53; Habermann, 93, 95, and 99; Eidelberg, 99, 102, and 108; Chazan, 225, 228, and 235. Revenge as a central motif in the anti-Jewish thinking of 1096 is emphasized by Riley-Smith, "The First Crusade and the Persecution of the Jews."

24. N&S, 47–48; Habermann, 93–94; Eidelberg, 99–100; Chazan, 225–226.

25. The centrality of Jerusalem to the crusading endeavor—reflected in both Christian and Jewish sources—is paralleled by the centrality of Jerusalem in the mental imagery of the Jewish victims of crusader violence, especially the martyrs.

26. For recent discussions of the importance of indulgences in lay crusader thinking, see Bull, *Knightly Piety and the Lay Response to the First Crusade*, 167–179; and Riley-Smith, *The First Crusaders*, 66–72.

27. N&S, 48; Habermann, 94; Eidelberg, 100; Chazan, 226.

28. N&S, 48; Habermann, 94; Eidelberg, 100; Chazan, 226. I have accepted a Habermann emendation, in line with the translation policy indicated earlier, prol. n. 10.

29. Note, for example, the remarkable speech attributed to the Jews assembled in the courtyard of the archbishop in Mainz, with its graphic imagery of

the otherworldly rewards to be enjoyed by the Jewish martyrs and the contrast between those rewards and the woes of this-worldly existence. See N&S, 53–54; Habermann, 100–101; Eidelberg, 109–110; Chazan, 236–237.

30. Albert of Aachen in his *Liber Christianae expeditionis*, 4:292; the *Gesta Treverorum*, in *MGH, Ss.* (34 vols.; Hanover, 1826–1990), 8:190–191.

31. Guibert de Nogent, *Autobiographie,* ed. and trans. Edmond-René Labande (Paris, 1981), 246–248 (Latin) and 247–249 (French trans.).

32. N&S, 48 and 2; Habermann, 94–95 and 25; Eidelberg, 100–101 and 22; Chazan, 227 and 244; Bernold of St. Blaise, *Chronicon, MGH, Ss.* 5:465.

33. N&S, 48–51 and 2; Habermann, 95–97 and 25–26; Eidelberg, 101–105 and 23; Chazan, 228–232 and 245–245; Bernold of St. Blaise, *Chronicon,* 5: 465.

34. N&S, 51–57 and 2–17; Habermann, 97–104 and 26–43; Eidelberg, 105–115 and 23–49; Chazan, 232–242 and 245–273. Albert of Aachen, *Liber Christianae expeditionis*, 4:292–293; the *Annalista Saxo, MGH, Ss* 6:729; the *Annales Wirziburgenses, MGH, Ss.* 2:246.

35. N&S, 17–25; Habermann, 43–52; Eidelberg, 49–61; Chazan, 273–287. Albert of Aachen, *Liber Christianae expeditionis*, 4:292.

36. N&S, 25–29; Habermann, 52–56; Eidelberg, 62–67; Chazan, 287–293. *Gesta Treverorum,* 8:190.

37. N&S, 29; Habermann, 56; Eidelberg, 67; Chazan, 293.

38. N&S, 29; Habermann, 56; Eidelberg, 67; Chazan, 293.

39. Cosmos of Prague, *Chronica Boemorum, MGH, Ss.* 9: 103; the *Annalista Saxo, Ss.* 6: 729. As noted earlier (chap. 5 n. 1), in the *Solomon bar Simson Chronicle,* there is reference to yet one more locale, identified with the three Hebrew consonants *Sh-l-'.* However, the story told about the Jews of Sh-l-' is of questionable reliability, and I have chosen to omit it from this catalogue of more-or-less reliably reported events.

40. Ekkehard of Aura in his *Hierosolymita, RHC, Occ.,* 5:20.

41. For the eyewitness narratives, see above, n. 2.

42. Emicho is mentioned frequently, specifically in the Hebrew narratives, in Albert of Aachen, and in the *Annales Saxo.*

43. Recall that there was pure burgher violence in Trier prior to the Pentecost outbreak. Recall also the story of Shmaryahu of Cologne, who successfully escaped from the refuge at Moers, prior to the forced conversion that took place there, wandered for a period of time, and then fell prey to vicious villager violence.

44. See chap. 5.

45. For some of the poetry, see Habermann, 61–71.

46. *Gesta Treverorum,* 190.

47. Jeremy Cohen, "The 'Persecutions of 1096.'"

48. In my earlier article, "The Facticity of Medieval Narrative: A Case Study of the Hebrew First-Crusade Narratives," I likewise emphasize the search for patterns of behavior, rather than the facticity of each discrete incident.

CHAPTER 9: THE TIMELESS

1. For broad and useful overviews of Jewish reaction to catastrophe see Mintz, *Ḥurban;* and David G. Roskies, *Against the Apocalypse: Responses to Catastrophe in Modern Jewish Culture* (Cambridge, Mass., 1984).

2. I have studied the medieval Christian argument regarding Jewish suffering and medieval Jewish responses in "Jewish Suffering." Some of the following discussion will be drawn from that essay. For a valuable analysis of twelfth-century Jewish thinking about the place and role of the Jewish people, see Haim Hillel Ben Sasson, "The Uniqueness of the People of Israel in the View of Twelfth-Century Jews" (Hebrew), *Perakim* 2 (1971):145–218.

3. For a recent and comprehensive discussion of the dating of the various segments of the New Testament, see Raymond P. Brown, *An Introduction to the New Testament* (New York, 1997).

4. The classic analysis of the critical period of separation is Marcel Simon, *Verus Israel: A Study of the Relations between Christians and Jews in the Roman Empire (AD 135–425),* trans. M. McKeating (Oxford, 1986).

5. Acts 28:24–28. I have used the New English Bible translation.

6. Isa. 6:11.

7. Eusebius, *The Ecclesiastical History,* trans. Kirsopp Lake and J. E. L. Oulton, 2 vols., The Loeb Classical Library (Cambridge, Mass., 1926–32), 1:7.

8. *Gesta Francorum,* 64. I have used Hill's translation.

9. This is surely a reference to the slaughter in Worms and Mainz that took place in May 1096.

10. N&S, 26; Habermann, 54; Eidelberg, 64; Chazan, 289–290.

11. N&S, 50; Habermann, 97; Eidelberg, 104; Chazan, 231.

12. N&S, 50–51; Habermann, 97; Eidelberg, 105; Chazan 231–232.

13. See a similar story told of the Jew David *ha-gabbai* of Mainz—N&S, 56; Habermann, 103–104; Eidelberg, 113–114; Chazan, 241–242.

14. N&S, 51; Habermann, 98; Eidelberg, 106; Chazan, 233.

15. N&S, 15; Habermann, 41; Eidelberg, 45; Chazan, 269.

16. N&S, 47; Habermann, 93; Eidelberg, 100; Chazan, 226.

17. N&S, 48; Habermann, 94; Eidelberg, 101; Chazan, 227. The biblical text cited is Ezek. 9:6.

18. N&S, 48; Habermann, 95; Eidelberg, 101; Chazan, 228.

19. N&S, 50; Habermann, 97; Eidelberg, 104–105; Chazan, 231.

20. N&S, 52; Habermann, 98; Eidelberg, 107; Chazan, 234. Third-person references to a divine decree can be found in N&S, 52; Habermann, 98; Eidelberg, 106–107; Chazan, 234.

21. N&S, 47–48; Habermann, 94; Eidelberg, 100; Chazan, 226.

22. N&S, 48; Habermann, 94; Eidelberg, 100; Chazan, 226.

23. N&S, 50; Habermann, 96; Eidelberg, 104; Chazan, 230.

24. See chap. 2.

25. N&S, 54; Habermann, 101; Eidelberg, 110; Chazan, 237–238.

26. See chap. 3.

27. The same basic stance can be discerned in the *Eliezer bar Nathan Chronicle,* with diminished emphasis on retribution.

28. N&S, 50; Habermann, 96; Eidelberg, 104; Chazan, 230.

29. Isa. 64:9–10.

30. N&S, 53; Habermann, 100; Eidelberg, 109; Chazan, 236.

31. N&S, 55; Habermann, 102; Eidelberg, 112; Chazan, 239.

32. Again, the *Eliezer bar Nathan Chronicle* deemphasizes divine vengeance.

33. The same combination of declaration and request can be found in the 1096 poetry as well.

CHAPTER 10: GOD, HUMANITY, AND HISTORY

1. The entire passage can be found in N&S, 49; Habermann, 95; Eidelberg, 102; Chazan, 228–229. The verse cited is Deut. 26:17.

2. The entire passage can be found in N&S, 53; Habermann, 100; Eidelberg, 109; Chazan, 236–237. The verse cited is Exod. 24:7.

3. N&S, 55; Habermann, 102; Eidelberg, 111; Chazan, 239.

4. N&S, 48; Habermann, 94–95; Eidelberg, 101; Chazan, 227.

5. N&S, 52; Habermann, 99; Eidelberg, 107; Chazan, 234. I have accepted a Habermann emendation, in line with the translation policy indicated earlier, prol. n. 10.

6. N&S, 24–25; Habermann, 52; Eidelberg, 61; Chazan, 287.

7. See chap. 3.

8. N&S, 4; Habermann, 27; Eidelberg, 26; Chazan, 248.

9. N&S, 47; Habermann, 93; Eidelberg, 99; Chazan, 225.

10. N&S, 47; Habermann, 93; Eidelberg, 99; Chazan, 225.

11. N&S, 50; Habermann, 96; Eidelberg, 104; Chazan, 230–231.

12. N&S, 55; Habermann, 102; Eidelberg, 112; Chazan, 239.

13. See chap. 11 for fuller comparison between the 1096 narratives and classical Jewish sources. As I emphasize there, the comparisons are not meant to be pejorative with respect to the classical sources. I understand that there are two different esthetics operating, each of them valid. My comparisons are simply meant to highlight the innovative in the 1096 accounts.

14. N&S, 54–55; Habermann, 101–102; Eidelberg, 111–112; Chazan, 238–239.

15. Recall the contemporary response of revulsion for these behaviors expressed in Halkin's review of my *In the Year 1096*.

16. Again, the central halakhic ruling can be found in T.B., Sanhedrin, 74a.

17. N&S, 50–51; Habermann, 96–97; Eidelberg, 104–105; Chazan, 230–232.

18. N&S, 53; Habermann, 100; Eidelberg, 109; Chazan, 236.

19. N&S, 56; Habermann, 103–104; Eidelberg, 113–114; Chazan, 241–242.

20. N&S, 50; Habermann, 97; Eidelberg, 104; Chazan, 231.

21. N&S, 49–50; Habermann, 96; Eidelberg, 103; Chazan, 230.

22. N&S, 53–54; Habermann, 100–101; Eidelberg, 109–110; Chazan, 236–237.

23. Lacey Baldwin Smith, *Fools, Martyrs, Traitors: The Story of Martyrdom*

in the Western World (New York, 1997), emphasizes the element of idiosyncrasy in many of the famous martyrs of the Western world.

24. N&S, 57; Habermann, 104; Eidelberg, 115; Chazan, 242.

25. N&S, 56; Habermann, 103; Eidelberg, 113; Chazan, 240–241.

26. N&S, 19; Habermann, 45; Eidelberg, 51; Chazan, 276. Again, I have accepted a Habermann emendation.

27. N&S, 56; Habermann, 104; Eidelberg, 114; Chazan, 241–242. Once more, I have accepted a Habermann emendation.

28. See chap. 2.

CHAPTER 11: THE 1096 NARRATIVES AND CLASSICAL JEWISH TRADITION

1. Biblical views of God, humanity, and history have been investigated thoroughly, and the conclusions of these investigations are regularly included in standard handbooks. The concern with biblical narrative style is newer. Precedent setting was the study of Robert Alter, *The Art of Biblical Narrative* (New York, 1981). Compare Adele Berlin, *Poetics and Interpretation of Biblical Narrative* (Sheffield, 1983); Meir Sternberg, *The Poetics of Biblical Narrative: Ideological Literature and the Drama of Reading* (Bloomington, 1987); Shimon Bar-Efrat, *Narrative Art in the Bible* (Sheffield, 1989). Parallel study of the rabbinic corpus developed later. Major efforts to identify key rabbinic views include George Foot Moore, *Judaism in the First Centuries of the Christian Era*, 3 vols. (Cambridge, Mass., 1927–30); and Ephraim E. Urbach, *The Sages: Their Concepts and Beliefs*, trans. Israel Abrahams (Cambridge, Mass., 1987). Study of rabbinic narrative style is quite recent. An innovator in this area is Yonah Fraenkel, *Darkei ha-Aggadah ve-ha-Midrash* (Tel Aviv, 1991). My colleague Jeffrey Rubenstein, who has been—as noted—most helpful with this chapter, has published a valuable new study, *The Complexity of Torah: On the Narrative Art of the Bavli* (Baltimore, 1999).

2. This is true for the great Near Eastern empires of Assyria and Babylonia, which dominated Israel and Judea, and for the small neighboring kingdoms with which the Israelites and Judeans regularly skirmished. There was some potential in the Egypt stories of Genesis and Exodus for persecution and martyrdom, but that potential was not realized.

3. Note, for example, the reign of King Ahab and Queen Jezebel, the evidence of persecution of those in religious opposition, and the resultant potential for highlighting martyrdom, a potential also not realized.

4. As indicated in the closing section of this chapter, Abraham—so regularly cited in the 1096 narratives—is in fact not a martyr figure.

5. On the book of Daniel, see any of the standard modern commentaries. I have found particularly helpful the insights of my former teacher, H. Louis Ginsberg, *Studies in Daniel* (New York, 1948). For an interesting analysis of the narrative techniques in Daniel 3, see David M. Gunn and Danna Nolan Fewell, *Narrative in the Hebrew Bible* (Oxford, 1993), 174–188.

6. Dan. 3:5, 3:10, and 3:15.

7. Dan. 3:19 and 22.

8. Dan. 3:23 and 25.

9. Dan. 6:18.

10. Dan. 6:24–25

11. Dan. 3:16–18.

12. The original version of the story can be found in 2 Maccabees. For a detailed commentary to this story, see Jonathan A. Goldstein, *II Maccabees* (Garden City, 1983).

13. See the important study of Gerson D. Cohen, "The Story of Hannah and Her Seven Sons in Hebrew Literature," in *Studies in the Variety of Rabbinic Cultures* (Philadelphia, 1991), 39–60.

14. The legal setting in which the rabbinic narratives is found is emphasized by Rubenstein, *The Complexity of Torah.*

15. The two stories can be found in T. B., Gittin, 57b.

16. Ps. 44:23–27.

17. T. B., Gittin, 57b.

18. N&S, 55; Habermann, 102; Eidelberg, 112; Chazan, 239.

19. N&S, 18; Habermann, 44; Eidelberg, 50–51; Chazan, 275.

20. N&S, 28; Habermann, 56; Eidelberg, 66; Chazan, 293.

21. The famous *'eleh 'ezkerah,* it should be emphasized, is a complex poem, with all that the poetic form implies.

22. T. B., Berakhot, 61b.

23. The verse in question, Ps. 17:14, is extremely difficult. Note the appearance of this verse at the close of the description of the second assault on Worms Jewry, effectively linking that group with Rabbi Akiba. See N&S, 51; Habermann, 97; Eidelberg, 105; Chazan, 232.

24. On the Abraham image, see the classic study of Spiegel, *The Last Trial;* and Jon D. Levenson, *The Death and Resurrection of the Beloved Son: The Transformation of Child Sacrifice in Judaism and Christianity* (New Haven, 1993).

25. This development is highlighted in the Levenson book.

26. N&S, 50; Habermann, 96; Eidelberg, 103; Chazan, 230.

27. For the linguistic usages, see above, chap. 2 n. 27.

28. The widely acknowledged greatness of this brief story buttresses the disclaimer made at the beginning of this chapter. I am not arguing the superiority of the 1096 narratives; I am, rather, arguing their innovativeness.

29. N&S, 50; Habermann, 96; Eidelberg, 103; Chazan, 230.

CHAPTER 12: THE 1096 NARRATIVES
AND THEIR MEDIEVAL SETTING

1. *Gesta Francorum et Aliorum Hierosolimitanorum.*

2. Secondary histories include, for example, those of Robert of Rheims, Balderic of Dol, Guibert of Nogent, Ralph of Caen, Hugh of Fleury, Robert of St. Remi, and Albert of Aachen. The last is special in depicting the popular German bands and mentioning at modest length the assaults on Jews.

3. I have argued this case in *European Jewry and the First Crusade,* chap. 4. For parallel argumentation, drawn from totally different aspects of medieval Jewish experience, see Ivan G. Marcus, *Rituals of Childhood: Jewish Acculturation in Medieval Europe* (New Haven, 1996).

4. *Sefer Yosippon,* ed. David Flusser, 2 vols. (Jerusalem, 1981). The first volume contains the text; the second Flusser's lengthy introduction.

5. *Sefer Yosippon,* 2:3–6.

6. Ahimaaz ben Paltiel, *Megillat Ahimaʿaz,* ed. Benjamin Klar (Jerusalem, 1974). There is an English translation by Marcus Salzman (New York, 1924), based on an earlier edition.

7. Note the interesting discrepancy: the archbishop could not promise to convert if he lost.

8. *Megillat Ahimaʿaz,* 24; Salzman trans., 80.

9. Steven Bowman, "Yosippon and Jewish Nationalism," *Proceedings of the American Academy for Jewish Research* 61 (1995):47 n. 49, seems to suggest the broad influence of *Yosippon* on the 1096 narratives. The present analysis acknowledges some linguistic impact, but ultimately rejects the notion of broader influence.

10. We have noted recurrently the image of the supernal light in the 1096 narratives. For the same concept in *Sefer Yosippon,* see, for example, 1:71, 75, and 424.

11. Recall the distinction drawn between the meanness of this-worldly existence and the glory of other-worldly existence by the Jew of Mainz in N&S, 54; Habermann, 100; Eidelberg, 110; Chazan, 237. Note the same distinction, for example, in *Sefer Yosippon,* 1:75 and 425.

12. *Sefer Yosippon,* 1:25–31

13. The entire set of incidents can be found in ibid. 66–75.

14. Ibid., 69.

15. Ibid., 70–75.

16. Ibid., 73.

17. The war with Rome fills slightly more than the last third of the book; see ibid., 275–431.

18. The original Josephus depiction of the war with Rome represents an interesting combination of time-bound and timeless objectives.

19. Once again, I have suggested that the Abraham image is not truly martyrological.

20. Rabbinic views of the rebels were seemingly quite negative. In fact, the rebels are not truly treated in rabbinic materials either halakhic or aggadic, perhaps the most striking evidence of negative views.

21. *Sefer Yosippon,* 1:423.

22. Ibid., 1:424.

23. *Gesta Francorum,* 9 and 97. Throughout this chapter I shall utilize the Hill translation.

24. Ibid., 97.

25. See chap. 10.

26. *Gesta Francorum,* 69.

27. N&S, 53; Habermann, 99; Eidelberg, 108; Chazan, 235.

28. *Gesta Francorum,* 62.
29. Ibid., 58.
30. Ibid., 59–60 and 65.
31. Ibid., 1.
32. Matt. 16:25.
33. *Gesta Francorum,* 7.
34. Ibid., 36–37.
35. See chaps. 2, 5, and 7.
36. *Gesta Francorum,* 19.
37. Ibid., 20.
38. Ibid., 21.
39. See chap. 9.
40. See chap. 9.
41. See above.
42. *Gesta Francorum,* 1–2.
43. Ibid., 17.
44. Fulcher of Chartres, *Historia Hierosolymitana,* 116–117; and the Ryan translation, *A History of the Expedition to Jerusalem, 1095–1127,* 58. I have used the Ryan translation. While Fulcher emphasizes miracles in a manner somewhat different from the style of the *Gesta Francorum* (and the Hebrew narratives of course), ultimately it is the willingness for martyrdom that signals the greatness of the crusaders. In this respect, he parallels the *Gesta Francorum* and the Hebrew narratives.

EPILOGUE

1. The so-called twelfth-century renaissance is generally dated from about 1070 to about 1170 and includes the First Crusade.
2. I have argued this case in *European Jewry and the First Crusade,* chap. 3.
3. This set of developments has been carefully investigated by Anna Sapir Abulafia, *Christians and Jews in the Twelfth-Century Renaissance* (London, 1995).
4. I have analyzed these developments in *Medieval Stereotypes and Modern Antisemitism.*
5. The new thrust in biblical commentary has been most fully studied in the various works of Sara Kamin. See especially her collection of essays, *Jews and Christians Interpret the Bible* (Jerusalem, 1991).
6. The fullest study to date of the Tosafists has been Urbach, *Baʿalei ha-Tosafot.* At a conference on 1096 held at Ben-Gurion University in 1996, Haym Soloveitchik delivered a revealing survey of the rise and decline of the Tosafist movement. I hope that his presentation will be published in the proceedings of that conference.
7. On this new pietism, see Haym Soloveitchik, "Three Themes in the *Sefer Ḥasidim,*" *AJS Review* 1 (1976):311–357; and Ivan G. Marcus, *Piety and Society: The Jewish Pietists of Medieval Germany* (Leiden, 1981). Some years ago,

I made some brief suggestions as to the linkage among the 1096 martyrdoms, the new pietism, and general religious developments in majority society in "The Early Development of Ḥasidut Ashkenaz," *Jewish Quarterly Review* 75 (1985): 199–211. I might well have added here some mention of the mystical speculation of the Hasidei Ashkenaz. However, despite the best efforts of my friend and colleague Elliot Wolfson, I continue to encounter serious difficulty in plumbing their idiom.

8. The underside of the "twelfth-century renaissance" has been studied by many recently. The fullest treatment is that of R. I. Moore, *The Formation of a Persecuting Society* (Oxford, 1987).

9. Again, see my *Medieval Stereotypes and Modern Antisemitism*.

APPENDIX

1. Such a survey was undertaken most usefully by Anna Sapir Abulafia in 1982, in the article cited below as number 11. The present survey is somewhat expanded. To be sure, not every study concerning the narratives is cited; studies that introduced no substantive innovation are indicated in notes only.

2. The sentence noted by Porges as indicative of missing sections reads: "Now I shall recount the development of the persecution in the rest of the communities that were killed for his unique Name and how they clung to the Lord God of their forefathers and proclaimed his unity to the expiration of their souls" (N&S, 1; Habermann, 24; Eidelberg, 21; Chazan, 243). As we shall see, others (correctly, it seems to me) viewed this sentence as an external introduction.

3. The four words are: *'ad henah shnat tatak* (N&S, 21; Habermann, 48; Eidelberg, 55; Chazan, 280), which would literally be translated "until now, the year [4]900 [=1140]." In N&S, the punctuation led to the connection of these four words with the ensuing phrase and resulted in the German: "Bis hierher. Im Jahre 900 habe ich Salomo bar Simon diese Begebenheit abgeschreiben in Mainz" (N&S, 123). This translation is problematic in many ways. The Eidelberg English translation takes much the same tack. Elbogen connected these four Hebrew words to the prior sentence, resulting in a description of a Jewess saved from death in 1096 who fasted "until now, the year [4]900 [=1140]."

4. Elbogen's reading makes it possible to understand the following sentence—"And I Solomon bar Simson wrote up this event in Mainz" (N&S, 21; Habermann, 48; Eidelberg, 55; Chazan, 280)—as a reference to the Altenahr incident only.

5. Sara Schiffman, in her dissertation, *Heinrich IV und die Bischöfe in ihrem Verhalten zu den deutschen Juden zur Zeit des ersten Kreuzzuges* (Berlin, 1931), accepted the views of Porges and Elbogen. She identified the author of the lengthiest narrative as Solomon bar Simson, rather than the Solomon bar Simon indicated in N&S.

6. The external sentence in the *Solomon bar Simson Chronicle* has been noted above, n. 2. The copyist sentence in the *Mainz Anonymous* reads: "I shall begin the account of the persecution of yore. May God protect us and all Israel

from persecution" (N&S, 47; Habermann, 93; Eidelberg, 99; Chazan, 225). That this is in fact the copyist's introduction is indicated clearly by the dots inserted above these words in the manuscript. The parallel dots over the closing copyist observations indicate the truncation of the source at his disposal.

7. In both the opening and closing copyist observations, the persecution of 1096 is called *ha-gezerot ha-yeshanot*, the persecution of yore, suggesting a substantially earlier date. Earlier researchers took this to mean that the *Mainz Anonymous* was composed well after the events. Sonne's insistence on distinguishing between the text and the copyist comments meant that these opening and closing observations imply nothing whatsoever as to the date of composition of the *Mainz Anonymous* itself.

8. A number of useful studies were published in the 1950s and 1960s that added nothing substantial to the discussion of the relationship of the narratives and their dating. See Ben Sasson, "The Objectives of Medieval Jewish Chronography and Its Problematics"; Salo Wittmayer Baron, *A Social and Religious History of the Jews*, 2nd ed., 18 vols. (New York, 1952–83), 4:94–106 and relevant notes; Shlomo Eidelberg, "The Solomon bar Simson Chronicle as a Source of the History of the First Crusade," *Jewish Quarterly Review* 49 (1959): 282–287; Moses Shulvass, "Historical Knowledge and Historical Literature in the Cultural Sphere of Medieval Ashkenazic Jewry" (Hebrew), in the *Hanoch Albeck Jubilee Volume* (Jerusalem, 1963), 477–486; Isaiah Sonne, "Critical Annotations to Solomon bar Simson's Record of the Edicts of 1096, Including a Fragment of this Text in Judaeo-German" (Hebrew), in *The Abraham Weiss Jubilee Volume* (New York: 1964), 385–405.

9. To be sure, the disparity observed by Hacker could be interpreted in opposite fashion. By the mid to late twelfth century, the later dating for the Worms attacks took hold, and thus no subsequent writer would have opposed that widely accepted dating. Thus, the alternative dating proposed in the *Mainz Anonymous* shows a date prior to crystallization of the normative tradition. In 1969, I published a brief essay—"A Twelfth-Century Communal History of Spires Jewry"—designed to clarify the external introduction to the *Solomon bar Simson Chronicle* indicated above, n. 2. I suggested that the *Solomon bar Simson Chronicle* was incorporated *in toto* by a later Speyer editor as part of a composite communal history composed toward the end of the twelfth century.

10. I discussed these issues in *European Jewry and the First Crusade*, 40–49, not moving beyond the conclusions noted in the studies cited above. In a lecture delivered in 1979 and published posthumously as "The Hebrew Crusade Chronicles and the Ashkenazic Tradition," in *Minhah le-Nahum*, ed. Marc Brettler and Michael Fishbane (Sheffield, 1993), 36–53, Gerson D. Cohen argued for a modestly late dating for the *Mainz Anonymous*, subsequent to 1161; see pp. 37–38. His case is based on two considerations. The first is the copyist's designation already noted. The second consideration is the suggested influence of Abraham ibn Daud on two phrases in the *Mainz Anonymous*. Both phrases, however, are standard rabbinic usages and need betray no ibn Daud influence. As noted in the preface, the commemorations of the nine-hundredth anniversary of the 1096 assaults brought me back to these narratives. I completed a number of studies, including: "The Trier Unit of the Lengthy Hebrew First-Crusade

Narrative"; "The Mainz Anonymous: Historiographic Perspectives"; "The Hebrew First-Crusade Narratives and Their Intertextual Messages"; "The First Crusade as Reflected in the Earliest Hebrew Narrative"; "Jewish Suffering: The Interplay of Medieval Christian and Jewish Perspectives"; "Jerusalem as Christian Symbol during the First Crusade: Jewish Awareness and Response"; "Christian and Jewish Perceptions of 1096: A Case Study of Trier"—to appear in *Jewish History*. Most—but not all—of these studies involve implications for dating the narrative units and the relationships among them. The conclusions of these studies will be found throughout the book.

Bibliography

PRIMARY SOURCES

Abraham ben Uziel. 'Arugat ha-Bosem. Ed. Ephraim E. Urbach. 4 vols. Jerusalem, 1939–63.

Abraham ibn Daud. Sefer ha-Qabbalah. Ed. and trans. Gerson D. Cohen. Philadelphia, 1967.

Ahimaaz ben Paltiel. Megillat Ahima'az. Ed. Benjamin Klar. Jerusalem, 1974. Trans. Marcus Salzman. New York, 1924.

Albert of Aachen. Liber Christianae expeditionis. In RHC, Occ., 4:269–713.

Annales Wirziburgenses. In MGH, Ss., 2:238–247.

Annalista Saxo. In MGH, Ss., 6:542–777.

Bernold of St. Blaise. Chronicon. In MGH, Ss., 5:400–467.

Cosmos of Prague. Chronica Boemorum. In MGH, Ss., 9:1–209.

Ekkehard of Aura. Chronicon universale. In MGH, Ss., 6:1–267.

———. Hierosolymita. In RHC, Occ., 5:7–40.

Eliezer bar Nathan. Sefer Ravan. Ed. Shalom Albeck. Warsaw, 1905.

Eliezer bar Nathan Chronicle. In N&S, 36–46; Habermann, 72–82; Eidelberg, 79–93.

Eliezer ben Joel ha-levi. Sefer Raviah. Ed. Victor Aptowitzer. Jerusalem, 1938.

Ephraim ben Jacob of Bonn. The Book of Remembrance. In N&S, 58–75; Habermann, 115–132; Eidelberg, 121–133.

Eusebius. The Ecclesiastical History. Trans. Kirsopp Lake and J. E. L. Oulton. 2 vols. The Loeb Classical Library. Cambridge, Mass., 1926–32.

Fulcher of Chartres. Historia Hierosolymitana. Ed. Heinrich Hagenmeyer. Heidelberg, 1913. A History of the Expedition to Jerusalem, 1095–1127, trans. Frances Rita Ryan. Knoxville, 1969.

Gans, David. Zemah David. Ed. Mordechai Breuer. Jerusalem, 1983.

Gesta Francorum et Aliorum Hierosolimitanorum. Ed. Roger Mynors, trans. Rosalind Hill. Oxford, 1962.

Gesta Treverorum. In *MGH, Ss.,* 8:111–260.

Guibert de Nogent. *Autobiographie.* Ed. and trans. Edmond-René Labande. Paris, 1981.

Hebräische Berichte über die Judenverfolgungen während der Kreuzzüge. Eds. Adolf Neubauer and Moritz Stern. Berlin, 1892.

The Jews and the Crusaders. Trans. Shlomo Eidelberg. Madison, 1977.

Joseph *ha-cohen.* ‘*Emek ha-Bakha*’. Ed. Meir Letteris. Cracow, 1895.

Mainz Anonymous. In N&S, 47–57; Habermann, 93–104; and Eidelberg, 99–115; Chazan, 225–242.

Monumenta Germaniae Historica, Scriptores. 34 vols. Hanover, 1826–1990.

Raymond of Aguilers. *Historia Francorum.* Ed. John Hugh and Laurita L. Hill. Paris, 1969. Trans. J. H. and L. L. Hill. Philadelphia, 1968.

Recueil des historiens des croisades, historiens occidentaux. 5 vols. Paris, 1844–95.

Sefer Gezerot Ashkenaz ve-Zarfat. Ed. Abraham Habermann. Jerusalem, 1945.

Sefer Yosippon. Ed. David Flusser. 2 vols. Jerusalem, 1981.

Solomon bar Simson Chronicle. In N&S, 1–30; Habermann, 24–59; and Eidelberg, 21–71; Chazan, 243–297.

Thesaurus of Mediaeval Hebrew Poetry. Ed. Israel Davidson. 4 vols. New York, 1924–33.

SECONDARY LITERATURE

Abulafia, Anna Sapir. *Christians and Jews in the Twelfth-Century Renaissance.* London, 1995.

———. "The Interrelationship between the Hebrew Chronicles on the First Crusade." *Journal of Semitic Studies* 27 (1982):221–239.

———. "Invectives against Christianity in the Hebrew Chronicles of the First Crusade." In *Crusade and Settlement,* ed. P. W. Edbury, 66–72. Cardiff, 1985.

Alter, Robert. *The Art of Biblical Narrative.* New York, 1981.

Andressohn, John C. *The Ancestry and Life of Godfrey of Bouillon.* Bloomington, 1947.

Baer, Yitzhak. "The Persecutions of 1096" (Hebrew). In *Sefer Assaf,* ed. M. D. Cassuto, 126–140. Jerusalem, 1953.

Bar-Efrat, Shimon. *Narrative Art in the Bible.* Sheffield, 1989.

Baron, Salo Wittmayer. *A Social and Religious History of the Jews.* 2d ed. 18 vols. New York, 1952–83.

Bartlett, Robert. *Trial by Fire and Water: The Medieval Judicial Ordeal.* Oxford, 1986.

Ben Sasson, Haim Hillel. "The Objectives of Medieval Jewish Chronography and Its Problematics" (Hebrew). In *Historionim ve-Askolot Historiot,* 42–48. Jerusalem, 1953.

———. "The Uniqueness of the People of Israel in the View of Twelfth-Century Jews" (Hebrew). *Perakim* 2 (1971):145–218.

Berlin, Adele. *Poetics and Interpretation of Biblical Narrative.* Sheffield, 1983.

Bowman, Steven. "Yosippon and Jewish Nationalism." *Proceedings of the American Academy for Jewish Research* 61 (1995):23–51.

Bresslau, Harry. "Zur Kritik der Kreuzzuzgsberichte." In N&S, xiii–xxix. Berlin, 1892.

Brown, Raymond P. *An Introduction to the New Testament.* New York, 1997.

Bull, Marcus. *Knightly Piety and the Lay Response to the First Crusade: The Limousin and Gascony c. 970–c. 1130.* Oxford, 1993.

Chazan, Robert. "The Blois Incident of 1171: A Study in Jewish Intercommunal Organization." *Proceedings of the American Academy for Jewish Research* 36 (1968):13–31.

———. "Christian and Jewish Perceptions of 1096: A Case Study of Trier." Forthcoming in *Jewish History.*

———. "The Deeds of the Jewish Community of Cologne." *Journal of Jewish Studies* 35 (1984):185–195.

———. "The Early Development of Ḥasidut Ashkenaz." *Jewish Quarterly Review* 75 (1985):199–211.

———. "Emperor Frederick I, the Third Crusade, and the Jews." *Viator* 8 (1970):83–93.

———. "Ephraim ben Jacob's Compilation of Twelfth-Century Persecutions." *Jewish Quarterly Review* 84 (1993–94):397–416.

———. *European Jewry and the First Crusade.* Berkeley, 1987.

———. "The Facticity of Medieval Narrative: A Case Study of the Hebrew First-Crusade Narratives." *AJS Review* 17 (1991):31–56.

———. "The First Crusade as Reflected in the Earliest Hebrew Narrative." *Viator* 29 (1998):25–38.

———. "The Hebrew First-Crusade Chronicles." *Revue des études juives* 133 (1974):235–254.

———. "The Hebrew First-Crusade Chronicles: Further Reflections." *AJS Review* 3 (1978):79–98.

———. "The Hebrew First-Crusade Narratives and Their Intertextual Messages." In *Ki Baruch Hu: Ancient Near Eastern, Biblical, and Judaic Studies in Honor of Baruch A. Levine,* ed. Robert Chazan, William W. Hallo, and Lawrence H. Schiffman, 465–480. Winona Lake, 1998.

———. *In the Year 1096 . . . : The First Crusade and the Jews.* Philadelphia, 1996.

———. "Jerusalem as Christian Symbol during the First Crusade: Jewish Awareness and Response." In *Jerusalem: Its Sanctity and Centrality to Judaism, Christianity, and Islam,* ed. Lee I. Levine, 382–392. New York, 1999.

———. "Jewish Suffering: The Interplay of Medieval Christian and Jewish Perspectives." In *Lectures on Medieval Judaism at Trinity University.* Occasional Papers 2. Kalamazoo, 1998.

———. "The Mainz Anonymous: Historiographic Perspectives." In *Jewish History and Jewish Memory: Essays in Honor of Yosef Haim Yerushalmi.* Ed. Elisheva Carlebach et al., 54–69. Hanover, 1998.

———. *Medieval Stereotypes and Modern Antisemitism.* Berkeley, 1997.

———. "R. Ephraim of Bonn's *Sefer Zechirah.*" *Revue des études juives* 132 (1973):119–126.

———. "The Timebound and the Timeless: Medieval Jewish Narration of Events." *History and Memory* 6 (1994):5–35.

———. "The Trier Unit of the Lengthy Hebrew First-Crusade Narrative." In *Between History and Literature: Studies in Honor of Isaac Barzilay,* ed. Stanley Nash, 37–49. n.p., 1997.

———. "A Twelfth-Century Communal History of Spires Jewry." *Revue des études juives* 128 (1969):253–257.

Cohen, Gerson D. "The Hebrew Crusade Chronicles and the Ashkenazic Tradition." In *Minḥah le-Naḥum,* ed. Marc Brettler and Michael Fishbane, 36–53. Sheffield, 1993.

———. "The Story of Hannah and Her Seven Sons in Hebrew Literature." In *Studies in the Variety of Rabbinic Cultures,* 39–60. Philadelphia, 1991.

Cohen, Jeremy. "The 'Persecutions of 1096'—From Martyrdom to Martyrology: The Sociocultural Context of the Hebrew Crusade Chronicles" (Hebrew). *Zion* 59 (1994):169–208.

Constable, Giles. "The Second Crusade as Seen by Contemporaries." *Traditio* 9 (1953):213–281.

Eidelberg, Shlomo. "The Solomon bar Simson Chronicle as a Source of the History of the First Crusade." *Jewish Quarterly Review* 49 (1959):282–287.

Einbinder, Susan. "Pucellina of Blois: Romantic Myths and Narrative Conventions." Forthcoming in *Jewish History.*

Elbogen, Ismar. "Zu den hebräischen Berichten ueber die Judenverfolgungen im Jahre 1096." In *Festschrift zum siebzigsten Geburtstage Martin Philippsons,* 6–24. Leipzig, 1916.

Erdmann, Carl. *The Origin of the Idea of Crusade.* Trans. Marshall W. Baldwin and Walter Goffart. Princeton, 1977.

Fraenkel, Yonah. *Darkei ha-Aggadah ve-ha-Midrash.* Tel Aviv, 1991.

Fram, Edward. "Perception and Reception of Repentant Apostates in Medieval Ashkenaz and Pre-Modern Poland." *AJS Review* 21 (1996):299–339.

Ginsberg, H. Louis. *Studies in Daniel.* New York, 1948.

Goldstein, Jonathan A. *II Maccabees.* Garden City, 1983.

Grossman, Avraham. "The Roots of *Kiddush ha-Shem* in Early Ashkenaz" (Hebrew). In *Kedushat ha-Ḥayim ve-Ḥeruf ha-Nefesh,* ed. Isaiah M. Gafni and Aviezer Ravitzky, 99–130. Jerusalem, 1992.

Gunn, David M., and Danna Nolan Fewell. *Narrative in the Hebrew Bible.* Oxford, 1993.

Habermann, Abraham. "Who Wrote Chronicle I Concerning the Persecution of 1096?" (Hebrew). *Sinai* 9, n.2 (1945):79–84.

Hacker, Joseph. "Concerning the Persecution of 1096" (Hebrew). *Zion* 31 (1966):226–231.

Hagenmeyer, Heinrich. "Chronologie de la première croisade." *Revue de l'Orient latin* 6 (1898):214–293 and 490–549.

Halkin, Hillel. Review of *In the Year 1096: The First Crusade and the Jews. Forward,* 26 July 1996, 9–10.

Kamin, Sara. *Jews and Christians Interpret the Bible.* Jerusalem, 1991.

Levenson, Jon D. *The Death and Resurrection of the Beloved Son: The Trans-formation of Child Sacrifice in Judaism and Christianity.* New Haven, 1993.

Levine, Baruch A. *The JPS Torah Commentary: Leviticus.* Philadelphia, 1989.

Marcus, Ivan G. "From Politics to Martyrdom: Shifting Paradigms in the He-brew Narratives of the 1096 Crusader Riots." *Prooftexts* 2 (1982):40–52.

————. *Piety and Society: The Jewish Pietists of Medieval Germany.* Leiden, 1981.

————. *Rituals of Childhood: Jewish Acculturation in Medieval Europe.* New Haven, 1996.

Mayer, Hans Eberhard. *The Crusades.* Trans. John Gillingham. Oxford, 1972.

Mintz, Alan. *Ḥurban: Responses to Catastrophe in Hebrew Literature.* New York, 1984.

Möhring, H. "Graf Emicho und die Judenvergolgungen von 1096." *Rheinische Vierteljahresblätter* 56 (1992):97–111.

Moore, George Foot. *Judaism in the First Centuries of the Christian Era.* 3 vols. Cambridge, Mass., 1927–30.

Moore, R. I. *The Formation of a Persecuting Society.* Oxford, 1987.

Munro, Dana C. "The Speech of Pope Urban II at Clermont." *American Historical Review* 11 (1906):231–242.

Poliakov, Leon. *History of Anti-Semitism.* Trans. Richard Howard et al. 4 vols. New York, 1965–85.

Porges, Nathan. "Les relations hébraiques des persécutions des Juifs pendant la première croisade." *Revue des études juives* 25 (1892):181–201 and 26 (1893):183–197.

Riley-Smith, Jonathan. *The Crusades: A Short History.* London, 1987.

————. "The First Crusade and the Persecution of the Jews." In *Persecution and Toleration,* ed. W. J. Sheils, 51–72. Oxford, 1984.

————. *The First Crusaders, 1095–1131.* Cambridge, 1997.

Roskies, David G. *Against the Apocalypse: Responses to Catastrophe in Modern Jewish Culture.* Cambridge, Mass., 1984.

Rubenstein, Jeffrey. *The Complexity of Torah: On the Narrative Art of the Bavli.* Baltimore, 1999.

Runciman, Steven. *A History of the Crusades.* 3 vols. Cambridge, 1951–67.

Schiffman, Sara. *Heinrich IV und die Bischöfe in ihrem Verhalten zu den deutschen Juden zur Zeit des ersten Kreuzzüges.* Berlin, 1931.

Schwarzfuchs, Simon. "The Place of the Crusades in Jewish History" (Hebrew). In *Tarbut ve-Ḥevrah be-Toldot Yisra'el bi-Me ha-Benayim,* ed. Menahem Ben-Sasson et al., 251–267. Jerusalem, 1989.

Setton, Kenneth M., ed. *A History of the Crusades.* 6 vols. Madison, 1969–89.

Shulvass, Moses. "Historical Knowledge and Historical Literature in the Cul-tural Sphere of Medieval Ashkenazic Jewry" (Hebrew). In *Hanoch Albeck Jubilee Volume,* 477–486. Jerusalem, 1963.

Simon, Marcel. *Verus Israel: A Study of the Relations between Christians and Jews in the Roman Empire (AD 135–425).* Trans. M. McKeating. Oxford, 1986.

Sivan, Emanuel. *L'Islam et la croisade.* Paris, 1968.

Smith, Lacey Baldwin. *Fools, Martyrs, Traitors: The Story of Martyrdom in the Western World*. New York, 1997.

Soloveitchik, Haym. "Religious Law and Change: The Medieval Ashkenazic Example." *AJS Review* 12 (1987):205–221.

———. "Three Themes in the *Sefer Ḥasidim*." *AJS Review* 1 (1976):311–357.

Sonne, Isaiah. "Critical Annotations to Solomon bar Simson's Record of the Edicts of 1096, Including a Fragment of this Text in Judaeo-German" (Hebrew). In *The Abraham Weiss Jubilee Volume*, 385–405. New York: 1964.

———. "Nouvel examen des trois relations hébraiques sur les persécutions de 1096." *Revue des études juives* 96 (1933):113–156.

———. "Which Is the Oldest Narrative of the Persecution of 1096?" (Hebrew). *Zion* 12 (1947):74–81.

Spiegel, Shalom. *The Last Trial*. Trans. Judah Goldin. Philadelphia, 1967.

Stacey, Robert C. "The Conversion of Jews to Christianity in Thirteenth-Century England." *Speculum* 67 (1992):263–283.

Sternberg, Meir. *The Poetics of Biblical Narrative: Ideological Literature and the Drama of Reading*. Bloomington, 1987.

Ta-Shma, Yisrael. "The Library of the Ashkenazic Sages in the 11th–12th Centuries." *Kiryat Sefer* 60 (1985):298–309. Addenda. *Kiryat Sefer* 61 (1986): 581–582.

———. "The Library of the French Sages." In *Rashi 1040–1090: Hommage à Ephraim E. Urbach,* ed. Gabrielle Sed-Rajna, 535–540. Paris, 1993.

———. "The Source and Place of the Prayer '*Alenu le-shabeaḥ*" (Hebrew). In *The Frank Talmage Memorial Volume*, ed. Barry Walfish, 1:85–98. 2 vols. Haifa, 1993.

Toussaint, Ingo. *Die Grafen von Leiningen: Studien zur leiningischen Genealogie und Territorialgeschichte bis zur Teilung von 1317/18*. Sigmaringen, 1982.

Urbach, Ephraim E. *Baʿalei ha-Tosafot*. 5th ed. 2 vols. Jerusalem, 1986.

———. *The Sages: Their Concepts and Beliefs*. Trans. Israel Abrahams. Cambridge, Mass., 1987.

von Oppolzer, Theodor Ritter. *Canon of Eclipses*. Trans. Owen Gingerich. New York, 1962.

Yassif, Eli. "The Hebrew Narrative Anthology in the Middle Ages." *Prooftexts* 17 (1997):153–175.

Yerushalmi, Yosef Haim. *Zakhor: Jewish History and Jewish Memory*. Seattle, 1982.

Index

Text:	10/13 Sabon
Display:	Sabon
Composition:	Binghamton Valley Composition
Printing and binding:	Thomson-Shore